Author! Author!

Author! Author!

TALES OF AUSTRALIAN
LITERARY LIFE

Edited by

CHRIS WALLACE-CRABBE

Melbourne

OXFORD UNIVERSITY PRESS

Oxford   Auckland   New York

Australia Council for the Arts

This project has been assisted by the Commonwealth Government
through the Australia Council, its arts funding and advisory body.

OXFORD UNIVERSITY PRESS AUSTRALIA

Oxford New York
Athens Auckland Bangkok Bogota Bombay
Buenos Aires Calcutta Cape Town Dar es Salaam
Delhi Florence Hong Kong Istanbul Karachi
Kuala Lumpur Madras Madrid Melbourne
Mexico City Nairobi Paris Port Moresby
Singapore Taipei Tokyo Toronto Warsaw
and associated companies in
Berlin Ibadan

OXFORD is a trade mark of Oxford University Press

National Library of Australia
Cataloguing-in-publication data:

Author! Author! Tales of Australian literary life.

Includes index.
ISBN 0 19 553608 8.

1. Australian literature – Anecdotes. 2. Authors,
Australian – Anecdotes. I. Wallace-Crabbe, Chris, 1934–.

A828.02

Edited by Cathryn Game
Text designed by Steve Randles
Cover designed by Steve Randles
Typeset by Solo Typesetting, South Australia
Printed by Kyodo
Published by Oxford University Press
253 Normanby Road, South Melbourne, Australia

Contents

Preface

This is not a scholar's collection: I have not scoured writers' archives in libraries across the country. But I have searched widely among books and journals, and called upon my fellow writers for gems. My task could not have been completed without the energetic assistance of Ronnith Morris, Lisa Jacobson, Mary Jo Pirola, and Toby Wallace-Crabbe. My thanks go to them, to the man whose brainwave this project was, Peter Rose, and to Cathryn Game for her meticulous editing. Among other people who have come up with suggestions for this book, I must thank Peter Alexander, Judy Armstrong, Kerryn Goldsworthy, Garry Kinnane, Jenny Lee, David McCooey, Ann McCulloch, Kevin Roberts, Alan Seymour, Ron Simpson, Lucy Sussex, Roly Sussex, and Marianne Wallace-Crabbe, whose patience is exemplary. Also Peter Steele, with whom I have had many a 'Small Super Special' at Papa Gino's in Lygon Street, Carlton, always returning inspired from our lunch. All these are partners in the enterprise.

My antipodean gratitude should also be expressed to James Sutherland, whose *Oxford Book of Literary Anecdotes*, published in 1975, showed me what it might be possible to do for Australian writers' yarns.

Introduction

Everybody loves anecdotes. They constantly form a staple of our conversation. They are, if you like, a junction where person meets story, character becomes narrative. At best, an anecdote captures a character, in the old sense of that word, as a person's defining quality.

As soon as you begin to tell any story about a life, let alone set forth on that dangerous voyage, a biography, you become aware that many of the molecular units with which you are dealing take the form of anecdotes. Indeed, the most vivid moments or hinges of your telling will commonly be little tales. Think for a moment about the sense we have of Doctor Johnson: it comes in pithy anecdotes with 'Sir' in them. Or think of Sir Walter Ralegh who, according to Aubrey, 'loved a wench well', even up against a tree. A good anecdote feels like an epiphany, a brilliant crystallisation from the flow of living. It gets the point.

All the more so if you are talking about writers. Dealers in words themselves, they are peculiarly prone to being captured in little webs of words. Tales are strung along their years. Glancing back or across at any of them, you tend to catch them in a phrase, a yarn, or a telling, as though a shaft of light had suddenly fallen upon the writer in question. I recall Vin Buckley suddenly telling a seminar that the greatest line in Browning was 'Guizot receives Montalembert'; and Xavier Herbert, skulking furtively in the night outside a Writers' Festival tent, asking, 'Are they after me?'

Some tales celebrate physical action, like Fay Zwicky's triumphal account of how a visiting American writer and a

Sydney female poet amorously smashed all the furniture in an Adelaide motel room. Too many turn on drunkenness and end in a standard comic blur. Others are hilariously indecent.

'Did you hear the one about ... ?' is a typical opening in conversation, but too many of those conversations, alas, are so apocryphal, hyperbolic, or lascivious — perhaps all three — that you just can't set them down in print. To make this anthology of literary tales reliable and respectable, I have had to insist that each tale has had a printed, or at least a written, form.

What is more, it has been necessary to have a rough-and-ready sense of where the limits of literary anecdotes might lie. Most of these pieces have a direct connection with the world of reading and writing, but in some cases I have been willing to admit tales of other events that have befallen writers of note, or that have sprung from their writerliness. After all, the hut of Australian letters has many windows.

Let me extend this overture with a personal anecdote; perhaps it shows how such a tale can illuminate a writer's career. In the early 1950s I bought a Faulkner novel in a Penguin edition. On the back cover it noted, among other things, that 'he wrote *As I Lay Dying* between midnight and 4.00 a.m. without changing a word'. Brooding on this amazing feat, as it seemed, and thinking of my own slow writing process, I realised that I would just have to stick to that short-distance genre, poetry. Misunderstandings are so important.

Being small, anecdotes can be read in lots of ways. Because they are so pungent, they appear — like good jokes, or like dreams — to be overdetermined. Or else it is precisely because they are overdetermined that we find them attractive. Brevity engenders wit, and we like to think that wit taps real knowledge, even the wells of wisdom.

Finally, I find myself wondering how far these selective tales of literary life reveal anything distinctive about Australian culture and its particular crystallisations. I can only hope that they do.

First fruits

Michael Massey Robinson (1744–1826) and the aptly named Barron Field (1786–1846) open our account with a double-headed anecdote about the beginnings of Australia's poetry, or at least our verse.

That year too the venerated bard, Michael Robinson, an ex-convict, whose witty, gay and classical muse had so often been the subject of general admiration and praise amongst emancipists and native-born, read his song for Anniversary Day. He had two themes: jokes about taking strong drink, which the Reverend Samuel Marsden, and General Darling and Archdeacon Scott would not have found funny:

> In Olympus, we're told
> The celestials of old,
> > In spite of morality's lecture,
> Would steal a sly sup
> From the festival cup,
> > And sometimes get mellow with nectar.

His other theme was the future greatness of Australia:

> 'Advance' then, 'Australia',
> By this thy proud gala,
> > Which no party *spirit* can sever;
> May thy shores and thy plains,
> Echo loyalty's strains,
> > And thy watch-word be 'FREEDOM FOR EVER!'

When Robinson died in 1827 the native-born and eman-cipists mourned him as the first poet laureate in the colony, and indeed as the only man whose productions had any pre-tensions even to the grade of mediocrity. Some said he would survive longer than Barron Field, who had insulted the locals with that line of verse in which he had prophesied that the kangaroo and not human beings would rescue

Australia from the fate of failure. Barron Field, it was said, would be preserved with as much sanctity of veneration as that extraordinary relic, the paring of the toe-nail of St Peter, was guarded by those fanatical devotees who boasted its possession.

C.M.H. Clark, *A History of Australia*, vol. 2, p. 166.

An artful dodger

James Hardy Vaux (1782–?) was a flash petty criminal who was transported three times to Australia and wrote the first autobiography to appear on this continent. Brian Elliott has dubbed him 'a literary rogue'.

... he stowed away upon the *Earl Spencer* Indiaman, lying in January, 1814, in Port Jackson, bound for Ceylon and Bombay. It would appear to have been a foolish venture after all; someone on board must have been extorting money from convicts with the promise of escape, but the operation was far too gross. When Vaux had already been in hiding four days, the Governor, alarmed at the number of convicts missing (Vaux mentions a total of twenty-seven), sent a band of thirty constables on board to search the ship; and thus he was betrayed by the false friend who had got him aboard.

> At length I heard voices approaching, and eagerly listening, I was convinced by the discourse which passed between the parties, that they knew exactly where I was concealed, and that I really had been, by somebody, most villainously betrayed. In a moment the mate advanced, as it were, mechanically, towards me, and thrusting his candle into the entrance of my hiding-place, desired me, in a peremptory tone, to come out.

'Thus,' he comments, 'were my fond hopes of liberty and happiness effectually destroyed.'

Brian Elliott, *James Hardy Vaux: A Literary Rogue in Australia*, p. 26.

Guying the flogging parson

William Charles Wentworth (1790–1872), born on the high seas between Sydney and Norfolk Island, became a substantial public figure, supporter of the emancipists and proponent of what his foes called a 'bunyip aristocracy'. While studying at Cambridge, he wrote the poem 'Australasia'.

By contrast the currency lads and the emancipists were turning, noisily, exuberantly and boisterously to embrace the world they knew. On the night of 26 January 1825 a party of them, with Wentworth as president, and Redfern as vice-president, met at Hill's hotel to celebrate the thirty-seventh anniversary of the colony. They drank toasts to many things — to the king, to the memory of Governor Phillip, and of Macquarie, to Sir Thomas Brisbane, who believed that all human striving was vain, to trial by jury, to a house of assembly, the freedom of the press, to commerce and agriculture, and to the currency lasses, for Wentworth was a man. There was much merriment, and much shouting when Robinson, an effective writer of doggerel verse for such occasions, called on them to drink the toast: 'The land, boys, we live in'.

A few months later copies arrived of the third edition of Wentworth's book on the colony of New South Wales. The emancipists hailed him as their historian and their advocate, a worthy native son of 'the land, boys, we live in'. John Macarthur was not greatly alarmed. The rhodomontade and the savage invective only confirmed what he had been telling himself for a long time about Wentworth — namely, that the man would offend grossly. But Marsden was deeply hurt. Wentworth, and his collaborator, Edward Eagar whom he, Marsden, had befriended in his early days of the colony, had held him up to public ridicule and contempt as a turbulent and ambitious priest, who had set his face against every philanthropic project. They had taunted him as an unctuous hypocrite whose reverence for the Lord's day was not such as to permit a windmill of his, which stood in full view of the very sanctuary where he officiated, suspending its profitable gyrations even during church time. They had written that he was as conversant with the points of a pig, a sheep, an ox, or a horse, as with the contents of the sacred volume which it should be the peculiar study and occupation of his life to inculcate. And, they had continued, 'tell it not in Gath, publish it not in the streets of Askelon', he had long been a private vendor in any quantity from a pint to a puncheon of those very spirituous liquors against which he had so righteously declaimed.

C.M.H. Clark, *A History of Australia*, vol. 2, p. 55.

Our first amazing surname

A mysterious wit of the 1820s, Betsey Bandicoot has never been identified. Her energetic style might be seen to prefigure the Ocker Baroque of the playwright Jack Hibberd in the following century.

Four years earlier in October of 1823 one Fanny Flirt had written some rather disparaging remarks about Australia and Australians to the *Sydney Gazette* — saying amongst other things, that riding through rows of gum trees was not to her taste, and, as for colonial conversation, why, nothing could be so sheepish. Young Arable's wits, she let drop, had gone a-wool-gathering, ever since he began grazing. As for music, well, as Fanny Flirt put it, you only had to ask for a song in Sydney town, and young 'wholesale' would promptly chant to you, over an invoice, of course, 'Money is your friend, is it not?'

This was too much for those with Australasian hearts. Two weeks later Betsey Bandicoot replied, with that magnificent, vulgar, cheeky confidence of those who loved the land they lived in.

MISTER EDITOR,

... every one knows their own liking; she [Fanny Flirt] might *prefer* the soft-singing notes of her Italian in his gondola (all the same as a boat, the *dictionary* says) to the loud *coo-hee* of a currency lad riding over the blue mountains. But our Bill [a currency boy] can play the flute, hunt the wild cattle, and shoot and swim with the best in the Colony.

It would do your heart good, Mister Editor, to see how Bill tucks in, when I've fried him a pan-ful of pork, *swimming in fat*, and a smoking hot cake from the ashes. O, it would make you shine your buttons, as the saying is, to see how Bill will swig off a pot of peach-cyder; and then he lounges like any *swell*, with a nice short pipe, and smoaks and whiffs, and whiffs and smoaks, all the afternoon. But ma'aps this woud'nt be to the liking of Miss Flirt; as she is so dainty as not to be fond 'of riding through rows of gum-trees;' but, la! she should see me galloping without a saddle, a'ter Bill, when he has a mind for a bit of a frisk; and as for shoes, I never thinks of putting them on, only when I goes a shopping to Sydney, at *Mother Marr's* or *Joe Inch's* for a bonnet; or a *Little* or *Big Cooper's* for a frying-pan; and I beg a wager, I could *swim* further and faster than Miss Fanny, and *carry my clothes on my head* into the bargain, without wetting so much as my comb, which cousin Bill paid for in 'tatoes at Josephson's last Christmas *hollidays*.

If Miss Fan's for a quiet life, Bill's her man; for I have made pounds, and pounds of butter, and never so such as heard Bill *out* with a word, but then he'd whistle. To tell the truth, whistling and smoaking is Bill's delight; and he likes to have a long *yarn* from the *cove*, who is sure to get a bit of tobacco, if he tells Bill a good 'un. Bill has plenty of stock, and will have a good farm, when father's off; and so Miss Fan, if she'd take a liking to Bill, she'd find, in the long-run, Bill no such bad chop neither. But I am running on at a deuce of a rate; but Mister *Scrollam* said I could always write better than father, but I never wrote so long a job before; and shoud'nt now only for that saucy minx, Fan Flirt, whose skits about the '*dummies*' of the Colony be only sheer envy, because she has'nt the dumps; and never you go for to mind her threats about throwing you into the tanks, for there's plenty of us, who will take your part, so long as you stick up for us *currency* girls. And,

                    I remain, dear Mister Editor,
                         your unworthy humble servant,
                              BETSEY BANDICOOT

Warragombie Creek

P.S. — Miss Fan Flirt is very much mistaken if she thinks because she has seen the *lions* in *Lunnun Tower*, that we don't know *what's what* for all that. She'd better go for to mind her own *P*'s and *Q*'s without troubling herself about her betterers; and I suppose she conceits there's never not one like her at the *pye-anney-foart*, but its all gammon after all — *boojeree* me if its anything else; but I won't be angry, that I won't. So yours again,

          B.B.

C.M.H. Clark, *A History of Australia*, vol. 2, pp. 157–8.

With voice and guitar

The English man of letters, R.H. ('Orion') Horne (1802–84), an associate of Dickens and Leigh Hunt, described himself as 'the most distinguished English poet ever to visit Australia'. Arriving in 1852, he began as commander of a gold escort and went on to try many occupations, among them standing for parliament, with great lack of success.

In such a predicament any work was welcome. At the start of 1861 he began a lecture tour, for lecturing was one of his few remaining marketable skills. Like a 'wandering minstrel' he travelled through Victorian provincial centres repeating his old lectures on Italy and Ireland and adding to his repertoire three new lectures: *Songs of Seven Nations* which he illustrated with his own voice and guitar; *Insane Kings* (insanity in historical figures having long attracted him); and *The Causes of Success in Life*, presumably modelled on Hazlitt's similarly named lecture. This last lecture, when reports filtered back to England, understandably caused mirth among his former friends, particularly Dickens. His few remaining friends only wished Horne himself could have followed his own sensible advice.

The tours were strenuous. Bad roads, draughty halls, draughtier hotel rooms, damp beds, and above all his advancing years made him complain of the physical misery. He caught bronchitis in one town and lost his voice; he returned with a 'villainous "something" at the hip joint'. Though his tours may have placated his restlessness and satisfied his urge to be busy and self-reliant, financially they were a fiasco. The public response was far from gratifying; the lectures were undeniably tedious. The towns, moreover, were often small and rough: at the mining town of Talbot, he complained, he was unable even to find a boy to snuff his stage candle and bring him a glass of water. After five months of intermittent touring he calculated both his profits and expenses at £12: the net result was a very bad cold.

Ann Blainey, *The Farthing Poet: A Biography of Richard Hengist Horne, 1802–84, a Lesser Literary Lion*, p. 222.

Not even a dog

Rural Victoria offered the poet few pleasures, Melbourne a handful more, and in 1869 he was to sail back to England. Horne did, however, plant the initial vineyard at Tabilk.

Novr. 19/61
MY DEAR BELL
Williams informs me, by the last mail, that he forwarded to you my MS. article entitled 'Descent into a Gold-Mine.' I am

very sorry that you should have the trouble of this matter — the more so as I subsequently sent another, in the same style, which I fear may share the same fate at the same hands. It shows how precarious it is to write anything at such a distance, unless by previous arrangement as to the subject and treatment.

My Australian autobiography having been placed by the *publishers*, at the beginning of my book, with a laudatory remark, I fancied that articles written in the same style of humourous egotism would be equally attractive — especially as they are not at all fictions — but *facts* — pleasantly put, as I thought.

Their non-reception is a sad mischance for me — unless you have kindly found a quarter for them, from which I shall derive remuneration.

I lost my Government appointment some three years ago (from Departmental changes, and no fault in me) since which every fresh Government has *promised* me another post — but meantime everything has been going out, and scarcely anything coming in. You are aware there is no field here for literature, but political, and the newspapers have their regular staffs, and are themselves in no very flourishing state at this time. The Colony is in a strange condition; and the continual changes of Governments, of course, make matters more insecure, if not much worse.

I have lived during these last two years at the seaside, in a little four-roomed cottage, two of which only are furnished, quite alone. Not merely have I been without a servant, but even without a dog, to receive me when I come home, or look after me, when I go forth.

Some time since I started on a Lecturing tour through the district of Rodney and the Goulburn River. It rained for five weeks, with scarcely a day's cessation. So, that I barely paid my expenses, being twice laid up for several days, with colds, and loss of voice. I was invited by some squatters, and other friends, to visit Warrnambool and Belfast (on the

Western Coast) and to lecture at the principal townships. My visits to one and the other extended over three months; but the wet weather you had on the other side of the globe found its way over here (the very *same* weather, I'll be sworn!) and we had incessant rains for twelve weeks! The only change was on the night I gave no Lecture, or when there was a hurricane of wind, with an interlude of thunder and lightning. Again, I returned to my cottage, as poor as I started.

'But,' said I, 'the "Cornhill Magazine" with my "Descent into a Gold Mine" will be due in a fortnight, and I shall then have a little to go on with!' Instead of which Williams writes a note telling me that it has been declined — and that 'All the Year Round' declined it also. Meanwhile I look about my lonely seaside cottage, asking myself the cause? The walls — the ceiling — the open windows? — but no idea of the cause comes to me. Yes — rather I should say, consideration presents to me all *sorts* of causes, and adds its tormenting shadows to the one, hard certain, remarkable *fact* of 'declined!'

One by one I am obliged to part with such things as I possess. My favourite old mare — my watch — lots of books and prints — are gone for what they would bring. Frequently I dine, when at home, on oatmeal and water. Since my loss of office I have never been able to send Mrs Horne any remittance — not that I believe she has needed it, or that she would receive it from me. At any rate, I have never had the means — but, no doubt, the usual odium. Surely I have a claim on the Literary Fund, or the Guild? In my very first work I suggested the latter Institution. During two years I helped poor Leigh Hunt. Can I find no friend to put forth a hand for me in this far-off country?

W.J. Fox said to a friend, the other day (i.e. two months ago — and five months when you get this.) 'Why, I have always fancied Horne had become a rich man!' Not very materially. My Australian book gives that impression. So do other things. The Articles I send. I have that elasticity, the

moment a pen is in my hand, that I forget troubles and difficulties of all kinds affecting myself. Also you may have heard
that when I lately went to Belfast, the late Government (just
turned out) wished me to contest the seat for this district. A
political Society guaranteed my expenses. The election was
gained by another candidate, through all sorts of dodges —
I was left with my expenses remaining after the contest —
and the society was dissolved! Also it is true that I am the
'laird' of a small township on the Goulburn River; but from
which I have never *yet* received one farthing of rent; but
meanwhile the grass grows so high, it may wave above my
grave, ere rent-day.

> I remain my dear Bell
> Under all circumstances,
> Yours, as of old
> R.H. HORNE.

R.H. Horne, letter to Robert Bell, in *Meanjin* 2/1954, pp. 243–4.

The last feast of reason

As befits a member of the Yorick Club, he left in style, at least.

Young George Macrae [i.e. McCrae], invited to visit Horne
for the last time, went down to St Kilda one afternoon in
March 1869. It was so memorable a visit that he afterwards
recorded it in nostalgic detail. On Mrs McGuirk's aggressive
directions he had gone into the garden that ran behind the
terrace houses to find Horne in his shirtsleeves, a broad-
brimmed hat on his head, sitting beneath an enormous fig
tree eating the fruit. On seeing Macrae he had given an elaborate start — he had forgotten he had made the invitation.
Then with great show he had begun to pull himself together
and organize their entertainment. He would give him
home-grown roast potatoes, done to perfection by Mother

McGuirk, and a tin of pheasant fetched by Horne with the aid of his library steps from among the confusion of the top bookshelves, and a glass of sparkling Moselle in Bohemian crystal glasses, produced from further confusion with numerous flourishes. Talking continuously, Horne arranged the meal. Their 'feast of Reason' concluded, he took up his guitar for the 'flow of the Soul'. Slipping the blue riband over his shoulder, throwing himself on the sofa with crossed legs, he 'poured out Spanish and Mexican songs with the greatest energy and enthusiasm, plenty of volume and all in excellent harmony'. That done, he produced his portfolio of line engravings — the celebrated Piranesi's of Ancient Rome among them — for Macrae's practised admiration, and finally a black quarto-sized case which he sprung open to show a magnificent miniature on ivory of a beautiful dark-haired girl. To Macrae's cries of 'Magnificent woman', he simply replied, 'My wife'. He snapped the case shut; the visit was over.

After wranglings over his treasures Horne finally sold them for £60 6s. 3d. at public auction. Probably the most extraordinary literary collection offered in Australia, it included first editions of Shelley, Keats, Hazlitt, the rare first edition of *Queen Mab*, presentation copies of Browning, Talfourd, Hunt, bound periodicals and lexicons, rare copies of Donne, the Decameron and the Koran: the artifacts of his mental life, along with guitars, trumpets, and violas.

Ann Blainey, *The Farthing Poet: A Biography of Richard Hengist Horne, 1802–84, a Lesser Literary Lion*, p. 239.

Sublimity

Louisa Anne Meredith (1812–95) migrated with her husband from England, briefly to New South Wales and then to Tasmania. A poet and watercolourist, she made use of a highly romantic prose style. It has what she would dub its own intrinsic lustre.

It is very common for people to talk and write of waves running 'mountains high', but I confess I always used to make a very liberal allowance for exaggeration and imagery in these cases; and I well remember once joining in the laugh of incredulity, when a gentleman told myself and other young people that he had seen waves of which two would fill the breadth of the Menai Strait, where we then were. I had not then been a long voyage myself; I had not looked and trembled at the scene I witnessed one Sunday morning after a two days' gale, during which I had remained below. The wind had abated considerably, but we could only carry a close-reefed mainsail, and were 'scudding' along. Any attempt to describe the vast, awful grandeur of the scene seems absurd — it is so impossible for anything but the eye itself to represent it to the mind; I feel dizzy with the mere remembrance.

When I came on deck, the ship lay as in an immense valley of waters, with huge waves, *mountain* waves, indeed (one of which would have flooded both shores of the Menai), circling us all around: then slowly we seemed to climb the ascent, and, poised on the summit of the rolling height, could look along the dark and dreary waste of ocean heaving with giant billows far and wide; then, plunging down into the next frightful abyss, the labouring vessel seemed doomed; — I fancied already the rush of water in my ears, when, with a violent pitch and shudder, the ship bounded along again, over another mountain, and down another valley, in long and slow succession again and again, till I grew accustomed to the scene, and could gaze without thinking I looked upon our vast and miserable grave.

There were the ghost-like albatrosses sailing solemnly above the tops of the towering billows, or diving beside us into the yawning gulf, — sailing about with the same unruffled plumes, the same quiet, wary eye, and majestic demeanour, that they wore in the brightest calm. Who could doubt their supernatural attributes? Certainly not a spirit-chilled landswoman, with Coleridge's magic legend perpetually repeating itself to her. I wish some of its good and beautiful lines were as familiar and impressive in the minds and thoughts of others as they are in mine:

'Farewell, farewell — but this I tell
To thee, thou wedding guest!
He prayeth well, who loveth well
Both man and bird and beast.

He prayeth best, who loveth best
All things, both great and small;
For the dear God, who loveth us,
He made and loveth all.'

Mrs Charles Meredith, Notes and Sketches of
New South Wales, pp. 29–30.

No novels called for here

More people have heard vaguely about Redmond Barry (1830–80) than know much about his career. An Irish judge, he sentenced the rogue hero Ned Kelly to death in 1880, thus helping to make famous the phrase 'Such is life'. He founded both the University of Melbourne and the Melbourne Public Library. Living as a bachelor, he kept a mistress and her children just around the corner for many years.

On the evening of 24 May 1871, the Queen's Birthday, Victoria's best-known opponent of modern fiction sat down to dine at Toorak House next to the Empire's most celebrated novelist, Anthony Trollope. In Australia to visit his younger son Frederic who had settled in New South Wales, Trollope was to publish a lengthy account of his visit two years later in which he spoke highly of Melbourne's clubs, the Menzies Hotel and Melbourne itself, but he made no comment about his dinner companion for that evening. Not, that is, in his descriptive accounts of the Antipodes. There his acute eye described Melbourne 'the undoubted capital, not only of Victoria but of all Australia' where 'Here and there is a grand public building — the Post Office and the Town Hall being very grand ... But the magnificence of Melbourne is not only external. The city is very proud of its institutions, and is justified in its pride. First amongst these, as being very excellent in the mode of its administration, is the Public Library'.

Trollope's faint praise of the Library, limiting himself to 'the mode of its administration' rather than commenting on the collection, suggests that he knew of Barry's implacable policy of refusing to acquire contemporary fiction. Barry had always disliked what he considered its frivolous nature: he feared the dissemination of moral laxity through the pages of the popular novel. So well known was this antipathy that anecdotes about his attitude were still in circulation in Melbourne some sixty years after his death. In a short article on 'Officialdom and the Novel', the *Argus* in 1947 retold one such story under the sub-heading 'A Judge condones Theft'. On this occasion Barry was conducting a visitor through the library when he was asked whether there were many works of fiction in the collection. 'Very few indeed sir,' replied the Judge, 'and I am thankful to say that those few are being rapidly appropriated by a few unscrupulous persons, and will not be replaced.'

Ann Galbally, *Redmond Barry: An Anglo-Irish Australian*, pp. 157–8.

Even a paranoid can have enemies

Charles Harpur (1813–68) was not a happy man. He was, however, a poet of great distinction, achieving long after his death something of his dear wish to be 'the Muse of Australia'. As well as lyrics and satires, he wrote long poems of narrative and metaphysical speculation. For some years he was a gold commissioner at beautiful Araluen.

To add to his woes, Fowler attracted another vehement public enemy — Charles Harpur. When the *Month* was first proposed Harpur had written to Fowler congratulating him on his lecture on Coleridge, and sending a subscription list for his proposed collection of poems, in order to 'break the ice' and get acquainted. 'It is true,' Harpur wrote modestly, '*my* poetry may not be up to his critical mark — but there may nevertheless, be enough in it to interest him — a little in *me*, as its author.' Harpur was evidently hoping to be invited to contribute his poetry to the *Month* and Fowler, it appears, just waited for him to send it. Harpur, not at all modest about his poetry, was always quick to take offence and this slight rankled. When he read in the February issue of the *Month* Fowler's grandiose statement that 'It has been his desire, ever since his arrival in the colony, to establish something like a national literature', Harpur exploded.

> It would appear from the eighth number of the *Month*, that its editor, Mr Fowler, has come hither, all the way from the Fatherland, for the express purpose of founding for us *natives a national literature* on a critical basis, and as I would fain have at least a finger-end in such a pie, however compounded, I have thus put forth this particular piece in an improved shape, as my contribution to the canonical foundation of it: that is, if aught may happen to appear out of the classical pages of the almighty *Month*, or that does not flow from the golden pen or flash from the lightning-tipt tongue of Mr Fowler himself, can in any wise contribute to the accomplishment of so towering a design. Be this, however as it may, W.C. Wentworth, Dr Lang, Martin, Norton, Parkes, Halloran, Deniehy, Dalley, my humble self, and all who have hitherto vainly endeavoured to lay down a few of the foundation stones of an Australian literature, are bound to be profoundly grateful for the generous 'intentions' of this *sovereign Londoner*. Yea, let us sing poems to the

Samson-like might of the man who has thus come to do for us the work we could not of ourselves.

Ann-Mari Jordens, *The Stenhouse Circle: Literary Life in Mid-Nineteenth Century Sydney*, pp. 63–4.

Local rags ...

Alfred Joyce (1821–1901) wrote a notable memoir of twenty-one years' squatting in Victoria. His two properties, Plaistow and Norwood, were lost to him during hard times in the late 1880s.

When in town with the last wool, I had an opportunity of looking about and noting the alterations and extensions since my visit before coming on the station. Its boundaries so far as buildings were concerned were still contained within the block bounded by Lonsdale, Russell, Flinders and King Streets, the large number of vacant allotments having been quite sufficient for its extension for the past year or two; but sales of town lands had been resumed northwards and blocks were being freely purchased. As yet, however, no country land was offered or had been offered except at short distances from Melbourne, such as the Moonee Ponds, the Merri Creek, the Plenty, the Springs, Heidelberg, and a few other places.

I saw very little of the Melbourne newspapers except when on my visit to town. We did not think it necessary to subscribe to any of them till our weekly post was established some time later; but I recollect the three, the *Port Phillip Patriot,* the *Port Phillip Gazette*, and the *Melbourne Herald*, and I distinctly recollect a strong slang-wanging encounter between two of them, the *Herald* one of them, which forcibly reminded me at the time of the Eatanswill episode in Pickwick.

Alfred Joyce, *A Homestead History: Being the Reminiscences and Letters of Alfred Joyce of Plaistow and Norwood, Port Phillip, 1843 to 1864* (ed. G.F. James), p. 80.

... *And gutter journalists*

James Edward Neild (1824–1906) was not only a prominent medico in Melbourne but also a leading theatre critic. As pugnacious as Yorkshiremen are expected to be, he readily stirred the pot with his stern reviews. Among his pseudonyms were 'Tahite' and 'Christopher Sly'.

For example, there is a fellow on the *Age* named Williams, whom once I kicked out of my house for coming to me drunk and insolent. I have traced the crawl of his slime ever since. In like manner that dirty twerp Collier has for years vomited filth at me, because he thought I cut him up when once he played Charles Courtly in 'London Assurance'. As it happens I did not write the notice about him.

Harold Love, *James Edward Neild: Victorian Virtuoso*, p. 199.

A hopeless Pom

Sir Frederick Pottinger (1831–65), an Eton product, was the very model of the English remittance man as dag. Vividly incompetent at catching bushrangers, he died young. He might well have been the original 'blind Freddie'.

On the other side of the legal fence, but equally advantaged by his rank, was Sir Frederick Pottinger, Baronet, a Pottinger of the Berkshire Pottingers, whose father was the first Governor of Hong Kong and whose cousin Eldred, 'Pottinger of Herat', was a celebrated hero of the Indian frontier wars. Sir Frederick seems to have been a true-born failure. Getting into money difficulties in his late twenties, in 1860 he resigned his commission in the Coldstream Guards and enlisted as a trooper in the New South Wales Mounted Police, employed in rounding up the outlaws known in Australia as bushrangers. Although very soon promoted to sub-inspector, when his baronetcy was inadvertently discovered, he was famously ineffective in this role, his failure to catch one popular villain being immortalized in a Sydney ballad:

> Sir Frederick Pott shut his eyes for the shoot
> And missed in the usual way.
> But the ranger proud, he laughed aloud,
> And bounding rode away!

But if Pottinger seldom succeeded in shooting a bushranger, in the end this hapless toff succeeded in fatally shooting himself, accidentally with his own revolver while boarding a coach. Through it all he remained the patrician anyway, and Sydney recognized it. His deathbed was in his own room at the Victoria Club, and his funeral was attended by the Premier of New South Wales.

Jan Morris, *Sydney*, p. 74.

An encounter in Castlemaine

Mary Fortune (c. 1833–?) left her husband behind in Canada for a picaresque life around the goldfields. Writing under the evocative sobriquet of 'Waif Wander', she was one of Australia's pioneer authors of detective fiction.

Coming almost directly from America, and being young you know, perhaps it was natural that, in a new land and among scenes in which law was of but little account, I should boom in the Poet's Corner as a thorough Democrat. At all events, some pieces of mine were printed in the sheet I have alluded to, of which Mr Saint (Charles, I think) was the editor or proprietor, or both. Some of the rhymes I have alluded to I have since reprinted, but with changes that redeemed them from the Republican taint.

The lines I write of were printed with my own initials attached, and just before I left the 'Flat' a line was addressed to me in the answer to correspondent's corner of the *Mount Alexander Mail*. The line was a request that 'M.H.F.' would call at this office at his earliest convenience. I was very much tickled at the personal pronoun, and curious too, so I took the opportunity of passing through Castlemaine to call at the office in question.

My recollection of the office is but slight, but I think it was even then a two storey building, and that from the desk in a corner of a large and almost empty room I was interviewed by a man who stared in open-eyed wonder at me and my youngster, whom I led by the hand.

'Are *you* "M.H.F."?' he questioned with evident disbelief. 'Yes.'

'I can hardly credit it. You had better see Mr Saint; but as for the request that M.H.F. would call, we want a reporter and sub-editor, and thought he might suit.'

I was fortunate enough afterwards to see Mr Saint, and to spend a very pleasant evening with Mr and Mrs Saint in their cottage home.

Lucy Sussex (ed.), *The Fortunes of Mary Fortune*, p. 52.

Schoolyard days

Although a suicide, Adam Lindsay Gordon (1833–70) is distinguished by a spot in Poets' Corner, Westminster Abbey. He is the only Australian poet to have been born in the Azores, but had a classical education in England.

It was a fighting school, and, notwithstanding strict supervision, combats were frequent. In these Gordon particularly distinguished himself, and I believe nothing gave him more pleasure than a fight, in which his long reach gave him great advantage.

Setting aside a fair amount of caning over the hand, the principal punishment was the committal to memory of some twenty to fifty lines of Virgil or Homer. This was a laborious task to most of us but to Gordon it was nothing, since his surprising memory enabled him to recite his lines after two or three perusals. He slept in the same room (there were seven of us altogether), and at night, after the lights were out, Gordon used to entertain us with long recitals from *Marmion* and *The Lord of the Isles*.

Many of Scott's novels he also related to us, several nights being required to go through one of these.

An unknown officer, quoted in Geoffrey Hutton, *Adam Lindsay Gordon: The Man and the Myth*, p. 26.

At the circus

Mad about horses, Gordon spent a couple of years in the South Australian mounted police. He was a plangent poet, as 'The Sick Stockrider' shows, but not necessarily acute about people.

Left to maintain order at a travelling circus which visited Mount Gambier, Gordon felt it his duty to arrest a drunken nuisance who was interrupting the performance. Gordon refused to listen to his excuses and it was not until they reached the station and the man undid his clothes to show his spangles and tights underneath that Gordon understood that he had made a mistake. Trainor was clowning the traditional role of the circus 'drunk' as part of his casual job.

Geoffrey Hutton, *Adam Lindsay Gordon: The Man and the Myth*, pp. 61–2.

Don't let a madman near a gun

In so far as we expect literature to be about extremities and adventures, Gordon had a great deal of raw material to draw upon. And it must have been Gordon above all, even more than 'Banjo' Paterson, who led one Australian writer to complain that our poetry was about 'Horses, horses, horses'.

He had been directed to conduct a lunatic to the nearest asylum, two hundred miles away. The madman was mounted on a young half-broken colt. The trooper, with his pistols and loaded carbine strapped to the saddle, curveted along on his excellent horse. At night they slept in the open air beneath the handiest tree, Gordon fastening his prisoner's hand to his own with the handcuffs, as the surest way of keeping him secure. The lunatic was very restless and Gordon's long day was followed by a sleepless night. Once or twice, after being awakened for the twentieth time, he uttered some awful threats in order to quieten his crazy charge, but in the morning the madman had a chance of turning the tables. Gordon with thoughtless good humour set the man on his own excellent horse, while he himself cantered on in front on the half-broken beast. But he had forgotten all about the loaded carbine in the saddle, and ere they had gone half a mile he had a sudden reminder in the shape of a bullet that whistled past him. Facing round, he became aware of the situation. The two were alone in the wilderness, and though he might have the advantage in sanity, the other had all the arms, and had, besides, the memory of that midnight score to wipe off. It was a trying juncture, and it required all Gordon's persuasiveness to get out of it.

Geoffrey Hutton, *Adam Lindsay Gordon: The Man and the Myth*, p. 66.

Disasters

Things only got worse.

Life began hopefully in Ballarat, but disaster struck very soon. On 21st March Gordon was schooling a jumper named Necromancer over fences in the country when the horse baulked. According to the *Ballarat Star*, the horse hit at the second attempt and fell on top of its rider. In struggling to its feet it trod on his face.

The accident occurred while Gordon was trying to jump from a paddock on to the road. He lay unconscious for a long time before Harry Mount went to look for him and found him lying on the road. He drove home for a groom, and together they lifted Gordon into a buggy, driving past his house on the way to the hospital. Mount had his midday dinner, then called on Mrs Gordon to tell her the news. She insisted that her husband be brought home, and four men carried him on a stretcher. When he saw his wife he was conscious and called out that he was not much hurt. In fact he had suffered a fractured skull (described in the paper as 'a bad scalp wound') besides a broken nose, jaw and several ribs. It was the most serious of Gordon's many serious riding injuries.

He lay in bed for weeks. To cheer him the Ballarat Light Horse marched past his house on a parade, stopped outside while a band played, and two officers called on him. This may have pleased him as a military man *manqué*, but a far worse blow fell while he was still convalescent. His daughter Annie contracted an infection, probably enteritis. Her condition rapidly deteriorated, she was seized by convulsions and on 15th April she died.

When Gordon heard the news he jumped out of bed, paced the floor and burst the bandages round his body. He was forbidden to attend the funeral but insisted, his head heavily bandaged.

Geoffrey Hutton, *Adam Lindsay Gordon: The Man and the Myth*, pp. 133–4.

Towards the end

The disarray of Gordon's life over his last months is registered in a phlegmatic account of his remaining books. All too soon he would go down to Brighton Beach and shoot himself.

In his restless movements from house to house Gordon's books had become scattered and almost entirely lost. His own catalogue of his library at Brighton ran:

> A Turf Register; half of a religious work that came into my hands I don't know how; a dilapidated dictionary; *David the Shepherd King*, with the author's compliments, which no-one will borrow or steal; and a volume of my own verses, which I cannot get rid of.

Geoffrey Hutton, *Adam Lindsay Gordon: The Man and the Myth*, p. 160.

Back to the beetles

Henry Kendall (1839–82) was a kind of melodious classic among early Australian poets; indeed, we had to learn his poems off by heart at school. Native-born, he wrote of the verdant bushland of the New South Wales coast. As a young man he served awhile on a whaling ship, a period of experience reflected in his coldwater poem, 'Beyond Kerguelen'.

The other major venue for educated discourse, the exchange of knowledge, and elevating cultural entertainment was the Grafton School of Arts, over which Michael presided when elected its secretary from September 1862. He, of course, relished live performances and a captive audience, but not so Henry Kendall. Even a decade and a half later at Cundletown, he was described by one eyewitness as being extremely nervous and self-conscious: 'his gestures were awkward, and he looked shy to the verge of childishness on being introduced to the audience'. This congenital unease amounted to virtual panic on the occasion of his maiden address in Grafton. Then, in the words of Victor Daley, 'he arranged to give a lecture on Australian Literature — an easy matter in those days one would imagine. When the time arrived he came upon the platform, glared at the audience, gasped — and fled. The chairman on the occasion [Michael] rose to the rescue with an address on beetles, or some other nauseous but interesting vermin, entitled "Under the Microscope".'

Michael Ackland, *Henry Kendall: The Man and the Myths*, pp. 69–70.

A critique of the Bible

As this acerbic passage might suggest, Kendall also wrote satirical verses. Not that it cheered him up very much; latterly appointed an inspector of forests (his old subject matter), he died, worn out at the age of 43.

Mrs Stenhouse has just presented me with a Bible. Poor lady — she wants me to swallow the dogma asserting its plenary inspiration. I cannot see it. Setting aside the grand poetry of the 'prophets', the magnificent myth of Elijah, the fine oriental wisdom of the Proverbs, and the sublime code of ethics laid down in the Gospels; it is about the most disappointing book I have ever read.

Michael Ackland, *Henry Kendall: The Man and the Myths*, p. 225.

Speechless

Much as Joseph Furphy (1843–1912) wove many tales and angles into the complex fabric of his pre-postmodernist novel, Such is Life, *the tales about him are numerous. A sandy, lanky autodidact, his literary gifts revealed themselves early, as did his chronic shyness.*

Joe had been away harvesting, and had not heard of the competition till the day before the closing of the entries. He went home, spent afternoon, evening and night in composition, and the poem was handed in. Mr Archer relates the remark attributed to the chief adjudicator, the Reverend C. Oakley Vance, M.A. (afterwards the Dean of Melbourne): 'The man that wrote this poem will become one of the most famous of men, or else sink back into oblivion.' The audience, reports Archer, went frantic and amid cries of 'Author! Author!' Joseph Furphy was pushed on to the platform. With a nervous glance at the crowd he began: 'Ladies and gentlemen — I thank you for the — for the . . .' and dashed wildly from the scene.

Miles Franklin, *Joseph Furphy: The Legend of a Man and His Work*, p. 21.

Joe was no Casanova

It seems that there was a real-life prototype for Mrs Beaudesart, the man-eating huntress who looms so large over Tom Collins in Such is Life. *Young Joseph escaped this time, although he was caught by a mother-and-daughter team a few years later.*

There is also, when he was travelling with the threshing plant, the account of a farmer's daughter who was smitten with him to the daring extent of suggesting unchaperoned meetings. Though Joe's vanity was flattered he remained Joseph indeed, and heard no more of the potential Mrs Potiphar until years later when he met a man from her district. She was then living up country, having married a Celt with a name which is used for the galoot connected with the horse Cleopatra in *Such is Life*. 'She said she knew you,' observed the man to Joe. 'Oh, what did she say about me?' inquired Joe, recalling the past. 'Well, she said you were the biggest fool she ever met.'

Miles Franklin, *Joseph Furphy: The Legend of a Man and His Work*, p. 20.

From Shakespeare to Whitman

The country schoolteacher Kate Baker became a fan of Furphy, fascinated by his gift of the gab and the range of his erudition.

The rain had made the October day chilly and after tea the circle round the ample kitchen fireplace consisted of father, mother, Joseph, Amy Vaughan and myself — Granny Furphy seated next to her beloved son, would now and then take a few whiffs from his pipe with the most beautiful expression I have ever seen on a woman's face. Her cup of love was full.

The talk was at first desultory — books, Bret Harte's poetry and his parodies. Joseph Furphy said how easy it was to parody Bret Harte and Walt Whitman, giving as an example of the latter — 'Oh! my fisherman with broad flat feet, my fisherman!' Then Joseph Furphy launched out on Shakespeare, developing a theory on the play *Othello* and the character of Desdemona, new to me, which later I worked out for myself.

The two days of his visit linger in my memory. I had, of course, heard fine speakers — the best — teachers, inspectors, professors, lecturers — these were always *ex cathedra*. But none spoke like Joseph Furphy. Like the householder in the parable, he brought out of his treasury things new and old, and with his lambent wit and mellow philosophy, flashed new light on hidden or obscure subjects. He had much the same style in speaking as in writing, discursive, breaking off into side issues, but ever returning to the main topic. At the time of meeting him I compared him in my mind to the gentle scholar in Longfellow's *Tales of a Wayside Inn*. Later, knowing him more perfectly, I likened him to Leonardo da Vinci … Joseph Furphy was no mere scholiast. He took nothing on authority. He dug, he delved, he probed, he tested, he experimented. To whatever science or art Joseph Furphy applied himself, in that he would excel.

The family dropped off to bed one by one. As Granny bade good night she said to Joseph and me: 'Make yourselves a cup of tea and finish your talk.' I made the tea and Joseph talked on till nearly 1 a.m.

He talked and talked, and I listened and questioned. In this opportunity to talk to a congenial listener he seemed like a thirsty man at a spring of cool water deeply quenching his thirst.

Next morning I was going in to breakfast when I met Joseph Furphy vigorously towelling his face. He had plunged his head into the cold water in a basin on a bench outside the kitchen door. 'You like to mortify the flesh, Mr Furphy,' I remarked. He laughed, but my remark made the occasion, at breakfast, for a dissertation on the origin of the cult of asceticism, which Joseph Furphy declared was against the teachings of Christ.

Miles Franklin, *Joseph Furphy: The Legend of a Man and His Work*, p. 9.

King of the kids

A combination of gentleness and humorous creativity marked Furphy out as a child at heart.

Joseph Furphy had a most engaging way with children. He would take a turnip or potato or a piece of soap and cut out quaint animals and houses &c., keeping up a whimsical conversation with the 'little fellows' — girls included in the term — as he worked. That was a habit of his. He would say to my brothers when they were taking him to see some sight, 'Well, what about these chaps?' — the 'chaps' being a group of girls. The chaps were pleased with the implied equality. Children responded to his charm and were always about him like bees round a blossom.

Miles Franklin, *Joseph Furphy: The Legend of a Man and His Work*, p. 41.

What's in a name

Furphy, who wrote as Tom Collins, was excessively fond of noms de plume, nicknames, masks, circumlocutions, and all manner of digressions. Your shy man is often your most elaborate stylist, as Tom Collins might well have said. In contact with the tougher sex, Furphy's demeanour was recessive to a fault. Only in his maturity was he able to form friendships with women: notably with Kate Baker and Miles Franklin, both ardent admirers and strenuous nationalists.

One of Furphy's idiosyncrasies was to subscribe himself in a variety of styles and to address his correspondents by names that he coined for them. His mother remained 'Dear Mam' except on rare occasions, but to her he signed himself in various terms: 'Prof.', 'Prodigal', 'Tatta, Prodigal', 'Very Rev. T. Collins', 'T. Collins, Esq.', 'Love to All, Riotous liver, Joe Furphy', or 'Your thriftless son (will that do?) Joe Furphy'; also 'Your affectionate son'. When he was revising *Rigby's Romance* he wrote 'Your plodding son'. His whimsical humour is in 'Riotous liver' and 'Prodigal' — two adjectives as wide of reality as the descriptions he made up for Misses Drewitt and Baker.

He would address Kate Baker formally as 'Dear Miss Baker', and through that to 'Baker of the Guards', or 'My Poor Child', 'MPC', 'MP¢', 'MP', and 'M', 'K', or 'Generalissimo'; and he would conclude 'for Australia' or 'Good night and benison'. Cathels was anything from 'Dear

Cathels' to 'My dear Fellow-squirmer', 'My Very Dear Friend', 'My dear Neglected and Neglecting Friend', 'My dear Fellow-Cynic', or 'Camarado'. To Cathels he subscribed himself with diversity, 'Your Old Man of the Sea', 'Your valley-de-sham', 'Yours in rustic simplicity', 'Your insolvent debtor', or 'Your most sincere friend', or 'Your fellow worm'.

Miles Franklin was 'The Tenth Muse' and to her he sometimes signed himself 'One of ten thousand Port Phillipers who are proud of you'. To A. G. Stephens he was 'Yours in the bond of iniquity' or 'in the hope of Australian literature'. The *Bulletin* varied from 'the immoral red rag', 'the heathen rag of George Street', or the 'Amalekite organ', to 'the invaluable B.', or the 'Washingtonian journal'.

Miles Franklin, *Joseph Furphy: The Legend of a Man and His Work*, pp. 20–1.

How many factors

The geometrical autodidact will always find room to construct a case …

Otto Brandon, Secretary of the Mechanics Institute in Shepparton, and his wife were retired actors. Owing to some temporary embarrassments Brandon shot himself dead. The distracted wife hurried to Melbourne to consult a spiritualistic medium and on her return begged Furphy's assistance. Every Sunday evening for three months Furphy, Mrs Brandon and one of her sons held a fruitless seance. Then began results, and Furphy wrote Cathels that he was finding mental recreation in threshing out the question. He argued that if there were three factors in the case 'the circle, the table and Something Else, it is a true science: if only two factors, it is merely a study in psychology'.

Miles Franklin, *Joseph Furphy: The Legend of a Man and His Work*, p. 123.

A young woman of talent

... and to build upon a disciple, in this case the faithful Kate Baker.

Furphy expressed himself in terms of such enthusiasm for her gifts and had such high expectations of her that she was embarrassed. He considered her literary attainments unrivalled, and told her that she reminded him of himself, of Marcus Aurelius, and also of Dean Swift and Daniel Defoe. The young woman struggling for self-support as well as for self-realization, with no encouragement for creative literary work, felt herself already too heavily handicapped by advanced political and other ideas; and to be likened to such heavy-weights frightened her into silence. One point she remembers is that Furphy insisted she would be a great man if she would only learn to hate.

Miles Franklin, *Joseph Furphy: The Legend of a Man and His Work*, p. 124.

Alas, poor skull!

Marcus Clarke (1846–81), a close schoolboy friend of Gerard Manley Hopkins, arrived in Melbourne in 1863 and rapidly established himself as a classy journalist and a sparkling figure on the literary scene. The huff recorded here did not last for long. Amazingly versatile and energetic, he more or less invented Australian literature, and coined the descriptive phrase 'weird melancholy'.

Clarke, who had a taste for black humour, borrowed a skull from Dr Patrick Moloney, then an intern at the Melbourne Hospital, and stuck a churchwarden pipe in its teeth as a reminder of the members' mortality. The first question was to find a name, and the members argued over a short list into the small hours of the morning. Clarke wanted the club to be called the Golgotha, and he was supported by Gordon, Henry Kendall and J. J. Shillinglaw, but their humour was too grim for the majority, and the club became the Yorick. Clarke left in a huff, taking his skull with him, and gave it to the management of the Theatre Royal, where it was used as the remains of poor Yorick by the celebrated tragic actor Walter Montgomery.

Geoffrey Hutton, *Adam Lindsay Gordon: The Man and the Myth*, p. 147.

The boy nuisance

As well as writing numerous works in many genres, Clarke still had time for squabbles at the club. He died young, worn out by literature.

The first Suggestions and Complaints book shows that the original Yorickers had some quarrelsome members, and none more so than the honorary secretary, Marcus Clarke. Because of his habit of rebuking members for misuse of grammar he acquired the name of the 'boy nuisance' and, although a member of the committee, he wrote a complaint asking why the club bought only one copy of his magazine, the *Colonial Monthly*. Thus, he added, 'five members are deprived of the pleasure and benefit of reading it.' The committee considered that one copy was sufficient. Clarke engaged in scratching contests with other members in the suggestions column, and when a more pacific clubman wrote a note asking members to keep their tempers, Clarke scribbled underneath that some of their tempers were 'not worth keeping'.

Geoffrey Hutton, *Adam Lindsay Gordon: The Man and the Myth*, p. 153.

One of Burns's heirs

This eccentric anecdote, largely couched in Standard Habbie, will serve as one illustration of what Les Murray has called 'The Bonnie Disproportion' in Australian letters. This Scottish demeanour appears to have made itself felt as far north as Rockhampton.

A Scotsman in Rockhampton, having been invited to attend the last Caledonian gathering at Warwick (Q.), on Boxing Day, sent his apology for absence in the following form:

BLYTHE

'Kind sir, I have received your letter,
And in the invitation matter,
Again I count myself your debtor;
    You are sae friendly,
Vexed am I, I can do nocht better —
    Thank you kindly.

Blythe could I be, to join your crew,
And wi' a quaigh o' mountain dew,
In social fashion wet my mou',
    And join the chorus
About the malt that Willie brew
    In tones stentorious.

But, ochance! this awfu' drouth —
That is in everybody's mouth,
I'm glad its no so bad doon south —
    Bears on us sairly;
O' misery we hae sic rowth
    Its dang us fairly.

Even my muse, puir silly thing,
She winna let me imp my wing,
And like a wee Cock Robin sing,

When things are wizened;
But yammerin' greets — the bonnie spring
    O' verse is gysened.

When Boxing Day comes roun' about
Or Cookaburras 'gin to shout,
May there be seen a blythsome rout,
    Wendin' your way,
O' winsome queans, and laddies stout
    To spend this day.

Settin' defiance to the clime,
Oh may they hae a happy time,
Not to be told in prose or rhyme
    Fu' crouse and cheery;
Till Auld Langsyne they canty chime,
    Tho tired an' weary.

And when around the social board
The barley bree is freely poured,
When rousin' toasts are loudly shared,
    Wi' rapturous glee;
Let 'Absent Freens', be not ignored,
    Keep mind o' me.

So fare ye weel, may gude attend ye,
May Providence, rich blessings send ye,
And frae misfortunes mony, fend ye
    In a time comin':
Sound wit and gear in plenty lend ye
    To keep ye hummin'.'

George Wallace Crabbe, *Scottish History, Songs and Lore*, pp. 127–8.

Imaginitis writ small

The world of letters certainly knocked people about in the nine-teenth century. J.F. Archibald (1856–1919: the initials came in time to stand for Jules François) was co-founder of the incomparable Bulletin *and later editor of* The Lone Hand. *He suffered a breakdown in 1906. As an editor, he stands behind the rise of Lawson and Paterson.*

It was an idyllic picture of health, productivity and rightness, written down in his own defence. He then gives his own version of the attack: it is a most precise account, with verbatim quote and incident detailed with as much care as he had put, more than twenty-five years earlier, into the reports of other men's executions. This was his own.

> One night I was at a table in the private sitting-room where I sat revising printed proofs; the typewriter at the other side of the table, when there a tap at the door and the face of my physician peered in. 'Hello doctor,' said I, 'delighted to see you — you are indeed a good fellow to have come so far. Sit down and have a cigar.'

The doctor — the one who had been thought to hint at syphilis and had diagnosed 'imaginitis' — requests the typist to withdraw, 'as he desired a private conversation'.

> 'I came here at the request of yr partner and am sorry to find you taking it out of yrself like this. You remember what I told you about night-work?'
> 'I forget nothing' I replied, 'but work agrees with me both by day and by night, if I knock off at a reasonable hour. When you came I was just finishing a proof and preparing to talk with some people in the corridor. Come & have a yarn with them. I will introduce you to a delightful girl from New Zealand who was out with us in the motor to-day and walked our legs off

during the return journey. She is a regular little horse.' Than which you can give no higher praise to any woman.

But he said no — it would be better for me to go to bed.

'Look here, doctor, I am off to the corridor. I hate to be interrupted. I thought we were going to have a friendly talk.'

'So I hope we are' he replied, 'but this you know is a very serious matter.'

'What is a serious matter? Please don't speak in enigmas. Talk right straight to me — I'm not afraid.'

'Well, I don't like to alarm you, my friend' he continued, 'but there are doctors in Sydney ready to certify to yr insanity and I have come here expressly to bring you away from this feverish work,' and

'Insanity!' I exclaimed derisively, 'and pray on what grounds am I considered insane?'

'Well', he answered with some hesitation, 'you have bn acting very strangely of late.'

'In what respect?' I demanded — 'tell me — I am mightily amused and would like to hear.'

'Well, for instance you have bn writing cheques for big amounts on little scraps of paper instead of on regular bank-forms.'

'My bank-forms have run out.'

Sylvia Lawson, *The Archibald Paradox*, pp. 224–5.

In vino veritas

Irishman Victor Daley (1858–1905) might be said to have brought the Celtic Twilight to Australia. He became a notable figure in Sydney bohemia.

Daley had the best of it. If his feet were in the gutter, his head was in the stars.

Yet I would venture a paradox [wrote Stephens]: Daley was respectable too. Not with the Respectability that is a capital crime; yet 'respectable'. He had an instinct for conventional decency, and abode by conventional canons. He shrank from foul or evil language, from gross stories, from violence of any kind — physically shrank and felt a physical nausea when the offence was serious. Yet often he risked such offence; for he hated solitude, was eminently sociable, and when he could not be sociable with somebody he was social with everybody. Dull souls sought him eagerly for diversion: 'I'm entertained at dinner and provide the entertainment,' he said quite truly. Part of his business in life was to exchange things spiritual for things material or spiritual; but he did not invariably admire his cohort of admirers. I found him once in the street, very sick, very pale. 'It wasn't the drink,' he said; 'it was the company.'

Vance Palmer (ed.), *A.G. Stephens: His Life and Work*, pp. 192–3.

Hannibal's cuppa

Daley, who also wrote as 'Creeve Roe', was both a lyric poet and a writer of radical verse. Tea was not what he drank in the evenings.

Victor Daley with his Saturday morning verses — three stanzas written overnight, three before breakfast, and three on the office counter. Daley's mind matched my own; we judged and valued by the standard of a similar taste; and the marketing was keen. So poetry was bought and sold subtly, weighed in the balance against silver, rarely gold, with seldom a difference in our scales. And still I can hear Daley muttering: 'I had to finish it here — didn't get a cup of tea when I woke up — I am no good in the morning without a cup of tea. I say to myself, "You poor creature! Did Hannibal have a cup of tea? Did Napoleon have a cup of tea?" No use!'

Vance Palmer (ed.), *A.G. Stephens: His Life and Work*, p. 27.

Sauce for the gander

It was typical of Randolph Bedford (1868–1941) to pick up the best stories. The goose tale is particularly light and charming. 'Cupid Quinn' was to become a New South Wales MP.

And then I met Victor Daley, and changed hero worship from Hammond. Victor knew 'the lot austere'. He wrote such things as 'The Rajah's Daughter', and a 'Sunset Phantasy', in a little old house in Abbotsford, almost quite unfurnished. Handsome Paddy Quinn, 'Cupid Quinn', Daley, Tom Durkin the artist, and I, sat in Daley's wilderness of a garden, watching foreign geese stringing thro' the broken fence to steal Daley's grass. Quinn watched the geese, and said, 'Not asking us to dinner, Victor?'

'There's not any dinner to speak of, Paddy.'

Quinn picked up a stone and said, 'It's an outrage, and I find that gander guilty of piracy.'

Saying which, he threw the stone and killed the gander.

That night we ate the gander, standing up and with our loins girded as the Israelites ate the first passover, because Daley had but two chairs.

Randolph Bedford, *Naught to Thirty-three*, p. 124.

Leaving Lolita

Havelock Ellis (1859–1939) was, as Muriel Spark would say, famous for sex. As a young man he came to Australia and spent four years teaching in a bush school at Sparkes Creek.

December 26th 1876

I have left Carcoar for good with a good deal of regret, though I should not care to stay there any longer. It has certainly been as agreeable a year as any I remember to have spent these last six years — and a very quiet, placid twelve months. 'I shall miss you' said Mr Platt, 'though we've not had much to say to each other.' And I, too, felt that I should miss a certain little face, and the laughing smile, and the roguish twinkle of the merry eyes and the irrepressible little tongue which has not yet learnt restraint. As I squeezed the warm little hand which had brought my plate of strawberries every day for the past three weeks, I longed to bend my lips. But this will never do. It was only today I was congratulating myself on possessing something of the Castilian faculty of silence; but (I never did) [Later note by H.E]. I shall rival Rousseau's confessions soon if I go on at this rate, though if M. Lallemand be correct in his supposition respecting the malady of that unfortunate man, perhaps that would not be surprising. Dear little Minnie. I shall not easily forget you. I shall see you, I hope, before I leave Australia though then perhaps, all that so pleased me will have fled — the childish coquetry, the struggle between the free romping nature of the child and the thoughtful consideration and reserve of the woman — when the charm of these has vanished, the result may perchance be a plain commonplace girl.

Yesterday was Christmas Day, my second in Australia …

Geoffrey Dutton, *Kanga Creek: Havelock Ellis in Australia*, p. 98.

Pissing on the nardoo

The saucy Miles Franklin has a swing here, first at the Irish-born 'Kabbarli', Daisy Bates (1859–1951), and then at poet Mary Gilmore (1864–1962), for their proclaimed closeness to Aboriginal culture. Both survived into their nineties, however; they must have got something right.

Wonders will never cease, Mary Gilmore got me on the telephone recently for a long call. It was about Daisy Bates, she was afraid I was going to join the boosting racket. Not on your tintype said I, that is a Catholic ramp. I knew it instantly when my butcher, who is not a reader, held forth about what a wonder Daisy was. He'd had word or a whiff of wind from the right direction. I leave Daisy to Prof Elkin et al. I never thought there was any sense in the way she went about out-ginning the gins without picking up anything deeply knowledgeable. Mary said that Ernestine Hill had ghosted Daisy's book, and Daisy took her name off it in the proof reading. I chuckled in the whiskers I haven't got, for leading journalists of whom I had no knowledge once called me up to tell me of Ernestine's capers for fear I might be dazzled by her, but she has made too much a mush of my beloved Flinders for me to go off on that tack. And the real fun of the thing is that even Mary's friends apologise for her Black fellow lore which is idealised fairy-tale stuff. For instance her yarns that because she was a delicate child her parents gave her to the blacks to nurture by their so-much-better health rules for dragging up infants. And the other about the blacks knowing the uses of ammonia in agriculture because when they planted out nardoo they got the little boys to wee-wee on it. Very funny. Wonder what they are telephoning behind my back.

Miles Franklin to Katharine Susannah Prichard, 25 May 1951, in Carole Ferrier (ed.), *As Good as a Yarn with You: Letters Between Miles Franklin, Katharine Susannah Prichard, Jean Devanny, Marjorie Barnard, Flora Eldershaw and Eleanor Dark,* p. 271.

A dashing air

Many writers have had a good start reciting poems in class, or trying to, as in this case.

When her turn came to recite the poem, 'The Sluggard' (the previous evening's homework), her memory, usually so reliable, suddenly deserted her. Dame Mary recalled the incident brilliantly in her childhood memoirs:

However I made a dash at it and began brightly 'Tis the voice of the Sluggard, I heard him complain You have waked me too soon, let me slumber again,' I carried those two lines through so well that Miss Galloway stopped me and said, 'You needn't say any more. I see you know it'. I sat down with perspiration running down my knees. It was the solitary occasion when an air of dash carried me through.

W.H. Wilde, *Courage a Grace: A Biography of Dame Mary Gilmore*, p. 38.

Her face was not her fortune

To be a character is not always to be a beauty, as Mary Cameron was well — if ruefully — aware.

I tried to get a photo taken for you. I took a photo to the photog. and asked to be taken 'Like that' (pose). He took me the other way and I came out with a face like a camel's upper lip. I objected, pointing out I had bared the lofty forehead wanting only a glimpse not a whole landscape view of it. He retorted with frightful emphasis — '*Mrs Gilmore!* If you want a pretty picture *I can't do it*. I can only take *likenesses*'.

W.H. Wilde, *Courage a Grace: A Biography of Dame Mary Gilmore*, p. 140.

Up country

Unlike many writers of the fabled 1890s, Mary Gilmore knew the bush well, having grown up in rural New South Wales and later lived back of Woop Woop, in western Victoria, not to mention her experience of the bizarre New Australia community in Paraguay.

I lived here in a constant state of shock and horror. Once saved a woman from getting her head smashed open when her lunatic husband got his gun to shoot me. I looked him down.

W.H. Wilde, *Courage a Grace: A Biography of Dame Mary Gilmore*, p. 50.

Johnson and the jackdaw

Beauty or not, Mary Gilmore dwelt among portraits of herself, as the dashing Hugh McCrae found when he came to visit her in her nest above Kings Cross.

A week ago, I visited Mary Gilmore, at her Darlinghurst flat … A cross between Doctor Johnson and the Jackdaw of Rheims: stubborn, curiously informed; and a collector of good stuff accidentally mixed with a great deal of rubbish. I don't mean manuscripts, but sticks and stones, the hair of 'Slippery Charlie', etc.

She has six or seven portraits of herself ranged along the wall, which she faces bravely, without any bandage over her eyes, all the while she stops at home.

I said '*This* one ought to be hung in the Gallery.' She said, 'If you think so, I'll present it to the Gallery.' Then she told me that Rayner Hoff was modelling her head: 'I daren't look! So far, I've only seen the back of one ear'; but, afterwards, she forgot; and emoted over the fact that R.H. had managed to cram the lineaments of all her ancestors into her face! (This makes me resolve not to go near Rayner until I can be quite certain he hasn't any Gilmore thingummies left.)

To finish off, Mary gave me an annotated copy of Neilson's *Heart of Spring*; and kissed me TWICE!!

Robert D. FitzGerald (ed.), *The Letters of Hugh McCrae*, p. 100.

Not effing potatoes

Gilmore had a great ear for the epiphanies of vernacular Australia, the more so when these were intensified by World War II.

A few days after that last outburst Mary called at the Lyceum Club where she found a precious gift (in those days of short-ages) awaiting her, a bag of potatoes from her friend, Captain

Fewen, who was a cousin of Winston Churchill. As the driver carried the potatoes to the taxi for her she informed him, somewhat proudly, that they had been grown by Churchill's cousin. The taxi driver swore what Mary said 'was a great oath', indicating that it was not — potatoes that Australia wanted from Churchill but — planes.

W.H. Wilde, *Courage a Grace: A Biography of Dame Mary Gilmore*, p. 357.

A fundamental question

Among the writers whom she befriended was the novelist Ruth Park, nearly sixty years her junior.

Ruth Park's friendship with Mary developed from a letter that Mary wrote to her (15 January 1947) deploring her use of the word 'bottom' when referring to males, Mary preferring 'backside', which she believed was the proper masculine word. In the same letter she compared Ruth Park with Dickens, but whereas Dickens moved his pieces by hand, meticulously and deliberately, she (Park) was always 'in the midst of a melee and, in a way, of it'.

W.H. Wilde, *Courage a Grace: A Biography of Dame Mary Gilmore*, p. 392.

The lineaments of poverty

William Dobell's 1957 portrait of Mary Gilmore was striking, hieratic, baroque: it certainly generated a great deal of public controversy, some viewers being quite appalled by it. On the other hand, Bernard Smith has written of the picture's 'air of spiritual grandeur' and 'queenly magnificence'.

An amusing anecdote about the portrait was told to the author by Walter Benson of Canterbury, Melbourne, at a chance meeting at the Mitchell Library's Dame Mary

Gilmore exhibition for Beverley Dunn's Sydney season of 'To Botany Bay on a Bondi tram' (February–March 1987). Mr Benson's elderly grandmother, Annie Wood, then living in West Wyalong, NSW, was reading a newspaper article on poverty in India. Alongside the article was a photo of Mary's portrait. The not-so-sharp sighted old lady thought the portrait was an illustration of the poverty article — 'Isn't it terrible how these poor Indians have suffered. Look at that poor old woman!' Another good story about the portrait concerns R.D. FitzGerald's reaction to it. Having viewed it for the first time at the Gallery, he and his wife hurried off to Kings Cross to 'see the original'. He is reported to have said, 'The portrait's like you, Mary, but thank God you're not like the portrait.'

W.H. Wilde, *Courage a Grace: A Biography of Dame Mary Gilmore*, p. 450, footnote.

The democratic queen

When Gilmore died at the age of 98, a state funeral wound through the streets of her adopted Sydney.

As the escort of police motor cyclists led the grey, flower-laden hearse and its stately procession along Macquarie Street, a small boy, standing by his mother's side in the crowd, tugged at her sleeve, and in clear tones that carried to the people around him, summed up his sense of wonder at the whole solemn spectacle with the question, 'Was she a Queen, or something?'

W. H. Wilde, *Courage a Grace: A Biography of Dame Mary Gilmore*, p. 4.

A Ruddy holiday

Rudyard Kipling (1865–1936) visited Australia and even stayed at Lorne, but without surfing there.

The leading paper offered me the most distinguished honour of describing the Melbourne Cup, but I had reported races before and knew it was not in my line. I was more interested in the middle-aged men who had spent their lives making or managing the land. They were direct of speech among each other, and talked a political slang new to me. One learned, as one always does, more from what they said to each other or took for granted in their talk, than one could have got at from a hundred questions. And on a warm night I attended a Labour Congress, where labour debated whether some much-needed life-boats should be allowed to be ordered from England, or whether the order should be postponed till life-boats could be built in Australia under labour direction at labour prices.

Rudyard Kipling, *Something of Myself, and other Autobiographical Writings*,
p. 58.

We are on the side of life

Scots-born playwright Louis Esson (1879–1943) saw in the work of the Abbey Theatre, Dublin, a possible model for the development of Australian drama. The Irish dramatist J.M. Synge (1871–1909) told Esson that we should have wonderful material for dramatic writing in Australia, with all those shepherds going mad in lonely huts.

I must get my boasting over, though it is necessary to state it. Yeats asked me up to see him and put me up for the night. I landed late afternoon, and he talked for an hour on my plays, theories, etc., before dinner. At dinner he told good stories.

After that we talked till past midnight. Next morning he took me into his study, and he was very sympathetic. I then took a walk round the town, had lunch with them, and returned.

He thought more of my little plays than I could possibly have dared to hope. He thought the dialogue excellent, the 'atmosphere' as suggestive as could be. I told him I didn't think much of myself as a 'plotter', but he said the four little plots were perfect. The only adverse criticism made was that near the end of *The Woman-Tamer* the woman might have pretended to relax to make the end more surprising. He said he thought the element of surprise was necessary in comedy, but not in tragedy. (He doesn't mean 'surprise' in the American magazine-editor's sense.) On the whole, he thought, I might do my best things in tragedy. There it doesn't matter if the end is foreseen, the emotion should carry the interest through. He thought success would come to me some day, though I don't believe that. I mention this not to skite, but to indicate the principle of sound literature.

Plays on really national themes, he said (not 'popular plays' in the ordinary sense) — and this is his important principle — help to *build a nation* in the spiritual sense; while the other type of play, so-called intellectual drama, abstract and cosmopolitan — Galsworthy, Bennett, etc., and the husband, wife, lover triangle (not on moral, but artistic grounds) will 'shatter a nation'. That is what our scholars fail to realize. Their arguments look good on the surface, rather difficult to meet sometimes, though they are quite unsound. We are on the side of life, and they ('they' means too many people in Melbourne) are on the side of death and desolation. And yet most people would be against us.

He thought we ought to get the theatre going, no matter how small. A good 50 enthusiasts are better than 500 indifferents. You must see Stewart Macky about this. He has a sympathetic philosophical personality. He will feel what is right. The plays we give should all be national. Academics will say we haven't got them. Well, we've got to get them: they'll never get them or anything else. At the beginning of the Abbey Theatre Miss Horniman wanted to do, with the local plays, the European masterpieces. That is what our repertory theatres have tried to do. Yeats said he wavered, but that 'inquiring man', Mr Synge, objected, and Irish drama was saved. *'A theatre like that,'* said Synge, *'never creates anything'*. Isn't that true? What did MacMahon create? What did Hilda's University Society that did Shaw, Galsworthy, etc., create? They should have discovered me for a start, but they didn't. What has Adelaide ever done, with all its list of plays?

The same applies to the writing of novels.

Stewart's English plays, if he does them, are all in vain. The local play, he [Yeats] says, will also produce a better type of acting; there are no bad models to imitate.

If Stewart's show is still going he'd better get a definite policy to begin with. A small sheet, stating some definite aims, needs to be drawn up. I would anticipate a startling success, not a failure, if some energy were put into the movement. But there must be no bloody lectures about it. They darken counsel. Also B. or people like that mustn't say anything until they're asked.

Yeats said they had to kill the pompous literary humbugs for a start. Their idiom was objected to as not being English; they retorted by showing that the professors couldn't write at all. It is really the same battle; it always is.

I wish I could give you the faintest suggestion of his intellectual power, the strongest I've ever met, even apart from his imaginative insight, vast erudition, and wonderful humour. In the midst of some elaborate discussion he'll drop in an outrageous story, but it always has an application and is not given for its own sake.

Among subjects touched on were early Egyptian art, Blake, Shelley, Browning and Balzac, whom he regarded as great medieval minds, all comprehensive and wise, as artists,

though they were futile, especially Balzac, in life; professional poets, George Moore's art criticism (which I told him
taught me a lot, and he thought they were Moore's best written books), sayings of Oscar Wilde, memories of William
Morris, Mrs Besant, some gorgeous stories of Dr Gogarty,
the great wit, Shakespeare, Ben Jonson's plays (when I mentioned the dialogue of Bartholomew Fair, Billingsgate made
classic, he said that play influenced Synge. Curiously enough,
I did think of Synge as I read some of Ben's speeches), a con-
tinuation of the Canterbury Tales, a remark on the phases of
Henry James (James the first, James the second, and the Old
Pretender), modern English poets, Tolstoy and the Saints,
Japan, the distinctive nationality of Australia — everything
deep, interesting, and all linked to his general philosophy of
art and life. That is only a meagre list. His chief theme, on
which he is writing a book (the book they told you about in
Dublin. What they said was true in one sense, but comically
exaggerated) is on unity of personality. He divides writers
into different classes — subjective, objective, half and
half, etc., the self — and the antithetical self — the writer
usually expressing his opposite, to realize the self. I could
explain all this fairly clearly, but it would take too long. Just
take it as a suggestion of something! Yeats seems to me to
have a mind as clear and penetrating as that of an old school-
man. There are a lot of things I'd like to tell you. Here are
the last two.

1. Why, in a Catholic country like Ireland, have most of the
   writers been Protestant? He said it was simply education. In the age of Huxley, etc., the Catholic Church had
   to be on the defensive. But now that age is passed; and
   probably in the future the Catholic education will be better than the Protestant, and the Catholics produce the
   best writers.

2. Is Australia a race yet? Could it develop a nationality in a
   hundred years? He said yes. It was so in Iceland. Iceland
   produced its heroes, conscious of their nationality,

though they had been on the island for a less time than we have been in Australia.

Louis Esson to Vance Palmer, November 1920, in *The Writer in Australia*
(ed. John Barnes), pp. 191–4.

Not quite a lady-killer

A.G. Stephens (1865–1933) was the dominant critic of his time, known as 'The Rhadamanthus of the Red Page' for his éclat on the Bulletin. *It was he who asked, 'Is there a single Australian who could pass an examination in Huysmans, Maeterlinck or Verhaeren?' This task might still find most of us wanting. Manly, bearded and well photographed, he had his weaker side, as this tale suggests.*

A.G. had devised his own stock formula of an approach to a woman. It implied a fluttered feminine in meek subjection to a dominant male, and I was given an account of it from a lady so approached. That was Eugenie Stone, who wrote the Melbourne Woman's Letter for the *Bulletin*. She was on a visit to Sydney; a big handsome girl even for those days, when big girls were the mode, and she dressed in its rich stylisms which emphasized an opulent femininity in breasts and bottoms. The *Bulletin* staff fell for her as one man, each member in turn taking her out to lunch or dinner. When it fell to A.G.'s turn for a lunch, he paraded her from the *Bulletin* as far as the Post Office in a state of paralytic speech-lessness. There only he got control of his vocal cords to exclaim[,] 'Why are you afraid of me?' Eugenie recounted this devastating assault by the male dominant with peals of raffish laughter.

Norman Lindsay, *Bohemians of the Bulletin*, p. 29.

A damp squib

Stephens could turn a good yarn or, better still, sketch a verbal portrait, as he does of this unidentified companion

So he is dead. Dead — and 'we shall see him no more until we meet with him beyond the mountains.'

Once I had the privilege of his conversation, once only. It was a dinner at the Trocadero — an excessive London restaurant that is possibly more familiar than fashionable. A notable London journalist had made his escape. He had fulfilled the London journalist's dream of becoming an advertising representative, and had been bought for a high figure by a Tobacco Trust. (It seems but yesterday, yet already these reminiscences are ancient; for the Tobacco Trust soon ended its ostensible career, and the advertising representative donned again his journalistic shackles, though in lighter metal.)

But in my London time he had escaped, and he was a good fellow, and he gave a dinner of celebration to half-a-dozen chosen comrades. His kindness added an invitation to me — the stranger, the sojourner. 'And', confided one of the comrades, 'don't miss it whatever you do! Charlie — will be there — the wittiest man in London! He's the one surviving journalist of the old school; he knew Charles Dickens. But Dickens hasn't his humour — no, in spite of reputation. I tell you that man has said the funniest things! Every paper in London knows him. There's not one that wouldn't be glad to have him on the staff if he would only stay with them. But he never will. He'll turn up in Fleet Street, after a week off. Nobody knows where he goes. Sit down anywhere and write an article that would make you die with laughing. But his writing is nothing: you must hear him talk. The things he says! just bubbles over with humour! He's getting old now, and shows it a bit. No wonder, after the life he's had! But there's nobody like him — nobody!'

I was duly astonished — and punctual. We sat down, half-a-dozen of us, to a private table, and waited for Charlie. Charlie was late. 'It's his way, you know,' volunteered somebody. 'He's a funny beggar. Never thinks of these things till the last moment!' So we waited, though the proprietor came up and greeted our host warmly, and suggested that the special dinner ordered was timed to a clock-tick. That could not be helped; we could not go on without Charlie. Everybody said what a good fellow he was — how during a generation his wit had pervaded London like garlic — like the subtle cook's garlic that is never tasted, scarcely recognised, yet gives the *plat* its crowning relish. Several guests tried to think of funny things that Charlie had said, but unhappily these had escaped their memory. So we sat around the table and waited — waited rather awkwardly. No one liked to tell a yarn or start a conversation. It seemed sacrilegious, somehow — as if it would have spoilt the flavour of Charlie. We waited and wondered what had kept him — 'good old Charlie!'

In a quarter of an hour the proprietor returned and whispered to our kindly host. The oysters were served and swallowed in a melancholy fashion; everyone was thinking of Charlie. Just then Charlie came in, looking red and flustered. Two or three of us were introduced; the rest welcomed him jovially. A whisper reached me: 'Be careful of him, will you, like a good chap? Something has put him out!' I was careful. The waiter cleared away our oysters and left a fresh plate before Charlie.

Charlie looked round with a discontented air. 'No rock-melon?' Our host was sorry: he had forgotten the rock-melon. 'You know I always eat a bit of rock-melon!' grumbled Charlie. 'Well, perhaps we could get some now —Waiter!' 'No!' said Charlie, and gulped his oysters, and sat brooding.

The fish came in. 'This fish is cold!' said Charlie: 'I hate cold fish!' 'I suppose they've muddled it while we were waiting,' suggested the host, timidly. Charlie grunted. He grunted afresh at every course, and glowered on us. Nothing pleased him. The wine passed round, and several times somebody attempted to start Charlie on a career of flashing anecdotes. We didn't venture to talk, for fear of disturbing Charlie and missing a good thing. Two guests whispered together, and one commenced, boldly, 'Do you remember that time with Archibald Forbes, Charlie, in the old Cheshire?' 'Yes, yes,' said Charlie; 'pass those olives, will you?'

Towards the end of dinner we gave up. Our host began a general conversation in the hope that Charlie might join in. He never joined in. When directly appealed to, he flung a contemptuous word at us. For the rest of the time he glowered.

Dinner ended rather sadly; and Charlie explained that he had an appointment, and left us at once. Somebody said, 'Poor old Charlie; he's often like that now; but when he's himself he's the wittiest man in London! Think of the things he has written! Remember that article he wrote about the Crystal Palace? or was it the Zoo? You remember that article, Jones? Devilishly funny, wasn't it?' Jones remembered devilishly funny articles by Charlie, and tried to remember enough to quote. Unfortunately nobody remembered enough to quote.

Vance Palmer (ed.), *A.G. Stephens: His Life and Work*, pp. 208–11.

Horses, horses, horses

There is an improperly close relationship between Australian literature and horses, particularly whenever 'Banjo' Paterson is in the offing. As Norman Lindsay notes, 'Steele Rudd' (Arthur Hoey Davis, 1868–1935) held simple views about horses and Wardour Street attitudes to prose style.

With the dinner over, 'Banjo' left us. He never did consort with any of our groups and none of us attempted to consort with him. Even when I got to know him fairly well, and that was only when I went riding with him occasionally, there was always a distance between easy exchanges. His departure from the dinner relieved it of tension, and we sat on till late over the wine, and there was a lot of noisy talk, in which Steele maintained his part as the reticent bushman. My brother Lionel, I may add, left with Paterson. At that time, Paterson was editing the *Evening News*, and Lionel was also on the staff of that paper, which *might* be held as an excuse for dropping our inferior mob in deference to the Boss.

When the party broke up, I got away with Steele, and we walked the silent streets till it was very late, which evidenced that Steele must have relaxed on his reticence. The discovery that I was a horse addict had a good deal to do with that, for I do remember that most of our talk had to do with horses. Of that talk, one item remains. Discussing colour as symptomatic of horse temperament, Steele said that all bushmen agree that the little brown horse was the most trustworthy, and that the ginger horse, the light chestnut, the most unreliable and bad-tempered.

But literature was not forgotten. Turning on me a slow smile, Steele said, 'You know, I'm beginning to get the hang of this writing business. In the past, supposing I was describing a picnic, I'd say, "Mrs So-and-so brought the cakes and Mrs So-and-so brought the sandwiches." But now I'd say, "Each guest brought the viands requisite for the occasion." '

Norman Lindsay, *Bohemians of the Bulletin*, p. 65.

Getting started ...

There are innumerable anecdotes about Henry Lawson (1867–1922) told by his old mates, his occasional drinking companions, and those from whom he tried to cadge a shilling. He got his start as a poet in the pages of Archibald's Bulletin, *that milch-cow of Australian writing.*

My mother started to publish *The Dawn*, in Phillip Street, then *The Young Idea* and *Young Australia*, which last was sacrificed in later years and is alive now I believe. Later on I edited and helped print, wrap and post a paper called *The Republican*, with William Keep, one time Tommy Walker's manager, and a sort of adopted brother of mine — but that was later on.

It was mostly house-painting now, and odd jobs about.

One wet night I was coming home through Hyde Park from working late on a job at Paddington. Rain and wind and swept boughs and sickly gaslights on the wet asphalt; and poles and scaffolding about in preparation for the Jubilee celebrations. I had sent a couple of attempts on the subject to the *Bulletin*, and had got encouragement in Answers to Correspondents. And now the idea of 'Sons of the South' or 'Song of the Republic' came. I wrote it and screwed up courage to go down to the *Bulletin* after hours, intending to drop the thing into the letter box, but just as I was about to do so, or rather making up my mind as to whether I'd shove it in or take it home, and have another look at the spelling and the dictionary, the door opened suddenly and a haggard woman stood there. And I shoved the thing into her hand and got away round the corner, feeling something like a person who had been nearly caught on the premises under suspicious circumstances and was not safe yet by any means.

I watched the Answers to Correspondents column as hundreds have watched it since — they'll understand. Here

is the reply: 'H.A.L.: Will publish your "Sons of the South".
You have in you good grit.'

I hadn't the courage to go near the *Bulletin* office again,
but used to lie awake at night and get up very early and slip
down to the nearest newsagent's on Thursday mornings, to
have a peep at the *Bulletin*, in fear and trembling and half
furtively as if the newsagent — another hard-life woman, by
the way — named Mrs Furlong, would guess my secret. At
last, sick with disappointment, I went to the office and saw
Mr Archibald, who seemed surprised, encouraged me a lot
and told me that they were holding the 'Song of a Republic'
over for a special occasion — Eight Hours Day.

Leonard Cronin (ed.), *Henry Lawson: Complete Works 1885–1900*, p. 34.

... *And married*

*Marriage was not one of Lawson's strong points. Bertha gives a
matter-of-fact account of their wedding.*

On 15 April he arrived early in the morning and begged me
to come to town and meet a dear friend of his. He said 'I
want you to look very very nice, so put on your wedding
dress to please me.' But I was horrified at the thought of
wearing my wedding dress before my wedding. However, we
finally agreed on my travelling dress — a green silk frock
with a brown hat wreathed in poppies!

We told Mrs Schaebel we'd be back by half-past three.
When we got to town Harry showed me another indignant
letter that he had received. He was very troubled and said
that he felt convinced that unless we married straightway, we
would be separated in the end. So he had arranged with
a clergyman to marry us privately that day, if only I was
willing. He showed me his special licence. But I told him that
it was impossible. Our wedding had been arranged, the
guests invited and all plans fixed for our Blue Mountain

honeymoon. In any case I thought Mrs Schaebel should be told. But Harry said we could be married and then go straight out and tell her. He was so afraid, in view of all the opposition, that something would come between us; he had a strong intuition that we might be parted. And loving him so dearly I felt that there was much truth in what he said and I consented. We went straight round to the clergyman's home and were married — a member of his family acting as a witness.

We started off afterwards for the Newtown tram, but Harry said no, we must go out in state in a cab as befitted the occasion — there were no taxis then. So we drove out to Newtown to find Mrs Schaebel very angry, because I was late. Harry bent down and kissed her and said, 'That doesn't matter, because she's my wife now. Here is our certificate.' Mrs Schaebel was most upset and asked him what she was to do about the bridesmaids and the guests. He said, 'Never mind, just say we are married.' She was very indignant, but because she was very fond of us both she forgave us in the end.

Bertha Lawson in *Henry Lawson by His Mates* (ed. B. Lawson and
J. le Gay Brereton), pp. 84–5.

Louisa

Henry's mother, Louisa Lawson (1848–1920), was a very strong figure in radical Sydney. Feminist, editor and publisher, she brought out his first book, Short Stories in Prose and Verse, *in 1894. Her Norwegian husband had long vanished from the scene, vanquished.*

I remember well when that book was issued. Lawson was on his way to the Public Library, with two samples which he intended to lodge there in accordance with the provisions of the Copyright Act, when he met me in George Street. 'Only one copy is really needed,' he explained, 'so you may as well have the odd one.' He was feeling very jubilant over that publication; 'but my mother's the hardest business man I ever met,' he said, with an appreciative grin.

J. le Gay Brereton in *Henry Lawson by His Mates* (ed. B. Lawson and J. le Gay Brereton), pp. 6–7.

The causes of brevity

Lawson's stint as a journalist in what he called Maoriland was brief. So, it would seem, were some of his reports.

It happened this way: a brewery and a butter factory were officially opened on the same day. As both were of paramount importance to the district, it was necessary that a reporter should attend each function. Baillie (our boss) 'decided' as part of a deep-laid scheme that I was to report the brewery, and Henry the butter factory. We left the office together bound for our respective jobs. There was, indeed, a sad look about Henry, although, up till now, he had given no hint as to the reason. We had only gone a little way when Lawson said: 'I think Baillie has made a mistake. I do not know too much about butter factories, and I don't think you know too much about breweries.' Being in the joke with Baillie, I agreed. We returned to the office to verify the order, stating that we were in doubt as to our respective jobs. Baillie replied: 'I thought I made it quite clear. You are to report the butter factory, and Henry the brewery. But, remember, I want the report for Wednesday's paper.' He had suspicions that something might go wrong. The brewery was opened with the usual speeches, and sampling of the amber-coloured product. Wednesday arrived, but there was no report, and no Henry.

On his return to the office Baillie said (in pretended wrath): 'I thought I told you I wanted the report for Wednesday's paper.' 'Quite true,' said Lawson, 'but as there are fifty-two Wednesdays in the year, you did not state which particular one.' When the report did appear, it illustrated brevity as the soul of wit, and was as follows: 'The Mangatainoka Brewery was opened one day this year. It was a gigantic success and ended in oblivion.'

Anthony Cashion in *Henry Lawson by His Mates* (ed. B. Lawson and J. le Gay Brereton), pp. 57–8.

Borax

Bertha Lawson plainly enjoyed telling this story about her tall, thin husband on a shopping expedition.

One day Harry went down to the village shop to get some borax for me to stiffen his old fashioned white starched shirts. Said the grocer, 'I'll send it up immediately, sir.' Harry leant his six feet of indignation over the counter, and, gazing down at the little man, said, 'Do you think I look delicate?' 'Well no, sir,' said the little man in surprise, 'though, perhaps, you don't look over-strong.' 'Well, do you think I look strong enough to carry half a pound of borax?'

Bertha Lawson in *Henry Lawson by His Mates* (ed. B. Lawson and J. le Gay Brereton), p. 113.

The tale of a stick

As lyricist Roderic Quinn makes clear, Lawson was an outstanding spinner of yarns, lightly embroidering the facts as he went on. This 1914 story of the stick that misbehaved shows him at his very best.

The stick was a friend's gift on the day the Big Trouble started in Europe. My friend said, as he handed it to me, 'I can't give you a sword, but take this and imagine it is one; at any rate, it will do as well as the best blade out of Castille to slay imaginary foes with.'

Being in a stickless condition, I accepted it with a salute, and he went away and bought himself another stick true to the type of that which he had given to me.

Thereafter, for many months that stick accompanied me, till contact with the hard pavements of the city wore its ferrule away, and ate into its hard wood. Having a crooked handle, wherewith to rest it on my arm, it was somewhat difficult to lose, and as it was just a plain, ordinary, valueless article no one would go to the trouble of stealing it.

So it stayed with me for a summer and a winter and an autumn, till Henry Lawson took a fancy to it. Why he should have taken a fancy to it goes beyond my wits to explain, seeing that it was nothing out of the way to inspire anyone to beg, borrow or steal.

One day while I sat writing in a newspaper office, he came along and silently appropriated it. I might have known from his noiselessness that something out of the ordinary was afoot, but, maybe, at the moment I was away in Europe slaying imaginary foes.

When I finished my writing and looked around and found my stick gone, I said, 'Lawson and no one else is the larcenist. Much goes to convict him. On a like occasion he walked off with my beloved pipe of carved bog-oak, but he won't get away with the stick — not if I know it; not unless I have read Sherlock Holmes in vain.'

Thereupon, seizing my hat, I set forth to sleuth Henry down. Although I knew his daily round of travel well, having been over it many and many a time with him, I failed on that afternoon and on many subsequent afternoons to track him. Yet, tantalizing me, ever and anon word would come to me that he had been seen here and there — at Angus and Robertson's perhaps, or at Tyrrell's, or at the offices of the *Sydney Mail* and *Australian Worker*. Wherever friends met him, they always saw him with my stick, and always saw him swinging it — swinging, swinging it always — as though to publish abroad his delight in possessing it. Now and again, when talking to mutual friends, he told them of how he had annexed it from me, and chuckling deeply, enlarged upon my wrathful pursuit of him.

Always, even to the end, with much of the boy in him, it was Lawson's delight to play tricks on his friends. Those who were not his friends, and who would not understand him, he treated with seriousness, but with his friends he took drollish liberties, expecting that they would make merry with him, even when the joke was against them, a thing which they seldom failed to do.

But to stick to the stick. I tired of pursuing it. I contented myself with its loss, comforting my soul with the thought that some day, when luck came my way, I would creep in on Lawson, as he had crept in on me, and steal my stolen stick back again. In the meantime, although fierce work was going forward on the frontiers of Europe, disarmed and powerless I was forced to refrain from slaying imaginary enemies.

Weeks passed, and then the hoped-for moment arrived. On a bright and breezy day, I met Lawson face to face.

'Henry,' I said sternly, 'where is it? Have you lost it?'

'What?' he replied; 'Lost what?'

'The stick,' I returned, still with sternness in my tones, 'the stick that I was told to imagine as a sword, and slay far-off enemies with.'

Deep down in Lawson's brown eyes rich humour dawned. 'Oh, the stick,' he said; 'oh yes. It's in the lock-up.'

'What do you mean?' I asked.

'It's all right; it's safe,' he chuckled; 'it's been arrested. It had dissolute ways with it,' he continued; 'didn't seem to have been taught to behave itself, and was too fond of being seen in public houses. Often when I was carrying it about with me, I felt that it would attract the attention of the police. It did in the end; last night, on its way to the Quay, it was arrested.'

Afterwards he told me how the stick came to be arrested. Chuckling, he said: 'Ever since I look a loan of it, I've been chasing you round and round town, so that I might return it to you, but I couldn't find you anywhere. I thought that, perhaps, you'd gone down to Ted Brady's place at Mallacoota, or were staying out with good old Fred Broomfield. Anyway, I got tired of looking for you in the end, and tired of the stick, too. It seemed to know too much; it seemed to have been in too many public houses for a sober fellow like me to be carrying round. If I went into a bar — it didn't matter what bar — the barmaid would say, 'Hang it there. It's often hung there before.' It was things like that that made me feel it wasn't a reputable stick; that in fact, it was a stick with a lurid and thirsty past. Failing to find you, I tried to give it away, but nobody would take it. Some said they didn't carry sticks. Others said they hated to be made conspicuous. Still others said that it wasn't fashioned out of good burning timber, and that, anyway, they used gas stoves at home. Do what I would, I couldn't get rid of it till last night. Starting out with me yesterday morning, goodness only knows on how many bars it hung by the crook during the day! Somehow or another, its environment seemed to affect it, seemed to make it merry, like a kid that wants to be swung round and round. And on my way to the Quay to catch the North Shore boat I swung it round and round. In a big crowd, when you're pressed for room, it's a good thing to have a stick, and swing it round and round. It makes people feel that it's safer to admire you from a distance. I got the stick to the Quay all right, but I didn't get it across the water. Near the ferry two policemen ranged up, one on each side of me. One laid hands on the stick, the other shook hands with me.

' "Get your boat, Henry," they said, "we'll take care of this." And they did. They took the stick away to the George

Street North lock-up. It didn't resist arrest — it went quietly — seemed to remember that it had been arrested before, and that it was better to go quietly.'

When his story was finished, I said, 'Well, disreputable and all as it may appear, I want that stick back.'

'In that case,' said Lawson, 'I'll go and bail it out.' And bail it out he did.

Roderic Quinn in *Henry Lawson by His Mates* (ed. B. Lawson and J. le Gay Brereton), pp. 184–8.

Small change

And he remembered what he heard in the streets of Sydney.

'Don't give me a penny, Mr Lawson,' a gutter tot one day shouted to him — the child world knew of his affliction — 'give me two 'aypunnies, 'cos if you give me a penny me muvver makes me put it in the gas meter.' And Lawson parted with his ill-afforded half-pence, according to instruction, and chuckled with a deep understanding of the tragedy of it all.

Vance Marshall in *Henry Lawson by His Mates* (ed. B. Lawson and J. le Gay Brereton), p. 284.

Beer for health

The latter years of Lawson's life were darkened by alcohol, deafness, and poverty. But even in those years, as his good friend Brady notes, a sense of humour flickered from time to time. Later Brady was to take Lawson away to his camp at Mallacoota Inlet, hoping to save him from urban damage.

I took him by the sleeve, looked into those brown spaniel eyes — there was a light in them I had never seen there before, the homing light — and said with a heartiness that I did not quite feel:

'You —— old sinner, you ought to have been dead long ago!'

'Why? Why did you think that?'

'The way you knock yourself about.'

He pretended to think it over very carefully — a way he had.

'Beer saved my life,' he said at last in a voice of simple conviction.

'Beer?'

'Yeth, Ted — *Beer.*'

'I cannot see how beer preserved your life.'

'Well,' he clinched, after taking a long pull, 'it *did*. If I'd been drinking hard tack I *would* have been dead long ago.'

E. J. Brady in *Henry Lawson by His Mates* (ed. B. Lawson and J. le Gay Brereton), pp. 132–3.

The double

English-born Brisbanite Will Lawson (1876–1957) got a good reception in Kiwiland as a result of being taken for Henry.

After we were introduced I was leaving the office, when Henry Lawson said, 'Wait for me outside.'

When he came out, we walked downstairs, and he laughed his dry, silent laugh and said,

'I just wanted to see the two Lawsons walking downstairs together.'

Some years later, when I was writing books about the west coast of New Zealand, my name became confused with that of Henry Lawson, and the newspapers and leading citizens made a big fuss wherever I arrived. I tried to explain, but it was useless. They insisted that I was the great

Australian writer. At one little village, the men had come in from miles around to meet me.

'Well, Henry,' one said, 'Here's jolly good health.'

'But I'm not Henry,' I said. 'I'm Will Lawson.'

'Well, here's to your brother then.'

'He is not my brother.'

'Well damn it, he ought to be. Well, here's to you, Bill.'

Will Lawson in *Henry Lawson by His Mates* (ed. B. Lawson and J. le Gay Brereton), pp. 266–7.

A cloth ear

Henry Lawson's sense of light self-mockery did not desert him, as in this quip about terrible eye-rhymes.

He never complained of his straitened circumstances or affliction of deafness. The latter, he said, had its advantages. It made men happier. It deadened the jarring notes.

'Awkward at times, though,' I still hear the soft, jesting voice. 'It doesn't give a rhymester a chance. Wrote some beautiful poetry on small-pox one day and then found it useless because I'd been making quarantine rhyme with steamship line at the end of each verse.'

Vance Marshall in *Henry Lawson by His Mates* (ed. B. Lawson and J. le Gay Brereton), p. 283.

A valedictory salute

Fred Broomfield's anecdote here serves as a dignified farewell to the lonely, deaf writer whose days of achievement were far behind him.

Ahead of us, some hundred yards or so, strode the tall, thin figure of one we both knew well. Presently he quitted the pavement, and, crossing the street, drew himself up before the electrically lit window of a cutler's shop on the opposite side. That man was Henry Lawson, the poetic voice of Australia. My wife, grasping my arm, said, ''Tis Henry Lawson!' I checked her. We waited, and watched. Hunter Street was deserted.

Instinctively I knew what had drawn Lawson to that window. The world was all agog in those days with a deed of wonderful heroism on the part of a boy (the sole survivor of the crew of a destroyer) a boy who had steered his vessel into the port of Dover, though he himself was wounded unto death. He reached the harbour just in time to breathe his last.

Photographs of the boat and of the lad were displayed in the cutler's window, and the electric lights were arranged to bring them into relief.

Thinking himself alone and totally unobserved, Henry drew his full, long length to a taut attention, and gravely came to the salute, holding his pose to the slow count of ten. Then he bared his head, and reverently bent it. Replacing his hat, he came to the salute and held it for an appreciable while; then, slowly, sadly, he turned and went his solitary way.

Fred J. Broomfield in *Henry Lawson by His Mates* (ed. B. Lawson and J. le Gay Brereton), pp. 74–5.

Political science

Jack Lindsay sums up aspects of the incomparable Randolph Bedford. On the other hand, Bedford sums up a good deal of parliamentary practice.

R.B. was a large genial journalist, story-teller, wildcat miner, and lots of other things; a personality from the spacious pre-war days, who had now become a member of the Queensland Legislative Council: a bulkily witty man, 'whose brain, polished in the shop of Minerva,' said the poet Hugh

McCrae, 'sent out sparks that made me wink'. Rather, perhaps, a generously overflowing beer tankard of a man, with a dangerous glint of mining shares in his right eye and only bluff humour in his left, whose sops of laughter made one amiably glow and whose slouch hat hid a rosy bald dome. Entering the House, he had shouted: 'Which way to the bribery department?'

Jack Lindsay, *Life Rarely Tells*, pp. 137–8.

Disposing of Rufus Dawes

By way of his gossip network, Bedford added a further strand to our understanding of Marcus Clarke and the different versions of His Natural Life.

I met portly lawyer Jim Maloney and his brother, Pat, the surgeon, and we talked much together. They had been close friends of Marcus Clarke, and they had the Irishman's love of literature and the drama. In fact, Jim dramatized life; the less excitable surgeon was the sonneteer. He wrote of Melbourne:

... the parallels of thy long streets
Like golden angels shining all arow.

In an evil hour he retired from the practice of a really eminent surgeon and went to London, where his daughter had married Boland, member of the House of Commons for Kerry. I met him in London about 1903 — a man dying for loss of occupation.

Jim told me the story of the altered ending of *His Natural Life*. Marcus Clarke had listened to his publisher, who required the usual and unnatural happy ending to the book.

'We were drinking and talking at Pat's surgery in Lonsdale Street,' said Jim Maloney, 'with Marcus Clarke and George Walstab, Tom Carrington, Grosvenor Brunster, Bob

Whitworth, and other village lads, who used ink and beer. At two in the morning Marcus and I went out to walk, past the gaol and into Carlton, and around by the University Gardens. I was determined that he should give the true artist's ending to the book, and I said to him, "Marcus, Rufus Dawes must die." '

'He pleaded for the life of Dawes as if Dawes were real. But we both thought of Dawes as real.'

' "I can't kill him, Jim," said Marcus. "He's been through the hell of Macquarie Harbour and Port Arthur, and now the heaven of his boyhood's home is waiting for him. His mother is waiting. I can't kill him." '

'And I said, "Marcus, it's cruelty to keep him alive. He's been through hell, you say. What is to cleanse him of the experience? He had grown away from manhood; his experience is indelible. In his old home he will be a stranger, alienated from decent life by the hell he has suffered. His innocence does not make him more capable of return — it makes him only more piteous. Give him a happy death. Let full recognition come in the last moment, and let him drown with Sylvia!"'

'And after an hour of argument, he agreed, and we came back to the studio at moonset ... I said to my brother, Pat, and the few chaps who had stayed, "We've killed Rufus Dawes." '

'And Pat said, "That's fine! Let's have a drink." '

Randolph Bedford, *Naught to Thirty-three*, pp. 231–3.

Stoushing with Meredith

Bedford provides a rattling good yarn about a fairly honest horse-duffer in gaol and his battle with George Meredith's elaborately wrought prose.

There was a bushman serving at Pentridge a sentence for horse stealing. He was a very honest man. He would not think of stealing a penny, but a horse was a different matter. A horse has four legs, and a back for a saddle, and a belly for the cinches; and this bushman could not help commandeering a horse when he needed to travel quickly. When he had tired the first horse, he turned it loose and commandeered another. For one demonstration of this method he was sentenced to three years' gaol.

While in prison he decided to 'improve' himself, reading all the prison library, if time permitted. He confessed that George Meredith's *The Egoist* had him guessing, but he said, 'I knew it was either me or the book for it. And I jist spit on my hands, and I said to that book, "Come on! we'll see which of us is the better man." I never let a book beat me.'

Randolph Bedford, *Naught to Thirty-three*, p. 160.

A sassy runt

Just once in a while Bedford met his match: with the impudent teenager Norman Lindsay, in this instance.

Bedford had decided to publish his verses in an illustrated edition and it was Lionel who intruded me on him as an illustrator. I recall him bringing Bedford to a little room I rented in Law Court Chambers, at the top of Little Bourke Street. I knew nothing of Bedford, or his established character as Randolph the Reckless, so I took over the job of illustrating his verses … as I did any other little jobs which came my way, such as commissions from printers for hair-restorer ads, or the labels on jam-tins or pickle-bottles, paid for at prices ranging from two-and-six to six shillings. The verses I set about illustrating were entitled 'The Ballad of Abel Tasman', and in the one illustration I perpetrated I went very wrong in my costume period, for I fitted out Tasman in Elizabethan trunk hose, a short cloak, and a velvet bonnet. Bedford's first glance at it exploded him into outraged derision. That prinking popinjay mincing on eggs the tough old seaman Abel Tasman! What the hell did I think I was doing, trying to fub off a lousy joke like that on him?

The eggs referred to were cobble-stones, or meant to be, but still even an incompetent art student may be aroused to defend his works from the sort of things Bedford was letting loose on them. My retort was automatic. 'I admit it's a lousy drawing, but just about on the level of your verses.'

The effect on Bedford was as if I had delivered him a punch in the midriff. He just glared at me a moment and ejaculated, 'Well, so help me God!' and stamped out of the room fuming. Such insolence from a runt of a lad of seventeen could not be dignified by combat in equal terms of truculence.

Norman Lindsay, *Bohemians of the Bulletin*, pp. 104–5.

The gift of the gab

The acute Nettie Palmer (1885–1964) discerns the difference between Bedford's wonderful conversation and his mildly disappointing effects on the printed page.

November 13th, 1928

Lunch with Randolph Bedford and a party yesterday on the balcony of Parliament House. For years I'd heard people talk of Bedford as a peerless storyteller, one who could hold you breathless in any bar or club, but I've never been satisfied with his published short stories. They have their fine splashes of vitality, humour, imagination; but something — is it in the connective tissue? — makes them emerge as flat and slightly false. There wasn't one of them I could remember except 'Fourteen Fathoms by Quetta Rock.'

But when Bedford tells his stories orally, it's really a different matter, as I'd guessed. They depend on so much more than his words — they're given life by his miming, the turns of his voice, a pause, a gesture, a glance around him. What a raconteur! Yesterday the party consisted mainly of members of his family. He sat at the head of the massive table on this balcony he has made his home and his club, entertaining royally, the light flickering through the jacarandas and playing upon his bald dome as he dressed the salad, mixing oil and vinegar liturgically, pouring out his stories one after another. Stories of mining, of journalism, of the youthful Lionel Lindsay and himself in the Europe of 1905, or thereabouts, when he was pursuing his haughty Explorations in Civilisation. Meanwhile he mixed the salad in its enormous bowl. Come, take, eat this story, he seemed to be saying; hear the green chlorophyll in these leaves dressed with epithets. And an iridescence, more than that twinkling from the salad-spoon, played over his talk. What a pity that all I can remember now of the longest and most dramatic of his stories is that it had to do with a Town Hall and a piece of string on the pavement outside ...

In a pause I asked him about 'Fourteen Fathoms by Quetta Rock.'

'Ah, that story,' he said, 'I can't get away from it. It's always turning up in magazines and anthologies. And it's true — at least it was founded on fact. Of course, the coincidence of the diver recognizing his wife's body in the cabin underwater by the pendant he had given her, and being overcome by the fact that she was with another man — all that I had to add. But the diver coming upon all those drowned people and being paralyzed by what he saw — that came straight from a Danish steward, talking about his brother in the Flores Sea and why he had given up the diving.'

In a moment he was creating the character of the Danish steward; the atmosphere of a night at Port Said, the foreign voice full of feeling, fumbling brokenly as they leant over the ship's rail:

'… Down there he move along slowly, feeling his way t'rough the passages of t' ship. A big shark move along, too, not far ahead of him. He burst open a cabin door and see t' people, all drowned — see t' body of a woman bobbing up against t' wires of a top bunk. He see their faces, how they are frightened. One little boy, he is afraid his father is being taken away; his arms around t' man's knee — his teeth are fastened in t' man's t'igh … I tell you, my brudder, he can't bear it. He just signal to be drawn up — quick, quick. A diver have a weak spot — his back. My brudder's back give way. He could be no more a diver. He see too much down there.'

Bedford, as he told the story, was not looking to right or left, nor down the table. His eyes were dazed with horror; he was the Danish steward, the steward's diver brother, the little boy, the father himself — and he couldn't bear what he saw.

A pause, then a click somewhere — two clicks. As if the power were turned off and ordinary light turned on. Bedford was now again the host, with largesse universal as the sun, sending us off with farewells and messages, bestowing patriarchal affection on his progeny, making appointments with one of the secretariat. By next week, with Parliament in recess, he'll be camping on the Diamantina, his gleaming great dome extinguished by his ten-gallon hat, his mind reaching out toward that Life which he always rather crankily asserts is superior to Literature — as if they were separate things.

Nettie Palmer, *Fourteen Years: Extracts from a Private Journal*, pp. 36–7.

Bottle-washing

Christopher Brennan (1870–1932) was a striking example of the Poet as Legendary Bohemian. From adolescence on he avoided the practical demands of life, although he seems to have been quite proficient at backyard cricket. Somehow, he acquired a remarkable education.

Fairly early in his undergraduate days they heard about the gown decorated with horse-shoes and jam tins. His father was so incensed that he took the drastic step of withdrawing Brennan from the University. (One wonders how he reacted when he heard about his son throwing stones into a lecture room — if he ever heard of it.) He also showed his anger by making a play of striking his grown-up son about the legs with a cane, though he had never in his life physically punished any of his children. Brennan was put to work in the brewery, washing bottles. But on the first day of his job, in a fit of absent-mindedness, he wandered away from the bottles and was nearly killed by a descending goods lift. His father sent him back to the University the next day.

Axel Clark, *Christopher Brennan: A Critical Biography*, p. 80.

His little oversight

Domestic bliss was an area in which Brennan lacked all proficiency, as his German bride found to her cost when she sailed into Sydney.

When Elisabeth arrived in Sydney on 12 December there were still several confusions, difficulties and unpleasant questions to be settled. It is said that Brennan forgot to meet the boat when it docked, and Elisabeth, knowing no English, had to search for him in a strange city.

Axel Clark, *Christopher Brennan: A Critical Biography*, p. 115.

Mallarmé and Cremorne

Brennan rejoiced in social occasions and could be very good company, as the poet Dowell O'Reilly found.

O'Reilly described an evening he spent at the Brennan home. Brennan offered an explication of Mallarmé's 'Toast Funèbre' until, at the time, O'Reilly said,

> I could follow the thread from end to end! And the good tempered little wife sits alongside the whiles interjecting quaint queries as to the 'price of land at Cremorne' and 'whether the rats will eat the chickens' and 'whether the balcony is too windy for the ferns', until the indulgent sage leans back laughing and says,
>
> 'There are nine questions my wife always asks any visitor — one evening when Delmer and I were discussing "Symbolism" my wife put all those questions to him — at intervals — just as she has put them to you! And he ticked the nine questions off on his gnawed finger tips. Do you remember?'

Axel Clark, *Christopher Brennan: A Critical Biography*, p. 124.

The need to practise conventionality

Then, as now, universities were not the place for bohemians. The job of a university, in this case the University of Sydney, is to interpret the works of dead bohemians while remaining as conservative as possible.

While congratulating Brereton very warmly on his promotion, MacCallum expressed surprise that senators had only raised trifling doubts about his unconventionality:

Your long hair + vegetarianism + (as I think) unwise leaning
to the pacif(ic)ists + other circles were not even mentioned, +
your hatlessness called forth only a good natured joke. All the
same, I might take the liberty of advising, I would recommend
you to become as conventional as your conscience permits. *My*
conscience tells me it is as conventional to be unconventional
as too conventional in small things.

Axel Clark, *Christopher Brennan: A Critical Biography*, p. 234.

A touch of magic

*For the handsome young poet, Hugh McCrae, Brennan's pub con-
versation was magical: he turned language into enchantment, like
the symbolists he so much admired.*

I adored Brennan. Sitting with me in a Woolloomooloo pub
one day, he said, 'A woman's skin is like music', and, from
that, he went on, better than I can repeat. The flyie pub, with
its pots of warm beer, plates of pigs' trotters, sawdust and
spittoons, disappeared in a moment; and I remembered, and
remembered, *and* remembered. He didn't intone 'the silent
note that Cupid strikes'; but it sounded through everything
he said.

Robert D. FitzGerald (ed.), *The Letters of Hugh McCrae*, p. 94.

Jovial nights

*Hilary Lofting was the Sydney brother of Hugh Lofting, author
of the immortal Doctor Dolittle stories. He, his wife, and their six
children were among Brennan's patient hosts.*

Hilary and the missus were always out of cash, but they
treated their guts royally: and both could cook. Chris

Brennan was a hardy visitor, sharing bed, woman, and board (the unfinancial side); and I've had merry evenings with them all. Madam, with her hair undone, filling up the sofa: Hilary, half in and half out of the kitchen, watching a procession of kids through a hot bath. Chris, seated over a black bag full of bottles (the cellar for the evening) translating Catullus aloud while the smoke from his rain-soaked breeches went up to the roof.

After an interminable dinner; bawdy stories — so that all could join in — and always, a song by Brennan (a low pitched half-voice) who sang it on his legs, turning his arse for the chorus

'Bum, bum, berry-bum, BUM!!'

Axel Clark, *Christopher Brennan: A Critical Biography*, p. 239.

Stop!

As a writer influenced by Mallarmé's concept of the livre composé, *Brennan gave his editors a hard time.*

He was also very meticulous about the use of punctuation marks in the printing of the titles of various sections of the volume. When the proofs were being prepared, he zealously deleted almost all the full stops from the titles. The printer made one heading 'INTERLUDE: THE CASEMENT.' Next to this, in red ink, Brennan wrote: 'NO FULL STOPS EXCEPT WHERE THE AUTHOR PUTS THEM: THIS IS THE AUTHOR'S BOOK'. At another place was printed: 'THE LABOUR OF NIGHT.' Brennan excised the stop and commented: 'THE LABOUR OF NIGHT IS NOTHING COMPARED WITH THE AUTHOR'S LABOUR TO CHUCK OUT THE PRINTER'S FULL STOPS'.

Axel Clark, *Christopher Brennan: A Critical Biography*, p. 209.

The appropriateness of blotto

When Brennan visited a girls school to talk to the French class he was able to give them the inside dope on adjectives describing drunkenness.

One girl later recalled the day they were translating a story by Maupassant:

> The character had imbibed overmuch and C.B. wanted the right translation. As students of a 'young ladies' college', with the compassion of youth, not wishing to hurt, we gave him translations from mild to middling. 'Inebriated?' we gasped. 'Drunk?' we half whispered. Still he was not satisfied — not until the daring worldly wise in the back row produced 'blotto'. The class crumpled, cringed in fear of the hurt to its hero, and a little ashamed of the slang. But no, 'blotto' was the translation and he smiled his satisfaction.

Axel Clark, *Christopher Brennan: A Critical Biography*, p. 285.

Shaven privates

The young A.D. Hope finally met the decaying Brennan in a Kings Cross pub and managed to communicate with him in gutter Latin.

Brennan himself I never met at all until a few months before he died. I was having a liquid lunch in the Marble Bar in Sydney with Ralph Piddington when he made some remark about Brennan — or perhaps asked some question. 'I don't know', I answered, 'I've never met him.' 'Never met him?' Ralph was surprised. Everybody knew or at least claimed to know Brennan. 'Well', he said, 'he's drinking himself to death at Kings Cross. I hear he isn't likely to last much longer. Look! Why don't we go up to the Cross and find him now?'

We finished our drinks and went out to find a taxi. None was to be seen but there outside the hotel was the last horse-drawn hansom cab in Sydney. 'This seems appropriate. Let's take it', said Ralph, so we clip-clopped up to the Mansions Hotel at the Cross, where Ralph said Brennan was usually to be found. Found he was, but he must have got there well ahead of us. He was seated at a table in an empty and half-dark lounge, one hand gripping a mug of beer and his head on his arms. Ralph tried in vain to stir him up so that he could introduce me. All we got was a few heavy grunts. He appeared to be too far gone, so we bought ourselves drinks and sat talking to each other, hoping the old man might stir. No luck!

After a while I got up and went off to the adjoining lavatory. I was standing in one of the two bays when to my surprise Brennan appeared and filled the other. I tried to say something to him but again only got a grunt in reply. So I took a pencil out of my pocket and leaning over began to write in capital letters just in front of him a well-known wall-inscription by a grateful client in ancient Pompeii: MULTO MELIUS QUAM GLABER FUTUITER CUNNUS PILOSSUS. Brennan glanced down, saw the inscription, recognised it, took the pencil out of my hand and finished it. 'Of course you know it's in Saturnian metre', he said. 'Yes', I said, not knowing anything of the sort. Then for several minutes, as we stood side by side, totally ignoring the sexual content of the line he gave me a fascinating account of Latin accentual metres from their origin right through the period of classical verse. Then he buttoned his fly and strolled off. I followed soon after, delighted at the prospect of having further talk with him. No such luck. When I got back to the table there he was as before, head on his arms and answering only in grunts. Ralph and I got up and left him to it. And that was my one and only meeting with Christopher Brennan.

A.D. Hope, *Chance Encounters*, pp. 57–8.

At the funeral

Brennan's funeral called for different kinds of testimony, the formalities being supplied by professor and poetaster John le Gay Brereton. A.G. Stephens had other ideas about what was called for.

The service at the graveside was conducted by Maurice O'Reilly, after which Brereton delivered an oration. Perhaps because of his position as a professor at the University, Brereton chose not to speak feelingly of Brennan as a friend, but instead spoke rather formally of Brennan as a poet: 'All the poets of Australia honour Christopher Brennan', Brereton said. 'They recognise him as a prince of their order.' Some people, such as Innes Kay, found Brereton's speech a disappointment. Kay said that A.G. Stephens, who expected to be asked to speak, stamped around the open grave, saying:

> 'Why the hell can't he say what a man he was, what a man? Just that. And how the Senate kicked his teeth in just to sate Mungo Maccallum's [sic] senile respectability. To hell with this burble! Jack Brereton's dropped his pants.'

Axel Clark, *Christopher Brennan: A Critical Biography*, p. 296.

A true crush

The novelist Henry Handel Richardson, born Ethel Florence Lindesay Richardson (1870–1946), spent much of her adolescence in the Victorian mining town of Maldon, where her widowed mother was postmistress. Now a pretty tourist village, Maldon was boring for the teenage HHR, except for the arrival of a captivatingly handsome vicar. Fortunately she soon escaped to the Presbyterian Ladies' College in Melbourne.

… For now I fell in love, desperately, hopelessly in love, with a man fifteen years my senior.

When we [the family] first lived in Maldon our Vicar was a very old man, considered by many of his congregation to be long past his duties. This feeling growing he retired soon after, and his place was taken by his son, till then curate at a fashionable church in Brighton. His father escorted him round the township, introducing him; but of the visit they paid us I remember only the two top-hats, then a droll sight up-country, that stood beside their chairs. It was not till the following Sunday that I had a real look at the new-comer — if look it could be called. Afterwards, an aunt who was staying with us let slip that he had asked who the brown-eyed little girl was, who listened so intently to his sermon. — Listened? I hadn't heard a word he said. My eyes had merely been feasting on a beauty of line and feature the like of which they had never seen — and, incidentally, were never to see in a man again.

Henry Handel Richardson, *Myself When Young*, p. 54.

In the merciless moonlight

Decades after she had left Australia, the memory of that hand-some clergyman could flare up in the novelist's heart.

Now when, in after life, I looked back on this youthful infat-uation, the one thing I complimented myself on was that I had had the strength to conceal my feelings. Nobody had known or even suspected what I was going through. Or so I believed for a matter of twenty years. But during the first world war Grace — by then the wife of Dr, afterwards Sir Henry, Maudsley — came to stay with me in Dorset; and as we sat over the fire in the evening we revived our memories of Maldon and its many associations. Jack's name naturally came up, and a fond, sisterly sidelight was shed on the affair of his marriage and all that had resulted from it. — At present he held a Bishopric in New South Wales; and I had long ago acknowledged fate's wisdom in baulking my young desires. As the wife of a Bishop I should indeed have been a misfit.

In the course of our talk, however, Grace dropped the casual remark: 'Of course, it was you, E., Jack really admired.' And this was more than I had bargained for. Its effect was to bring my age-old defences of time and oblivion toppling down. In a flash I was back in the old days, the old surroundings, a prey to the old misery. Again I tossed in a hot, crumpled bed, my little heart swollen with an ache that was much too big for it; again I paced round the dam, staring into its muddy yellow depths and wondering if they were deep enough to drown in; mocked at everywhere alike by the merciless southern moonlight. What wouldn't I *then* have given to know what was now so casually asserted. Even his marriage would have lost some of its sting. — Under the uprush of these supposedly extinct feelings I sat confused and silent. And when Grace went on to disconcert me still further by adding: 'You cared for him, too, I think, didn't you?' all I could get out was a weak and mumbled 'Yes.' — I have often laughed at myself since for my inability to come into the open. After close on the third of a lifetime, and with a friend like Grace! What I ought to have said was: '*Cared?* I would have lain down for him to walk on!'

Henry Handel Richardson, *Myself When Young*, pp. 60–1.

Nice little girls

Writers often begin by asking the questions that seem improper. Perhaps all of us remember having done so, as HHR did here.

About this time I went, by special invitation, to visit a quiet new baby that had arrived to a lady we knew at the Bank. 'The youngest baby *you'll* ever have seen!' announced my cousin. It certainly was, being only two hours old. Its mother lay sick in bed, and I thought how nice *she* looked, with a strip of her white chest showing. But the baby! Carried in on a pillow and presented for our inspection, it seemed to me not only the newest but the ugliest thing I'd ever set eyes on. Quite bald, the colour of underdone meat, and with a face like an old, old man's, all creases and wrinkles. I regarded it with extreme distaste; and firmly shook my head when urged to touch its twitching fingers. — And there was Mother declaring enthusiastically: 'Oh, what a lovely boy!' Lovely indeed! I was glad to get away from it.

But this was not the only effect of the visit. Something overheard in its course must have set me ruminating on matters till then unthought-of. For a day or two later, I approached my cousin with the inquiry whether women could have children after their husbands died.

I can still see the look of stupefaction on her broad, mobile face.

'What on earth ... Good gracious, you mustn't *ever* ask questions like that!'

'Why not?' from me, in innocent surprise.

'Why? Because you mustn't, that's all. Nice little girls *never* do!'

'But *why*?' I persisted.

'Because they don't, because it's naughty. Now let me hear no more about it!'

Even my mother, when informed, raised her eyebrows. 'What next, I wonder!'

I withdrew red and discomfited, conscious that I had disgraced myself, but quite unable to understand how.

Henry Handel Richardson, *Myself When Young*, pp. 30–1.

Passionate concentration

After her husband's death in 1933, Richardson moved to Sussex, living close to William the Conqueror's Battle Abbey. Nettie Palmer, who had long failed to realise that HHR was a woman, let alone a fellow Old Collegian of PLC, Melbourne, visited her there. During World War II, Green Ridges was directly under the main flight paths of the Battle of Britain.

December 19th, 1935

Just back from another couple of days at 'Green Ridges'. H.H.R. is perhaps more revealing, because more concentrated, in midwinter. The chunky house, with its central heating, cut off from the creeping cold of the Downs and the sea-mist, seems a little dynamo, humming with long-stored energy, carefully husbanded. We went out, drove along the foreshore, then inland to the glorious town of Battle, returning through countless other little country places they had visited before H.H.R. decided on 'Green Ridges'. We walked to the highest ridge above the Lane, heard the fog-siren on Beachy Head a dozen miles away, saw the nothingness of distance over the Channel. Always I felt her tautness, like a coiled spring.

She is working now on another book, highly documented. Nothing to do with Australia this time. Her general ideas on writing have never changed. More than ever she is determined, for her part, not to interfere with her characters but to let them work out their own destinies; to keep the author out of it. It was the same when she began, in 'Maurice Guest'; to the confounding of the critics who wanted, for instance, to represent the controversial passage on Mendelssohn as her own opinion. Later on, people quoted Richard Mahony's view of Australian life, people, and landscape as her own; this in spite of the brief aside at the opening of 'Ultima Thule' where she speaks as a 'native born'.

I listen to her out-of-doors, where she shows me, on the misty Downs, some grand stuggy horses, Suffolk Punches, actual importations of a farmer who had once travelled abroad to Suffolk, or indoors, in the study all the evening, the mild central heating quickened by a fire, the mental atmosphere warm and fluid. She asks me about some Australians on her shelves. What is this novelist likely to do next? Hasn't that one rather the over-emphasis of a journalist? What poems are to be expected from So-and-so?

So much of my life has been spent watching writers at work, reading in manuscript their poems, stories, novels, listening to their ideas — or guessing at them; trying to come to some conclusions about the special nature of each. But what makes up the special nature of this writer, H.H.R.?

First of all, concentration: her life planned to fertilize those hours of creative work. But concentration to what end? Economically free, she has never thought of writing for money, never been tempted to please a publisher by writing a novel for the new season. Her impulse to create has all along come from a passionate interest in human relationships and character; perhaps a lifelong absorption in a few figures that have touched her feeling and imagination. Her need for human contacts is mainly satisfied by the people in the world she builds up. She seems to have few close friends, and has no love at all for large groups.

To write is her joy. Suggest to her that a writer's life is a hard one, an agonizing struggle with intractable material, and she will deny it. 'But I love every moment at my desk. How else could I have kept on writing all these years, getting nothing for it but starvation-fees and obscurity?'

Success, immediate and retrospective, came, ironically, with 'Ultima Thule', her most intransigent book (one that had to be published privately). It might never have come in her lifetime. She would have kept on without it. She is a writer.

Nettie Palmer, *Fourteen Years: Extracts from a Private Journal*, pp. 193–5.

Pellets of curry

John Shaw Neilson (1872–1942) lived with poverty, hardship, and ophthalmia for much of his life, most of which was spent in the Victorian Wimmera. For much of the time he lived near the appropriately named Nhill, where a plague of mice ate many of his poems.

I remember getting some treatment from an Indian oculist at Sea Lake. He put some little pellets (made of curry I think) into my eyes. He charged £27 & of course the treatment did no good whatever. I had to knock off reading altogether. For twelve months or more I never looked at print. I had to get my sister Jessie to do all my writing for me. I got out a good deal of stuff but very little of it was worth print.

The Autobiography of John Shaw Neilson, p. 70.

Stick to the tears

Neilson grew up in a house where both Gaelic and English were spoken, but received very little schooling and was self-conscious about his ignorance.

At times I have shown some of my light verse to my friends. Many of them seem disinclined to express an opinion. Generally speaking I think they disapprove of it. A man needs a good knowledge of English for doing light rhyming & my knowledge is of course very slight. I have got the reputation of being rather a tearful kind of fellow & perhaps it is best to stick to it.

The Autobiography of John Shaw Neilson, p. 75.

Citrus

Picking fruit in the Sunraysia district gave Neilson a taste for Botticelli's Primavera.

While on this few weeks' rest I finished 'The Orange Tree'. I would have liked to have got it out in time for the book but there was no chance. I think a man writes better when he is having a complete rest after toil or any form of worry. I have said before that I got some of the ideas when I was weeding oranges at Merbein. There was also something which I tried to drag in, some enchantment or other. I cannot well describe it. I have seen Prints of Botecelli's wonderful picture 'Spring'. I think that is its name. It has lovers, it has maidens & greenery & I think a robber in the background. Of course I know nothing about art at all but anything of Botecelli's I see fills me with emotion. Prints of other great pictures seem to leave me cold.

The Autobiography of John Shaw Neilson, pp. 105–6.

C'est la vie, hélas!

One of the more remarkable evenings in Australian literature was a Saturday night in Sydney when Neilson dined with Stephens, Brennan and J.J. Quinn. The farm labourer was so tolerant that he seems not even to have minded the others conversing in French.

One Saturday night J. J. Quinn took Neilson with his work-swollen hands to a French café (probably Paris House); Stephens and Brennan were also in the party. Neilson thought himself the only one there who could not understand French, but the itinerant labourer had no vanity and did not resent sophisticated display in others. The following evening he went on a ferry ride with Stephens, Brennan and others. The party passed a few hours listening to Brennan talk. At nightfall,

Neilson, Brennan and Stephens went to Stephens's rooms for conversation, then Brennan and Neilson walked back together towards King's Cross (Neilson was staying at Paddington). That night Brennan showed neither bitterness in his adversity nor condescension in speaking to the unlettered navvy. Neilson later said: 'Although he had such knowledge & such achievements, he spoke as simply to me as though we had been mates in the bush together'. Perhaps Brennan, who had known Neilson's work for some years, sensed that this humble man was his superior as a poet.

Axel Clark, *Christopher Brennan: A Critical Biography*, p. 270.

Hard times

Neilson's autobiography is distinguished by what we like to think of as a typically Australian stoicism and dry humour.

The fifth Letter draws to a close. I am calling it 'The Worst Seven Years', because it is a navvie's joke to comfort a new-comer who is feeling the work with the guide. — The first Seven Years are always the Worst Mate.

The Autobiography of John Shaw Neilson, p. 119.

The poet's sandwiches

That writer of luscious prose, Hal Porter (1911–84), records an autumnal lunchtime walk with Neilson who, by this stage, had a menial public service job, the nearest thing then available to a Literature Board pension.

John Shaw Neilson the poet is as old as I now am ... I'm then twenty-four ... when we walk together, last time, Exhibition Gardens, Melbourne, 1935, windy sunny Autumn.

I've met him outside the Exhibition Building where he works (I think to remember) as a runner, some sort of messenger with — would it be? — the Country Roads Board. It's his lunch-time. I'm at a loose end, school holidays perhaps, for in 1935, year of the first-ever quiz programme, of early Swing, of Führer Adolf Hitler banning Negro and Jewish music on the wireless, I'm a junior teacher at North Williamstown State School 1409.

As we walk he takes crude isosceles sandwiches (mutton? pork German?) thickly bloodstained with tomato sauce (White Crow? — *Hot?*) from a brown paper bag with pinked edges which, when it's empty, he neatly folds, and puts in a waistcoat pocket. As he eats, he politely slightly averts his face. Has he made the sandwiches himself? I don't know if he has a wife, or a looking-after sister, or even an antique mother, but he has a bachelor air. They're certainly not sandwiches to be dealt with while vertical, and in motion along a public path, but while sprawled, wearing bowyangs, in a quarry or a hay-field. Had he not been too timid and mannerly to put me off he'd surely've chosen to eat them alone, on a seat in some restlessly dappled corner where one of the injured statues which, then, lurked among the gunnera and acanthus, stares elsewhere, disdainful of mortal gaucheries. Yet here he is, half-blind, shy, monosyllabic, awkwardly eating while walking *and* being hounded by an unshy and inquisitional pest.

Oh, my intentions are of the sweetest and selfishest, my love of his poetry intense and almost sincere. 'The Orange Tree', I recall, particularly tantalises me yet, though I know it by heart, has me flummoxed. It's like reading smoke. Full of the poem and a dreadful alertness, I fire unrecallable questions into his diffidence, and can't recall any of the answers. Only two of his remarks stay with me. One's that he can't recite 'The Orange Tree' or any other poem of his, even mentally to himself. This strikes me as extraordinary: I can rattle off any of *my* adjective-choked verses anywhere, to anyone. Neilson's inability no longer seems extraordinary. Today, neither thumb-screws nor threats of the stake could make me remember the first two lines of a poem written last week, nor the opening sentence of a short story written yesterday.

John Shaw Neilson's other unforgotten remark is:

'Like a cup of tea?'

Hal Porter, *The Extra*, pp. 156–7.

The professor's trousers

Walter Murdoch, who also wrote under the pen-name of 'Elzevir', was a most influential essayist and scholar. Here he laments the earthly transience of trousers.

My dear, I posted a parcel to you this afternoon … It contains only fragments of what were once my best trousers, now made into covers for hot-water-bags and a few pot holders. I may tell you I was very fond of those trousers, & much resent their disintegration. I bought them in London in 1927. I was having lunch, at a restaurant near St Paul's, with [a man from] the Oxford University Press. He came here to see me when he was in Australia on business, so when he went to London I went to see him and he asked me out to lunch. After telling me of many curious things I ought to see in London, he looked at me as if I was a curious sight myself and said, 'I can tell you the address of a very good tailor.' The tailor, it turned out, was his uncle. His place was in Chancery Lane & he really *was* very good though rather expensive. He made me a suit of a then fashionable sort, now incurably démodé — black coat & waistcoat and striped trousers. The Coat & waistcoat are about as good as ever; the trousers, alas, are covers for hot-water-bags! So the earth passes and the glory thereof. The grass withereth, the flower fadeth. Nothing lasts. Change and D.K. in all around we see. A sad world …

John La Nauze, *Walter Murdoch: A Biographical Memoir*, p. 86.

In the shrubbery

For a man with such style, Hugh McCrae was remarkably shy.

[McCrae] had no confidence in his ability to conduct any sort of conversation. 'I can't *talk*,' he would shout. If, when he was staying with us, the gate clicked, he would leap from his chair and hide in his bedroom or sneak down to the bottom of the garden. Occasionally visitors would ask to see the garden, and then Hugh would spend an agonized ten minutes on tiptoe dodging them round bushes and trees. Ethel Anderson was no stranger, and he admired her and her writings; but her erudition and wit and especially her familiarity with and disposition to discuss modern poetry terrified him. He had a favourite rocking-chair in our sitting-room. One day he saw her entering the gate, catapulted from his chair, and shut himself in his room.

'Ah!' she said, looking around the sitting-room, 'this is the nearest I've got to meeting your father for years. You see, it's *still rocking*!'

Robert D. FitzGerald (ed.), *The Letters of Hugh McCrae*, pp. xix–xx.

Purple socks

Hugh McCrae had a gift for verbal portraiture. Here he has captured a visit by the young Kenneth Slessor in a few deft strokes.

I had a visitor the other day in the person of young Ken Slessor: a boy not yet twenty-one who writes leading-articles for the *Sun* and is so well-paid that he was enabled to turn down the Editorship of *Art in Australia*.

His presence is hardly a pleasing one, but what seems at first to be bad temper proves only to be shyness which wears off. He has a cold German face at top, finished off below with purple socks and little shoes. Yet he writes like an angel.

Robert D. FitzGerald (ed.), *The Letters of Hugh McCrae*, pp. 55–6.

I did

Westralian novelist Mollie Skinner (1876–1955) collaborated with D.H. Lawrence on The Boy in the Bush. *The 'I' in this extract is Olive Pell, writing to R. Guy Howarth.*

Mollie is in hospital, very sick after an operation for gallstones, where I visited her. 'I thought I was going to die', she told me.

'There were spectres round my bed and I was talking to them. If that isn't near it, I don't know what is. I don't know what's the use of going on living. Except to justify Lawrence.' She feels he has been badly misrepresented which she must correct from her knowledge of him. That — when she was so miserably sick.

At that time the woman in the next bed told us that the doctor came in and suddenly said loudly, 'Who wrote *The Boy in the Bush?*' and Mollie sat bolt upright and said, 'I did.' I think perhaps that was her turning point. I was dumb-founded when she thanked me for coming to see her when she knew I hated visiting sick people — for it was true.

Brian Dibble, Don Grant & Glen Phillips (eds), *Celebrations: A Bicentennial Anthology of Fifty Years of Western Australian Poetry and Prose*, pp. 62–3.

Jobs for a bachelor girl

*Mary Grant Bruce (1878–1958) was one of our outstanding
writers for children. Famous for the Billabong books, she published
in all thirty-seven novels for young readers.*

I was twenty when I left Gippsland to seek my fortune in
Melbourne, much against my father's will. There were not
many bachelor girls then, and he feared all kinds of disasters
for me; but my mother begged that I should have my chance,
and so, at last, I went — with a heart full of assorted ambitions, and £5 in my pocket. I had at that time no thought of
earning my living by writing — daily teaching was what I
sought to obtain, so that I might have my evenings for literary work. But a temporary secretaryship came my way, and,
before it ended, the *Leader* asked me to run its Children's
Page. The salary was not great — writers were poorly paid
in those days — but I saw that I could live on it somehow,
and the teaching project vanished for ever — leaving me one
deathless memory of a lady who wished me to teach in her
school, prepare her eldest daughter for the University o'
nights, and 'share our highly refined home' — and all for
£12 a year!

Mary Grant Bruce, *The Peculiar Honeymoon and Other Writings* (ed. Prue
McKay), p. 203.

Don Juan

Here we have a 1942 encounter between the sardonic Miles Franklin (1879–1954) and a swaggering Xavier Herbert (1901–84), author of the incomparable Capricornia. *Elusive, peripatetic Stella Miles Franklin also wrote as Brent of Bin Bin, an amusingly squattocratic pseudonym.*

Well, I had Xavier H here lately had a long talk. He kept saying 'You and I Miles are the only two great Australian novelists.' I suppose when he is with others they and he are the only two great and I derided. He is a colorful personality. I enjoyed him. Told me his liaisons and all.

Miles Franklin to Mary Fullerton in *My Congenials: Miles Franklin and Friends in Letters*, vol. 2 (ed. Jill Roe), p. 79.

The curve of a floruit

Miles Franklin reflects ruefully on her own career when confronted by the young novelist Catherine Gaskin, who did indeed go on to produce a string of bestsellers.

There was present a girl named Gaskin (?) who at sixteen has a novel accepted by Collins — the age I started with *MBC*. What a bore I must have been to my elders who had to take notice of me! Well, *time marches on*, I took notice of Katharine (I believe her name is) and gave her my bouquet, the loveliest thing of yellow pansies and autumn leaves. I hear she comes from a convent, and the book is set in England whence she came as an infant. So I hope her career will be the reverse of mine — upward to prosperity and popularity by means of orthodox best-sellers, not just getting nowhere because of sticking to one's own ideas.

Miles Franklin to Katharine Susannah Prichard, 5 July 1946, in *As Good as a Yarn with You: Letters Between Miles Franklin, Katharine Susannah Prichard, Jean Devanny, Marjorie Barnard, Flora Eldershaw and Eleanor Dark* (ed. Carole Ferrier), p. 140.

Five big swabs

Come in Spinner *was a prizewinning if scandalous novel about the 'American Invasion' during World War II. Miles Franklin gives a sketch of how the book was concocted by Dymphna Cusack and Florence James and how the shoals of publication were negotiated. Franklin's contempt for Ruth Park's* Harp in the South *is made quite clear.*

I'll tell you about the *Telegraph* competition because Dymphna and I feel it is not be kept from such as you, and you are please to *keep the secret as tightly as it has been kept.* Dymphna and her friend Florence James (Mrs Heyting) took that cottage in the Mts and set to work deliberately to produce a novel. The comps were not going at the start, I believe. Well, they put a vast story into the *Daily T* Competition. I read it in rough draft. They sent it to me in five big swabs. I got the first one, then the third one, then the two last, and then the second. Much over 200,000 words. I said it, (judging from that irregular rushing-through), could not be ignored, and I considered had a great chance of being first. I felt more sure after the Bugs of the *Syd M Herald*, as the *Telly* would wish to go one better. Well Mrs Heyting and two young daughters sailed last July to rejoin her husband in London, with no news of Comp. Some time later Dymphna was called-up before Penton, a lovely story of his peremptoriness, and said the story called for certain changes, as otherwise it wd involve the publishers in libels and would be banned. Wd they be ready to do this? Their main critic, Stewart Howard, furnished a report, and D went down to his home for a week-end, and went through the thing. Said there were no unreasonable demands and that, in an edition revised since the first one put in the comp, she had done some of the things they indicated, and cut out 70,000 words. So she got the MSS, and Florence James Heyting had to do 10,000 words on her portion and returned same, and the cut-about MS went in. Howard told D secretly that he considered it wd get the prize, but it was up to Penton finally, and he had timid publishers to consider. No word for weeks till D got a hint, I forget how, that the MSS were at Consolidated, being set up. So with this knowledge she went into the business mgr on the other count of her and FJ's children's book, which they published. While there, she said to Mr Walsh, 'How are you getting on with the printing of *Spinner*?' He was taken off guard and gave the show away. (We are not skilled in Gestapo duplicity yet.) So, he said, you know Sydney Wyborne? (That was the nom de plume.) D said yes. Then he went on and said the MSS was such a mess he did not know how to tackle it, that he was going to send it back to Penton to put more in order. You have no idea, said he, and it is in two different typings. Florence's machine has that little type — is it called brevet? Then he got scared at his admissions, but D calmed him by saying she too shd not have said anything, and wd keep the confidence. She says she doesn't know how she'll face him when she comes out as co-author. It gave her great confidence to know it was actually to be set up: she wd be in a stronger position about contract. Penton had told her at first interview that he did not care how long the comp result remained unannounced. They were determined to have a first-rate novel — no slush like *Harp in the South* wd satisfy them.

Miles Franklin to Katharine Susannah Prichard, 4 May 1948, in *As Good as a Yarn with You: Letters Between Miles Franklin, Katharine Susannah Prichard, Jean Devanny, Marjorie Barnard, Flora Eldershaw and Eleanor Dark* (ed. Carole Ferrier), p. 197.

What price popular fiction?

Here Miles Franklin's scorn is shared with novelist Jean Devanny (1894–1962) as they look down on those two popular favourites of mid-century, Ion L. Idriess (1889–1979) and E.V. Timms (1895–1960).

Jean Devanny has been down from Townsville, brought MS of her autobiography. It is inchoate. She does not realise the work it will mean to lick it into shape. She stayed a week with me. 5 years ago we went to Sydney Royal together so we went again. A great day. She said when she went to the show she wanted to see everything, and as I know every nook of it and love it that suited me. She cried crack first. I took her through the Hall of Industry and said there is A and R's stall. A fine display, mostly of course dictionaries and general books — they cd not take all the shop to a show. Only two novelists on display, two high shelves that caught the eye splendidly, one a line of Idriess, the other of Timms. Jean bowled up and rapped out 'It is disgraceful, a great firm like this displaying nothing but such trash as that!' The man, whom I don't know, got snakeheaded at once and said as roughly as a police sergeant, 'What nonsense you talk Madam, the concensus of all the editors and critics for 20 years is that they are the 2 greatest writers in Australia' !!!! Glowry and Glammer be!

Miles Franklin to Dymphna Cusack, in *Congenials: Miles Franklin and Friends in Letters*, vol. 2 (ed. Jill Roe), p. 321.

On the Dorking Olympus

The crossing of generations is always something to make you catch your breath. In this longer anecdote, the young Melbourne novelist Katharine Susannah Prichard (1883–1969) travels to the heart of the British Empire and meets the aged ironist, George Meredith (1828–1909). An apprehension of decay and death overwhelms her.

The great event of my first year in London was meeting George Meredith.

We lived on the hill at South Yarra before I left home, not far from the Deakins. Alfred Deakin, who was Prime Minister of Australia at the time, and my mother were old friends. I walked into town with him sometimes, through the Domain and along St Kilda Road; he tall and stooping, already worn and disillusioned, I full of idealistic illusions and of my determination to become a famous writer as soon as possible.

One morning when the deciduous trees along the road were yellow and shedding their leaves, Alfred Deakin said: 'Words are like those falling leaves. What are they worth? Very little.' He talked of the seeming futility of words and of my trade as a weaver of words. We discussed the way writers used words, drawing Carlyle, Walter Pater, Anatole France and George Meredith into the argument. I had a passion for Meredith at the time.

Later, when I told Mr Deakin that, like the gosling in the old rhyme, I was 'off to the world so wide', he sent me two letters of introduction: one 'To whom it may concern', with the red seals of the Prime Minister's office attached, and the other to Meredith.

In my ignorance of 'the world so wide' I had decided not to take any letters of introduction to England, intending to stand alone and to take London by assault of manuscripts.

That I would fail to do so never occurred to me, or that the MSS would be returned in shoals, as they were at first.

Mother wanted me to promise to say with our cousins in Huntingdonshire; but when Mr Deakin's letters arrived she was sure that, armed with them, no evil could befall me. 'How like him,' she said. 'He is always so kind and thoughtful.' Alfred Deakin and Mother had many happy youthful memories in common, I knew, although for years they had not seen much of each other.

I did not use the letter 'To whom it may concern' on that first visit to England; but the letter to George Meredith was like an introduction to one of the high gods of Olympus.

Meredith was then the great man of English letters. I had read most of his novels and poems. I loved *Diana of the Crossways*, *The Egoist*, *The Tale of Chloe*, their exuberant vitality, intellectual brilliance, the exquisite quality of irony that informed them. Above all, I was impressed by Meredith's form of expression, his unusual approach to a subject, his vigorous usage of words. 'Love in the Valley' I knew by heart, and many other poems of his. I had attended a series of lectures on Meredith given by Walter Murdoch at the University of Melbourne, and thought that as a humble worshipper I might approach the master.

So I folded a small note over Alfred Deakin's introduction, and eventually a letter arrived saying that Mr Meredith would be pleased to see my on a day named. The letter instructed me what train to catch to Dorking; but all the clocks in London whirled that morning. I arrived at Charing Cross station two hours too soon and took the wrong train to the wrong Dorking, not realising that there were then two Dorkings, each with a different railway station. A row of shabby open carriages and old coachmen stood outside the Dorking at which I got out of the train. 'Drive me to Mr Meredith's place, please,' I said to the nearest coachman. His face crumpled dubiously. 'Meredith? Meredith?' he muttered and consulted another old man. They came back to tell me they didn't know anybody of that name round about.

'George Meredith, the great writer,' I gasped. 'You must know him. He lives here at Dorking.' The coachmen looked glum, shook their heads, and eyed me suspiciously. Then another old man came from the end of the row of carriages. 'Party o' the name o' Meredith lives up be Box Hill,' he said.

Box Hill was three miles away. My old man climbed up on to his high front seat, whacked his stolid horse and we rattled off across cobble stones through the street of a dull smug township that looked as if it did not know or love George Meredith.

But the road after leaving the town turned lazily between green fields and rounded hills, past an inn by a brook which ran into the shadow of trees. It was a glorious day, warm and sunny, with the hawthorn in blossom and dandelions gold in the grass.

To be driving in state in that ancient shandrydan, with the old coachman and fat white horse, seemed so comical that I wondered what everybody at home would say if they could see me. There had to be a white horse, of course: this was rural England, and Meredith the first really great writer I was ever to meet. I was too thrilled and excited to bother about anything else.

It was so summery that I had put on a light dress and was wearing a big straw hat. I began to wonder whether I looked nice enough for such a visit. And what should I say? I tried over several speeches, but none of them seemed quite right. Should I bow or curtsey? Would I be awed and stupid, embarrass Mr Meredith by my gaucherie? Would he resent this intrusion of a young person from Australia and secretly curse Mr Deakin for his letter? Or would I perhaps remember Mother's instructions about natural grace and composure?

The carriage stopped on the rise of the road up a broad hillside. A red brick house, flat-faced and suburbanish, with gravelled paths and round flowerbeds, flanked by pines, sat behind a picket fence. I gave the coachman his fare and went through the gateway, stood before the door, lifted the knocker.

The door opened and an elderly woman showed me into a room which seemed dark and dingy after the sunshine outside. A small fire was burning in the grate. An old man, like Whistler's portrait of Carlyle, was seated on a chair before the fire, with a rug across his knees.

What happened in that moment, as I stood in the doorway, I've never been able to understand. A curious communication seemed to pass between us as Meredith's eyes reached me. I was aware of a magnetic personality, of desolation and tragedy. The realisation was so swift and devastating that I forgot to be shy and self-conscious. We seemed not to be strangers.

I remember that I went towards him quickly, as he apologised for not rising. We began talking at once, as if we were old friends who had not met for a long time.

'Here I am,' Meredith said, 'chained to this old body, though my spirit is as young as it ever was. Carlyle was right. He used to say a man should not outlive his physical usefulness.'

A passionate sympathy overwhelmed me. Meredith talked as he wrote, with the same brilliant, ironical exuberance. Yet age had crippled him — he was partly paralysed — and I became almost dumb because of his bitterness and despair.

Trying to arouse me, perhaps, Meredith asked what I had written. I told him about the short stories, some sketches of the back country of Australia, newspaper articles, but added that I had not yet done anything of importance. I had never been able to write as I wanted to: my work was too restrained and anxious, and I corrected and revised too much.

'Oh, throw it off,' he said. 'Get rid of what there is in you.'

I told him how I loved his poetry and *The Tale of Chloe*.

'Poor Chloe,' he said sadly, as if Chloe were someone he had known and cared for. Then: 'Do they read my poetry in Australia? People don't in England, you know. They don't like it.'

I told him about a holiday in the Dandenong Ranges, when a party of boys and girls had read 'Love in the Valley' together — a golden sunshiney Easter, with pears ripe in an abandoned orchard beside the homestead, and of how we had gone about quoting verses to each other for days.

Meredith said that he thought 'The Day of a Daughter in Hades' was his best poem. He murmured as if to himself:

For he said: A glad vision art thou!
And she answered him: Thou to me!
As men utter a vow.

His housekeeper brought in afternoon tea and he talked to me about the chalet where he had worked, in the pine wood behind the house.

Then it was time to go. A letter from home that day contained a piece of wattle blossom. I had brought it as a greeting from Australia and now left it beside Mr Meredith.

As he held my hand to say goodbye, the grief which had oppressed me all the time I was with him surged. A tear or two dripped on his hand. He patted mine. 'There, there,' he said, as if he understood what was distressing me. Then he kissed my hand with a gentle gracious gesture — and I fled.

I was crying as I went down the garden path. The old housekeeper came after me with the sprig of wattle blossom. 'Mr Meredith thought that as it had come in a letter from home you might attach a special value to it,' she said.

Somewhere along the path, downhill out of sight of the house, there was a hawthorn bush. I sat down under it and wept and wept. Why I didn't quite know — except that I had an overwhelming sense of tragedy, and my youth seemed a reproach to me. I felt that I should not be young and

Meredith old: that I should not have gone from the sunshine into his darkened room and stood in the doorway in my light summer dress. Perhaps I had stirred some tender memory — or merely my youth and being on the threshold of my life's work had intensified the realization that his was nearly over. He was waiting for death, and I somehow had broken in on him, like his Daughter of Hades.

Katharine Susannah Prichard, 'Contrasts: Meredith and Marchesi', in *Meanjin* 3/1961, pp. 388–91.

Out in the noonday sun

Prichard's longstanding membership of the Communist Party made her a natural object of interest for the police and ASIO agents, some of them ham-fisted or comically misinformed.

Prichard challenged her watchers a second time a year later when she returned from a tour of the eastern states to find that her house had been broken into by officers of the Commonwealth Investigation Branch and had been left open. As well as being unnerved by this invasion of privacy in her absence, Prichard also had to contend with disturbing rumours circulating about the reasons for the raid. A complaint had been made by a neighbour that signalling had occurred at Prichard's home. The offending object turned out to be a biscuit tin on a stump which caught the midday sun.

Fiona Capp, *Writers Defiled: Security Surveillance of Australian Authors and Intellectuals 1920–1960*, p. 63.

Making western eyes?

Dorothea Mackellar (1885–1968), she of the sunburnt country, was born posh. Her shipboard diaries are wonderfully flapperish, two decades before the international heyday of flappers.

Wednesday January 31

Read Conrad's *Under Western Eyes* … Mr Rome played a very fine game of deck-quoits. **It is absurd — he's making a dead set at me**. He danced eagerly and talked for hours in the moonlight on the upper deck — with and without Nina, and he talks down to me, nice old thing, and **he said I had an innocent face**! Never have I been treated as such an ingénue before.

Friday February 2

Sports and cricket matches and avoidance of **Mr Rome**, until evening when that was not possible any more. Fancy Dress Dinner Dance and Gymkhana. People usually wore operatic costumes, and looked extremely well. Nina wore a white wig and black hat, patches and rouge, and looked simply ripping. Mr Garrard very attractive as Trilby. I wore a semi-oriental gipsy dress (from Traviata with additions of my own) and it looked well, so about forty of the passengers told me. I'm thinking they mostly were of the opinion of the Cannibal Island man, who said, 'You look quite different to-night, absolutely charming. I didn't know you!' Mary lent me a crimson silk tie with which to bind my head. The dress was a tunic of gauzy greenery-yallowy stuff with tiny Magyar sleeves embroidered in red sequins like the stiff dark-blue broidered band across the breast: there was a quaint short red-sequinned zouave jacket, and a stiff skirt of any mixed rainbow of colours, tied round the hip with a fringed scarf of dull cream that had crimson roses on it. As I wore the golden Spanish shawl, crimson roses, green macaws and all, between the dances … I was rather like a macaw myself. I wore no stays, but just now my waist is springy and muscular, so it didn't matter. **Mr Rome** was rather trying, though he *is* a good sort … **he kept on suggesting marriage more or less scotchly** — Oh dear! …

Jyoti Brunsdon (ed.), *I Love a Sunburnt Country: The Diaries of Dorothea Mackellar*, p. 107.

Mice absorb literature

In another of Nettie Palmer's adroit portraits, we look upon Neilson in the light of his dealings with A.G. Stephens and get a glimpse of the great Wimmera mouse plague, along the way.

When Furnley Maurice dropped in about five, Neilson was talking of the few poets he had been able to read. In his good days, he came on Padraic Colum's 'Wild Earth' and it meant a lot to him, perhaps giving him confidence to use naive rhythms and simple themes that suit him. But through the years the bulk of his reading has undoubtedly been the letters pouring in from A.G.S. Blessing and cursing, admonishing, praising — and sometimes bringing models to his notice, so that he knew what Heine had written, and Victor Hugo, and something of other poets whose names meant nothing to him.

'And you've kept all those letters?' I asked anxiously, knowing Neilson had had to move about and travel light.

'I kept them for years,' he said, 'but in 1917, you know, there was the mouse-plague over the Victorian wheat country. Every scrap of paper went. The only letters of Stephens I own now came during recent years. I haven't been able to take all his advice, but he's been a wonderful friend to me — sometimes a bit awkward, though, when he knocks someone else down with the idea of building me up.'

He made this remark at large and 'to whom it might concern.' It was an honourable disclaimer of agreement with all

Stephens' long-standing hostilities or sudden slaughters. If there was anyone in the room who had suffered … Peace!

Nettie Palmer, *Fourteen Years: Extracts from a Private Journal*, p. 57.

Of frocks and fish

Nettie Palmer, in this Paris memory, catches Christina Stead's idiom strongly, as well as her preoccupation with appearance and style.

June 21st, 1935

Talks at odd intervals with Christina Stead. I feel rather ashamed of having brought her, with some others, to this Hotel des Grands Hommes, just because I knew it and they asked for a suggestion. It's suddenly burning midsummer, and the Panthéon makes this the hottest square in Paris. Christina, who knows her way everywhere, would have chosen better. But it has meant that we've seen a good deal of one another, going out for meals and walks, as well as sitting together in conference sessions. Her voice is easy to remember:

'My father wanted me to be a scientist like himself. When I was very tiny he used to tell me the names of what interested him most — fishes with frightening faces. It was all right, but when he saw I learnt easily he took me to science meetings. I suppose I was about ten by then. I wasn't frightened of fish with ugly faces, but those science women who didn't know how to do their hair or put their clothes on! I ran away from science forever.'

Nettie Palmer, *Fourteen Years: Extracts from a Private Journal*, p. 155.

Poor old New Zealand!

In one of her most brilliant pieces of characterisation, Nettie Palmer captures F.R. and Queenie Leavis at the top of their form, in their native Cambridge. After World War II the Leavises were to have a powerful moral influence on literary studies in Australia, comparable to that now exerted by that hybrid monster, Theory.

April 5th, 1936

Yesterday met Jean Young in Cambridge, and she took me to see her old friends, the Leavises. Mrs Leavis, a friendly, dark, young spectacled woman, welcomed us and, after we had dropped our cloaks, ushered us in to the sitting-room where Dr Leavis was handy-man, watching the tea-kettle on the fire. He was tallish, baldish, with brown hair and side-whiskers; brown, sensitive humorous eyes, with a droop at the corners. Mrs L., with her high, very rapid utterance, and Dr L. with his slight drawl broadening his vowels, were both of them fatigued, and utterly aware of it all the time — admitting it in words.

Coming along, I had asked Jean Young about their position, which is known to be unfortunate. She explained that Mrs L. had been L.'s most brilliant student while he held a University post as English lecturer for six years. Then they had married. At the end of the six years the post came up for revision: L. had expected re-appointment for another period, thereafter permanently. Nothing of the kind. Through some hostility of the academic authorities he lost the post and has now to live on giving lessons, though he has also a tiny post as lecturer in a specially hard-up college. Yet he publishes *Scrutiny*, which is eagerly read by his old students all over the world, and he is overwhelmed by students who make their way to him for advice and training. As for his wife, she wrote her brilliant, searching book, 'Fiction and the Reading Public', as a thesis years ago, but has not had leisure to do anything else except articles for *Scrutiny*.

Dr L. has fluency and pungency in talk, though he finds writing a slow, difficult matter. 'My wife's the making of *Scrutiny*, you know. She's a born journalist, and comes to the rescue, especially when a promised article fails to turn up at the last moment. Incredible to me how she can write straight off like that. With me, writing's a long struggle ...'

Again and again he confessed: 'But I'm so tired. I'm undertaking too much. Even now I can't speak as I should because I've got my eyes on that boy over there. There's no need, as his mother's here and at leisure. But we're so used to the need for watching him.'

The boy was little Ralph, terribly nervy and delicate, physically unable to 'tolerate fats' and mentally alert enough for the age of six instead of two. He didn't sleep, his father said, and he had been very ill.

While Jean and Mrs L. talked on the sofa about their common friends, I asked about *Scrutiny*, in which (March) I had just been reading his grand revaluation of Keats. What relation was *Scrutiny* to the two volumes called 'Scrutinies', collected from files of the *Calendar of Letters*? He said it was in direct descent. He had immensely valued the *Calendar* while it lasted, and had admired the critical intelligence of the young men — Edgell Rickword, Garman, and Bertram Higgins — who had run it:

'The *Calendar* was an important review, and I couldn't help regretting it should be forgotten and unused. It was very little known or circulated at the time, and complete sets are now unobtainable. I had my set bound and kept it safely; but I thought something could be done about it and, two years ago, I got Wishart to publish a volume compiled from the *Calendar* — "Towards Standards of Criticism".'

He showed me a copy, with an essay by Bertram Higgins in it, which he much admired; said Bertram was a wonderfully sound and shrewd critic and wondered how that little *Calendar* group had got themselves 'educated' — had they educated one another by good conversation? He asked me how old Bertram was, and when I told him thirty-five said that made him think all the more of him — he must have been under twenty-five in the days when he had followed him and found him so sound.

'As for Rickwood and Garman, it seems they've gone all to pieces. Call themselves marxists, but are really just Bloomsbury, knocking round at cocktail-parties and not doing any thinking.'

I told him I thought he was misinformed — that Garman was in poor health, lived in the country and came to town every week to deliver a careful literary lecture, while Edgell Rickword had just taken over the managership of an important publishing business. But L.'s apt to suspect a young writer of turning Bloomsbury, which means for him — I asked for his definition — 'an acceptance and bandying about of current fashionable notions on literature.' He complained that the Indians he had seen lately were hopelessly Bloomsbury, and I found he meant Iqbal Singh and Anand.

'I've known Singh for years and have been disappointed in him. After a term at Cambridge he decided to leave. He was to be a genius; the University could give him nothing. Then lately he brought me his long story, 'When One is In It' — you've seen it?'

I certainly had: a tense, imaginative story of life among the cotton-spinners of Bombay.

'Well,' said Dr L., 'that, of course, was so hopeless I hardly knew how to tell him. He has no sense of writing at all. It's not as if he were a beginner. He's quite twenty-five and doesn't know more than that.'

(Leavis's tha-at has a dying fall; he never bites his words off with a snap. He is tired, neurotic, never indecisive, though; the dying fall finds its angle of repose.)

I demurred about Singh, admitting some turgid passages in the story but insisting on the strength and pattern and sincerity; L. said he would read it again, but I'm afraid he knows the answer. From Anand he seemed to hope for nothing, though he knew that E.M. Forster had prefaced his 'Untouchable.' When it comes to new material, entirely new material, I feel, L. is just as academic as the other academicians. He told me, innocently, that when he found a New Zealand student of his, named McCormick, doing a thesis on Tudor literature that bored him, he proposed that he should investigate something nearer home — 'The Reason Why There is No Literature in New Zealand.' An investigation with the answer known beforehand, $x = o$! The little modern continuity he admits in literature is nearly all very safe — Eliot, Forster, Virginia Woolf, Lawrence, Joyce and (I hear incredibly) Charles Morgan!

Nettie Palmer, *Fourteen Years: Extracts from a Private Journal*, pp. 204–7.

Epistolary crises

Anyone who is truly interested in punctuation is on the side of the life forces.

These interested people, so far as I have met them, may be of all ages. I have met one, aged five, and have received entrancing letters from another aged ninety-four. The person aged five was just beginning to read, and what was more, to write: and better than all her words she liked the little marks she learnt to put beside them. She liked the question mark you could make out of a pothook, with a little ball underneath it, when you wrote down important questions out of games like, 'O say, what is she weeping for?' There was another mark, though, more interesting still. It was just a stick balanced upright in the air, with a little ball underneath it, and you called it a wonder-mark. It came in when some grown-up might say, 'She's got her shoes muddy.' The person aged five liked putting the wonder-mark directly against the most surprising word, even if it made a bumpy-looking sentence. This way: 'We climbed that hill in ten! minutes.'

I think she was right to experiment. My correspondent aged ninety-four was perhaps less revolutionary, but his punctuation was elastic and expressive enough. With him a comma was a comma, never a mere casual concession to habit. He used no promiscuous pepper-castor to distribute his full-points. His colons and semi-colons, sparingly used, had their separate purposes. He could even use a dash, and he did, saving it up for that kind of epistolary crisis when nothing but a dash will serve.

Nettie Palmer, 'On Stops' in *Nettie Palmer* (ed. Vivian Smith), pp. 448–9.

War in Catalonia

Nettie and Vance Palmer made their way into Barcelona during the Spanish Civil War, where their elder daughter Aileen was serving with the medical service of the International Brigade.

Next morning, before dawn, the firing in Barcelona began again, and, for want of definite news, things seemed worse than before. A village woman, who did our cleaning, came with stories that had leaked through. Barcelona was just a heap of ruins, she said. The hospitals were crowded out with wounded, and dead were lying in all the streets. It could not be worse. She sat crying in the kitchen, wondering how she would ever get news of her parents, who lived in an alley near the centre of the fighting.

There was a sense of dreadful things happening everywhere. The milkman told about a heart-breaking affair not far along the road where two lorries carrying eager militiamen had mistaken one another for enemies in the dark.

During the morning I heard shots, and looked from the balcony. Our next door neighbour, who had been reading under a eucalyptus tree in the lane, was stretched behind a stone seat, protecting his head with a newspaper. Down the main road a couple of well-dressed motorists, one curiously like Trotsky, had been turned out of their car and were standing with their hands up. Lorries and cars full of armed men came racing up from both directions. There was a rattle of questions, and it looked as if there might be a gruesome execution there at the bottom of the garden. But after a long examination, the car was allowed to drive on.

Lying awake that night we determined to get to the city at all costs. We knew that General Goded (the insurgent leader, whose execution was reported yesterday) had been captured, so that the worst of the fighting was over, but the district was full of fugitives and suspected Fascists.

While we were having our breakfast, there was a loud banging on the front door. There had been some firing on a military lorry at the end of our lane, and armed peasants were searching every house for firearms.

No, it was not at all harrowing, just a little unreal, those heavy, tired men doing their duty solemnly and even courteously. The leader was blunt in his refusal to accept our word, and his 'off-sider', a tall, quiet boy, was careful to say, 'We will not bother you long. We have to search the whole street, but if we don't find anything, we will go away immediately.' Downstairs and upstairs they ransacked cupboards, earnestly peering into my harmless diaries and notes on Spanish literature.

Nettie Palmer in *Nettie Palmer* (ed. Vivian Smith), pp. 524–5.

A man of the world

Critic and novelist Vance Palmer (1885–1959), best known for The Legend of the Nineties, *had the opportunity while in London to meet the flamboyant philanderer Frank Harris.*

People have often wondered how Harris, with his scandalous record as liar, swindler, profligate and libeller, could yet hold the loyalty, even the affection, of such men as Shaw, Yeats, Bennett, and Max Beerbohm. The answer lay in his generous impulses which were quite as marked as his vices. He protested violently against public injustice; he gave money away freely to those who asked for it; he made unusual gestures, such as carrying off Ben Tillett, the wharfies' leader, every year for a recuperative holiday at his villa in the Riviera. Personally there was an attraction in the mysterious vitality of the man and the tones and undertones of his great voice; an attraction, too, in his democratic easiness. I was astonished once, when I had sent him a short story, to get a friendly, informal note saying he didn't quite like the end of it and asking me to come in and talk it over. All he was concerned about, I found, was the particular poison I had used for a character's suicide!

'Why lysol?' he greeted me. 'Lysol! Good God, man, you don't need to be as brutal as that, do you? Why not — well, laudanum?'

And with this particular point settled he was ready to bring out the decanter and hold forth on a number of things — his own short stories, his early experiences as a sand-hog working on the foundations of Brooklyn Bridge, his first invasion of London when he had bearded the proprietors of *The Fortnightly Review* and asked them peremptorily for the editorship. It was a monologue that went on for a couple of hours. Leaning forward over the table, jumping up to pace about the carpeted floor, he talked as if he could not stem the flow of that compelling voice of his which, as someone said, sounded as if he had been granted an extra organ; and he passed easily from witty description to obscene rhetoric directed against the British aristocracy. Harris was small, gipsy-dark, deep-chested, and formidable. His own conception of himself seemed to be, now that of a powerful bandit, now a genius like Shakespeare, now a Man of Sorrows.

'Christ goes deeper than I do', he is reported to have said once, 'but I have had a wider experience'.

Vance Palmer, 'London Days' in *Meanjin* 2/1959, p. 220.

A romantic ending

Vance Palmer was close to Clem and Nina Christesen and to the literary journal, Meanjin, *for which he once played cricket. He can be seen as having had an operatically romantic death.*

Meanjin was still temporarily being produced out of the house in Carlton when Clem's signs of relief were cut short by the personal sorrow of Vance Palmer's death. On 15 July Vance had invited Nina to his house to read a play he had written, in which he thought one of her student protégées might act. When he moved to give the fire a poke, he suffered a sudden heart attack and died — sagging backwards, caught by the woman he adored.

Judith Armstrong, *The Christesen Romance*, p. 131.

Concerning decadence

A.R. Chisholm (1888–1981) was one of that line of Australian scholars who carried forward Brennan's line of scholarship in French symbolist poetry. As we can see from his anecdote here, his Sydney colleague G.G. Nicholson did not share their enthusiasm.

His lectures on philology were good, but rather too schematic, with long lists of sound changes in the transition from Latin to French. I discovered only several years later that he was exactly the opposite, as far as philology was concerned, of what we had thought him to be. To us as undergraduates he seemed a hard and fast conservative; whereas actually, in books that he was then preparing, he turned out to be a brilliant revolutionary. So much so, indeed, that he wrecked more than a few etymologies which had for a century or more been taken for granted.

His weakest point was literature. It was not that he lacked insight or appreciation: he almost had tears in his eyes when he spoke of his idol, Lamartine. But he would not or could not believe that anything of real value was produced after the Romantic period. Many years later, when I sent him an off-print of an article on Baudelaire, he praised my method, but added that he looked on Baudelaire as a loathsome personality; that he had never read his poetry, and that he never intended to read it.

A.R. Chisholm, *Men were My Milestones: Australian Portraits and Sketches*, p. 51.

Kissing the shark

The naturalist A.H. Chisholm was no relation of French scholar A.R. of the same name. Ion L. Idriess, later an Australian bestselling author, tells here of his first meeting with Chisholm and with publisher George Robertson.

Well, this chap, the birdman bloke, he was then the editor of the Sydney *Telegraph*, he was a bigshot, one of the big men of the city, and I wrote up to tell him about a funny little bird I'd seen hopping about up there. Chisholm didn't know that bird so he wrote to the *Bulletin*. 'This mad bloody wanderer who sometimes comes down to Sydney and writes things, will you send this letter to him?' So I got this letter, saying when I came to Sydney to come and see him [and tell him] whatever I knew about this bird. He spoke to me and I told him about where I'd come from and about the island, and he said, 'You ought to write a book.' I said, 'I have written a book, I wrote it up on the peak of Hammock Island. There you are, it's here.' He took me straight across the road to Angus & Robertson's, right up the stairs, still holding on to my arm, and away at the end was our lovely old Miss Betty, she was a dear old girl, boss of all the young girls, and even in those days they needed a boss. She was a lovely old girl.

Beside her was standing a great big long giant of a man with a great big black Ned Kelly bloody beard and a very austere, severe, distrustful-looking countenance. Chisholm ran me up beside him and said, 'Here you are, George, I've got your dream, what you wanted, at last. The great Australian novel.' I looked at this bloke, and this was George Robertson of Angus & Robertson, the founder and all. I told him my little story and I said, 'I'm buggered if I know whether it's a book. I reckon it is. What do you think?' He said, 'I've read many a bloody story like that.'

Mind, I'd just come down from the bush, down in the city I suppose I looked — of course, they thought us bushies were, you know, half nuts.

Anyway, he took the manuscript to read. [Eventually] he said, 'I'm a bit interested in that awful manuscript, it really is.' Mind, I fully accepted that, because it was written with a stub of a pencil up on top of a bloody hilly peak out in the wild bloody sea. He said, 'One condition.' So I said, 'Yeah?' And Chisholm said — he was true blue, he was very keen on Australian literature — 'No conditions.' 'No conditions, with a manuscript like this?' he says. 'Look here, young fellow,' and he spoke to me, 'no book would ever sell, particularly in our Australia, unless it's got love in it. It must have love.' I said, 'What do you think I could do, make love to a tomtit or a tiger shark?'

So I went home, and I thought it out. So I brought in a girl from Cairns and it's just like a love story written by a young lad, sandwiched in between primitive, red hot stuff, you see.

Ion L. Idriess in *Self Portraits* (ed. David Foster), p. 78.

A demurral

Novelist Martin Boyd (1893–1972) was the gentlest of imaginable narrators; sugar would hardly melt in his tea.

H.H. Champion, a publisher in Melbourne, who had been concerned with Bernard Shaw and others in some pre-war political activities which led to disturbances in Trafalgar Square, gave me letters of introduction to several celebrated writers. I sent three of them to Cunninghame Graham, Galsworthy, and to Bernard Shaw, who, Mr Champion told me, would fall on the neck of any friend of his. Cunninghame Graham asked me to dine at his club, Galsworthy asked me to tea, but I only had a curt note from Bernard Shaw's secretary.

Galsworthy's invitation was to his delightful old house in Hampstead. To my surprise I was received in a drawing-room gay with Queen Anne lacquer. I had somehow imagined him in a setting of thick brown carpets, dark mahogany, and book-lined walls. Both Mr and Mrs Galsworthy were charming to me. He showed me his old glass, told me that he liked 'Reynard the Fox' best of Masefield's poems, and after tea we went into the garden where he threw sticks for the dog. I mentioned Mr Champion. He hesitated, smiled faintly, and said: 'Actually, I don't know Mr Champion.'

Martin Boyd, *Day of My Delight*, pp. 115–16.

Silence is golden

Bill Harney (1895–1962) was a latter-day outback version of Randolph Bedford and, as 'Bilarni', a good friend to Aborigines of the Centre. When he and Herbert got going together it must have been like a meeting of Titans.

One of my favourite Harney stories is of an incident which, Bill told me, never actually happened. I think you will agree, however, that it carries the ring of truth, like the tale of King Alfred and the cakes. As a professional collector of memories, verbal impressions, and the gossip and hearsay of our day, I ascribe to these surface manifestations a validity which the more pedantic might hesitate to endorse; and in spite of Bill Harney's denial I insist that this story is true — because it deserves to be.

The story is that some years ago Bill visited Xavier Herbert who was living in the Queensland bush. He followed a track from the railway station, plugging uphill on his fat little strong legs, and in due course sighted a cottage ahead of him. As he approached, Xavier appeared on the verandah. The two old friends shook hands, but Xavier held up his left hand like a traffic cop and said: 'Don't speak! Not a word!' Still holding Bill by the hand he led the way into the cottage and steered him into a chair. 'Not a word, not a word!' he repeated, and he picked up an alarm clock. It must of course be appreciated that the human species can seldom have produced two talkers more tireless, more inveterate, than Bill Harney and Xavier Herbert. The latter repeated his injunction — 'Silence, please. Don't speak!' — while winding and setting the clock. He then plunked it down, sat himself at the table, and said: 'Now, you old bastard, the first hour's mine!'

John Thompson, 'Remembrance of Things Past', in *Meanjin* 1/1964, p. 98.

Micks and Prots

The old warfare between Catholic and Protestant children has pretty much faded away, but the versatile historian Sir Keith Hancock (1898–1988) calls it back from his boyhood days in the Melbourne suburbs.

It would be agreeable if I could now record a genuine and enduring amendment of my character but all I can say honestly is that I learnt prudence. Although I was a strong little boy I was not really brave; indeed, I am inclined to think that my outbreak of brutal exhibitionism had expressed a hidden desire to bluff not only my fellows but myself. Billy à Pack taught me to recognize my limitations and frame my behaviour accordingly. Although I still fought when I had to, fighting ceased to be my trade.

About this time I found myself in a gang of Protestant heroes who used to exchange taunts and threats with a Roman Catholic gang. We would chant:

Cathlick Dogs
Jump like Frogs
Eat no meat on Fri-ee-days.

And they would sing:

Proddy Dog, Proddy Dog,
Sitting on a well,
Up comes the Devil
And pulls him down to hell.

Then we and the Catholic boys would pelt each other with cow-dung. There was plenty of it lying about on the river bank, some of it too new and wet to pick up, some of it too dry and light to hurt; what every boy looked for was a piece that was dry and hard outside but with a centre of green sticky muck. But even when we scored or suffered a hit or two with these stinking bombs we never threw stones, nor, so far as I can remember, fought with our fists. When we had flung enough cow-dung we chanted our doggerel again and went our separate ways jeering.

Keith Hancock, Country and Calling, p. 50.

Jacobean considerations

Like many a word child, Norman Lindsay's prolific son Jack (1900–90) remembers one of those embarrassing occasions when he put a schoolteacher right.

I grew conceited in my reading. When the brown-tweeded master commenting on the *Epitaph on the Countess of Pembroke*, took a look at the notes at the back of his book and told the class, 'That is by Ben Jonson,' I interjected, 'No, it isn't, it's by William Browne of Tavistock.' The class laughed and I was ordered outside. After, the master called me in. 'Look here, Lindsay, probably you're right, blast you, but don't contradict me in front of the class, do you hear?'

Jack Lindsay, Life Rarely Tells, p. 36.

The silky opalescent sheen

Historian Jack Lindsay wrote three colourful volumes of auto-biography, informed by adolescent bohemianism and mature Marxism. He begins here in Brisbane, with the lurid life of Fortitude Valley.

And once, taking a short cut near the shopping centre of the Valley, I stumbled on a day-street of such unashamed bitchery. I was in a hurry and my pace gave offence to a blowsy wench lounging broad-bosomed in a doorway among the strings of a bead curtain. She shouted an insult or a proposal, and when I hurried faster, she shouted yet more loudly. Scarlet-mouthed trollops in frowsy lace petticoats or slack dressing-gowns came out yawning and puffy-eyed to watch the fun. I suppose they thought I was trying to bilk one of the sisterhood. Anyway they joined in the noise, and I ran, dodging into safety, into the normal traffic of the Valley, past a girl who opened her kimono to hedge me in, showing swollen breasts with the silky opalescent sheen of a Rubensesque *Kermes*.

Jack Lindsay, *Life Rarely Tells*, pp. 5–6.

A word child

In the best Lindsay tradition, Jack found himself caught between the world of reading and that of young women. His bookishness was something of a puzzle to an old digger.

We ourselves were still in the boarding-house near the rowing club. The proprietress, an efficient hard-faced woman with a scar over one eye, had taken up with a discharged soldier who had been wounded in the left arm. He sat drooping on the piano stool, picking out tunes with one hand or playing with the ginger cat. He was proud of being able to roll cigarettes with his one free hand. Once, as I sat on the verandah, waiting for the factory girls to go noisily by, he stood over me, 'What the devil do you keep on finding to read?' He scowled, 'Your mother says you write things? I'll tell you my life some day and let's see if you could write that up. Nobody'd believe it. I could make a pot of money if I had the patience to write it all out. But I can't read for ten minutes on end, let alone write. Anyone who can stick it must be a bit potty.'

Then the girls came pouring out of the galvanized-iron gates and saved me from his suggestions.

Jack Lindsay, *Life Rarely Tells*, p. 79.

On the astral plane

One does not normally associate the world of the medium, the planchette board and the communicating spirits with scholarly questions about classical metres. However, Jack Lindsay hoped that his stepmother's psychic powers might help him with some research.

Only once however I participated in the board business. Norman believed that in Rose lay the force which brought the messages into our time-space. He asked her if she thought I might hold the stick with her. I had the feeling that she wasn't pleased, but she agreed.

That evening in the water-colour studio we held the stick, which pointed out various letters, words. Nothing very impressive happened. It seemed an off-evening in the spirit world, with the more important characters gone roystering off into some yet remoter sphere. However, I asked various questions, to which I did not receive illuminating answers. For instance, I asked if the Homeric hexameter was much older than scholars suspected and if its roots lay in the Mykenean world. (I already had a notion, on general grounds, that the Greeks had much earlier origins than the textbooks said and that their culture had close links with the Mykenean and later Minoan societies, as has now been proved by the reading of Linear Script B.) If there was anything one would expect Apollo to be well up in, it was such matters. But I got no clear reply; I was told that the subject would have to be gone into.

Jack Lindsay, *The Roaring Twenties*, pp. 304–5.

The doomed beauty of Sydney

Anne Brennan is an almost mythical figure in Australian culture. Daughter of the poet, she was beautiful and highly intelligent. Turned out of her mother's home, she was for a while a prostitute. She died in her thirty-second year.

One Saturday night I went to an Italian café, the Roma, then popular with us all, accompanied by a girl I was getting around with in those days. To my surprise, there was Anne seated alone at a table, looking very tired and ill. I had not seen her for some time; I believe she had been in Melbourne. As we passed her, I wished her good evening and she replied with that slow, grave, sweet smile of hers. When my girl and I were seated, she excitedly asked who Annie was. I told her and she exclaimed how beautiful she was. 'You should have seen her a couple of years ago,' I replied, unconsciously quoting Hugh's remark to me when I first saw Anne. But my girl could not take her eyes off Anne and said that I must introduce them as she wished to kiss her! (My girl was perfectly normal, let me say.) I was horrified and told her not to be silly, not to dream even of doing such a thing as Annie was by that time rotten with T.B. and God only knows what else. However, when we had finished our meal and were leaving the table, she rushed over to Anne, introduced herself, and asked if she might kiss her. I looked on, stricken but entranced. Annie, with all the dignity and grace of a princess, gave that irresistible, beautiful smile of hers and accepted the kiss as her rightful homage. I never saw her again.

Jack Lindsay, *The Roaring Twenties*, pp. 380–1.

Clean bowled

For all his versatility, Jack Lindsay recalls his culpable unaware-ness of Test cricket.

Having acquired a beard, I needed a new photo in my pass-port; but as I knew no clergyman, etc., I went to Australia House to ask someone to vouch for me. The official I saw was sympathetic, though concerned to find out why I had grown such a luxuriant beard. He chatted on, and happened to bring up the fact that the Australians were playing cricket at Lord's. My blank ignorance of this world-shattering event must have made him doubtful of my Australianism; however he signed my photo.

Jack Lindsay, *Fanfrolico and After*, p. 536.

The woman within

Always concerned with the state of the human heart, Manning Clark records an interview with novelist Eleanor Dark (1901–85) and with sublimity.

There was so much to discover, so much to explore. The glow of those years was like the effect of music on the mind: it made me believe I was capable of things I was not really capable of. In that glow I wrote to Eleanor Dark, the author of *The Timeless Land*, one of my teachers on the influence of the spirit of the place on all those who live in Australia, the creator of Wunbula and the image of the 'winged bird' sail-ing on the bosom of the 'very vast sea'. I asked her to speak to the honours class in Australian history. She came. She was shy with the class until David Bennet, the grandson of John Monash, but as different from his illustrious grandparent as Melbourne is from Sydney, asked her to tell us why she wrote such beautiful prose poetry about the Australian landscape. Words gushed out of her, her eyes, hitherto dim, lit up as though the woman within had switched on a light. The discussion became lively.

She invited Dymphna and me to visit her at Katoomba. There it was like resuming a conversation which could never have an end. After tea, and that exchange of those special looks which acknowledge a bond, and the inner confidence nourished by such an awareness, she took us for a walk to a place in the Blue Mountains where we could see not a mark of man's presence or interference, but only the gaunt rocks, the steep valleys, the ridges clothed with trees which did not move, one of those views in Australia which seem to me to convey a message of vast indifference to all human striving, all human hopes. She sat on a rock, her face as much a riddle as that universe down below us. She quoted from one of the diaries she had read for *No Barrier*. 'The country ahead appears to be not easy of access.' I got the message that the human heart was even less easy of access.

Manning Clark, *The Quest for Grace*, p. 174.

Deciding on Mordecaius

The learned poet Bertram Higgins, often seen as a pioneer of modernist poetry in Melbourne, is caught here in the creative act by Nettie Palmer.

September 26th, 1931

Went across this afternoon to see Bertram Higgins, convalescent from a broken ankle. He was on a chaise longue, in the garden of the old family home, a roomy rambling villa. Three or four people on the lawn — mostly disciples who look upon him as a rare visitant from the world of Eliot and Valéry. Weeks of enforced quiescence have made Bertram's mind keener than ever, even in daytime — usually he begins to warm to a long complete discussion about midnight.

Today his slight figure looked fatigued, his face fine-drawn, though he is grimly amused by his mishap.

He was letting people assist him in 'assembling' some background details for a long poem that is taking months to write. 'Not,' he said in a firm severe aside, 'not that the poem is entitled to any special consideration on that account.'

So far as I can gather, the poem's to be in free verse — his own variant of it. A kind of rhapsodic monologue by a Jew, old enough to have witnessed the Crucifixion and to be now experiencing the eruption of Vesuvius at Pompeii. The present darkness over the land recalls to him the darkness of a day forty years earlier. In the darkness of death he feels his way alone, toward an illusory safety, still, *in extremis*, chiefly concerned with the meaning of life for himself.

But the man's name? That's very important. It must show him as what he is — a Jew of Rome, a Romanised Jew. Would he change his original name to Gaius, Caius? But that would obliterate all his origin. Could a Latin ending be put on some Jewish name — David, Absalom? There was Josephus about the same time. Someone ran through great Jewish names: Moses, Nehemiah, Ezra, Daniel, Mordecai ... Mordecaius! The last part overlapping to give the appearance of a pure Roman name, it makes a wise pun fit for Joyce.

It was forthwith decided; the title of the poem would be 'Mordecaius.' The name need not be used in the actual lines, nor will Mordecaius ever say plainly, 'I am a Jew, now a Roman citizen. I was at the Crucifixion; now I am at Pompeii.' All this will underlie his soliloquy, and the title, 'Mordecaius', will have the task of making what revelation is allowed.

Nettie Palmer, *Fourteen Years: Extracts from a Private Journal,* pp. 70–1.

The nose-picking waiter

There are many anecdotes about bow-tied, plump clubman Kenneth Slessor (1901–71), some of them speculations on why he gave up poetry at 40. Humorist Alex Macdonald recalls here a debate about the scansion of a vaudeville quatrain with poets Slessor and Douglas Stewart.

And now seemed an ideal time to have a little chin-wag about the Muse. Beers were lined up, and I said my piece.

'I'd like your critical opinions of a short sociological poem written by a friend of mine.'

Slessor and Stewart eyed me as if I'd turned into a death adder, but I pressed on: 'It goes as follows:

"What will you have?" said the waiter,
Reflectively picking his nose.

"I'll have two boiled eggs, you bastard,
You can't put your fingers in those." '

I was gratified to hear a couple of appreciative snorts from my audience.

'Not bad,' said Slessor. 'Who wrote it?'

'Our mutual friend, the late George Wallace, senior, the celebrated Tivoli Thespian.'

'I think the third line could be improved, though,' said Stewart. 'Better would be — "Two hard boiled eggs, you bastard".'

'I don't agree,' said Slessor. 'The anapaest gives a cumulative effect which — '

'Oh, come off it,' said Stewart, testily. He dipped his finger in the beer and made marks on the bar counter —

$$\cup \; — \; \cup \; — \; \cup \; — \; \cup$$

— "Two hard boiled eggs, you bastard" improves the whole — '

'Yes, yes,' said Slessor, dipping his finger in beer. 'But to counterbalance the first line —

— ' "What will you *have?*" said the waiter' you need —

∪∪ — ∪ — ∪ — ∪

"I'll have *two* boiled eggs, you bastard", with the stress on "two".'

'Rubbish!' said Stewart. 'The stress should be on hard! "*hard* boiled eggs, you bastard!" This gives hardness to the idea of the invulnerability of the eggs from this bastard's fingers, see?'

(They were now starting to raise their voices slightly, and exciting not a little attention from the good burghers of Mittagong who happened to be standing around.)

'No I don't see at all,' said Slessor.

Alexander Macdonald cited in Geoffrey Dutton, *Kenneth Slessor: A Biography*, pp. 311–12.

The marmalade pineapple

In a memorable vignette, almost a prose poem, Hal Porter records his first meeting with Slessor, in the company of Angus & Robertson editor Beatrice Davis and academic anthologist Guy Howarth. Porter is disappointed, to put it mildly.

Slessor?

You first see and hear him at Sydney University. He's on the last stretch of an evening lecture on Christopher Brennan of whom you know nothing, haven't even heard. As the taxi-cab draws up among neo-Gothic towers and creepered walls, a small wind, hissing between its teeth, untidily scampers every which way. There's a full moon speeding through a spume of clouds. Now so near a hero, your heart is holding its breath, and you're mutely counting down.

Eight ... seven ... six ...

Are we too late? Beatrice Davis and Guy Howarth, with you in tow, scuttle under Gothicky arches. Beatrice wears a Michael-Arlenish Garbo hat of bottle-green velours. Guy Howarth, about forty-eight, plump, not tall, effervescent and sprightly — he, as Nan McDonald does, somehow matches in appearance and manner his poems. You're about to find out if Slessor does. Quick down this last corridor.

Five ... four ... three ...

We sidle into the back of the lecture room.

Two ... one ...

You look towards the ...

Zero!

Where's your highwayman?

This is he.

The moon outside skids to a halt. The room too. It becomes colourless, odourless, silent. Next, all the world's clocks begin again to tick.

One-*one*. Two-*two*. Three-*three*.

This is he. Standing at the lectern is a — how to write it? — marmalade cat. That, truly, is your first impression. Not tall at all, your highwayman. Solid as a pineapple, more male than masculine, gestureless, pink-full-faced, with short, slicked-down gingery hair, pale eyes. The dandy touch alone tallies with prevision. The marmalade cat's well-licked, sleek, diligently immaculate, fastidiousness made flesh in raiment. Always easy to spring when a man's clothes are chosen by a woman. There's none of that women's magazine colour-chart taste here. He wears, as it were, his own inevitable fur. The voice you could've had the idiocy to imagine metallic yet sonorous is without timbre, grog-abraded, cigar-kippered.

' "O desolate eves along the way ..." ' it quotes, flat and unpoetic, ' "Desperate eves, when the wind-bitten hills turn'd violet along their rims ..." '

After the performance, mentally making the picky motions of a man collecting bits of himself after a detonation, you go with Beatrice and Slessor to Guy Howarth's … chambers? room? study? office? … whatever-it-is a Reader in English Literature occupies in a university. This, at the age of forty-four, is the first time you've set foot in a university, and it's consoling to find a 1930s film, *A Yank at Oxford*, with Robert Taylor, Maureen O'Sullivan, and delicious new actress called Vivien Leigh, has prepared you for what to expect architecturally. That's about all, though. From somewhere among the ceiling-high bookshelves and scholarly furniture, Guy exhumes what you've hitherto only associated with penurious artists or blackfellows on the rantan, a flagon of liver-coloured Australian wine, a half-gallon of it. CLARET announces the label. As the level sinks, *they* talk much of the Christopher Brennan person at whose Johnsonian and drunken feet Slessor, you gather, spent many a rumbustious night when gaslight, tango teas, Gaby Deslys figurines, and unmixed bathing are on the way out, and 1923 on the way in with the donkeys and camels of Oscar Asche's *Chu Chin Chow* traipsing through Sydney.

Listening to the trialogue, you're content to devote yourself to inconspicuousness, to let the grass grow under your tongue. What do you know about the backstairs life of Sydney's literati or of Brennan, of these local legends told in the voices of people reciting from Homer?

Perhaps to entertain the foreigner, now as lively as a tin of camp pie, some Brennan relics, of which Guy Howarth (or the University) has a small collection, are brought out. They're so miserably pathetic, so morbidly similar to the Lafcadio Hearn ones you saw at Matsue, Japan, in September 1950 (a darned sock, grey flannel combinations with armpits curdled by old sweat, two dumb-bells, a tooth-glass, a decrepit frock-coat) you're jolted alert. There's a mange-blotched top-hat with a blob of mud on it from, they tell you, the last gutter the sozzled Brennan ever fell in. The Well-known Literary Characters dismay you. To your own amazement you burst out:

'You ghouls!'

The succinct quack doesn't discompose your companions or cause an earth tremor.

As though you've just become visible, Slessor says:

'Hal, where are you staying in Sydney?'

Hal Porter, The Extra, pp. 93–6.

A card

Slessor specialised in farewell gestures: they crystallised his stylish dissatisfaction with the universe.

As for his career as official war correspondent, Slessor has the last word. Some time after his resignation, Slessor met the journalist and humorist Alexander Macdonald at a pub called the Bells at Woolloomooloo, recently taken over by the famous boxer, Jimmy Carruthers. Slessor said someone ought to write a ballad about it. He had already begun one:

> God help the man who starts a blue
> In the Bells Hotel in Woolloomooloo…

He then produced his card, one of those Noela had ordered long ago in London. Macdonald recorded that under the words ' "Kenneth Slessor, Official War Correspondent", he had written in his small, crabbed hand, "Retd, Hurt" '.

Geoffrey Dutton, Kenneth Slessor: A Biography, p. 251.

Ham on the floor

The baroque, or perhaps rococo, prose of Hal Porter here captures the misogynist Slessor punishing his second wife, Pauline.

By half-past nine we're in Elizabeth Bay. Pauline, surprised at our before-midnight arrival, and rattled, quite properly, by the request for a meal, nevertheless sets about preparing it. Bowls and plates appear, German, very white white. Soon a tureen of vichyssoise appears, ham, a salad. Conscious that the ice is wafer-thin, some delicatesses anaesthetised, and the room shot through with misery-coloured inklings, you attempt — friend's friend — guestly quips and cranks. As well might a muezzin ululate from his minaret above a plaza seething with Christadelphians. Something's up. Slessor picks a slice of ham, a square slice like flexible laminex, from his plate, and holds it up by one corner.

'I said,' he says, tonelessly yet pentametrically, 'always buy ham cut from the bone.'

You agree entirely but are appalled at his saying it thus, in front of you, his eyes frozen steady yet having the perfidious glitter of a scalpel.

When Pauline, as wives must, begins, rationabilissima, some explanations — a boar strike? a plague in the delicatessen? — milord lets the slice fall to the floor. The crash is noiseless but deafening. Without a word he grinds the sole of his shoe on it. This seems, headman's blade quivering in the block, to close a subject. He begins again to walk the waters of politesse. You're blushing like the Swiss flag. Should men over forty blush? Still blushing, you start to chatter vivaciously as if men and women pursuing a goal you can't see aren't a riddle to you, as if you've not twigged the mother in the vinegar.

Poor Pauline, her face sacked of vitality, swimming truly now in a mirror on the wall.

Poor Slessor, time-vexed, his own rather tedious hero, in the Harbour-blue shirt, the dead-centre pussy-cat bow tie, polka-dotted if you please.

Hal Porter cited in Geoffrey Dutton, *Kenneth Slessor: A Biography*, p. 289.

Debating the skylark

Slessor crushes a fellow journalist and friend.

I remember this particular party was December 1966. In addition to Ken, Alex Macdonald was there, Douglas Stewart, Ross Campbell.

And the thing that sticks in my mind was that Ken and Ross got into a terrible bloody argument. It started off innocently enough, they were talking about poetry and Shelley's 'Ode to a Skylark' came up. And Ross said, 'That's verbal twaddle', or words to that effect. Whereupon Ken took to him, his face got red and the cigar jutted out of his mouth. And he said, 'It is a supreme lyric.' And then he turned around and said 'That Campell, he wouldn't know a poem from a donkey's arse!' And they were working together on the *Telegraph*.

Geoffrey Dutton, *Kenneth Slessor: A Biography*, p. 318.

How like you this?

Ian Mair was a literary wit and long-time Age *reviewer, notable for his gnomic utterances. He long ago described the present editor in a review as one 'for whom no pittosporum hedge is opaque'.*

I went to lunch with Mair in his old age. The venue was his favourite South Yarra pub. Conversation turned to my mother's old friend, the lovely Irma Janetski, long since dead. 'Oh, yes, beautiful white skin, she had,' he said. Then he went on: 'Alwyn Lee wrote a sonnet on her. Literally on her. We were all at a party and Alwyn told her that he wanted to write the sonnet. And that it was to be *on* her. So they went into the bathroom and she stripped off to that lovely white skin. Alwyn wrote the sonnet on her back. The lucky devil!'

Chris Wallace-Crabbe, 'Character Isolated by a Deed', p. iii.

A touch of luck

Nina Christesen, who, with Clem, was a good friend to Christina Stead (1902–83) on her return to Australia after many years abroad, reports on Stead's powerful sense of her own childhood and of an overwhelming father.

She talked about her father again, his reticence about sex, his and her own strong sexuality. Also repeated the story of how her stepmother sent her once for some milk which she spilt on the way home and how, foolishly trying to scoop it up from the sand, she stumbled on a gold coin. 'Things that are bad always turned to my advantage,' she said. 'If I didn't have such a bad time at home I shouldn't have developed my capacity to observe.'

Quoted in Judith M. Armstrong, *The Christesen Romance*, pp. 198–9.

The king of sweets

From Nettie Palmer, again, by way of the writer Brian Penton, comes this glimpse of the distant relations between the world of letters and a captain of industry, famous for his chocolates.

Had expected Brian Penton up for the day, but his Sydney paper suddenly gave him an assignment for the weekend and his wire included a 'curse it' that the postmistress kindly let through intact. He is over here describing the personalities of the Victorian Centenary and he does it as if he were sure of an audience that could read between the lines and understand all the implications. In a way his technique is like that of Dorothy Parker in her relentless stories; he gives people in their own terms, putting hardly a word into their mouths that they wouldn't acknowledge and even admire, yet achieving a sardonic portrait.

There was, for instance, the interview with Sir Macpherson Robertson he told me about when we were having lunch in town the other day. Wearing his professional-vestigial white coat like a sacred vestment and smoothing his wavy, silver hair the millionaire was talking about the £10,000 he had given in prizes for the air-race. Penton congratulated him on his public spirit and innocently remarked how much larger his prizes were than those given for literature. He received a curious stare.

'Literature? What do you mean by that?'

'Well, original writing. Prizes were offered for novels, stories, poems, you know.'

'Oh, books. I never read them.'

Nettie Palmer, *Fourteen Years: Extracts from a Private Journal*, p. 137.

In dreams begin responsibilities

A.D. Hope (1907–) has been the doyen of terror and violence among Australian poets. In this filmed interview with Ann McCulloch, Hope reveals how far back his fears go, as he does elsewhere in that wonderful poem, 'Ascent into Hell'.

The first dreams I can remember were about lions and tigers and they were attacking the house I lived in. I could only see their paws. Because of the attack we were abandoning the house and for some strange reason we were getting into chaff bags to be hauled into a cart and driven away. My father wanted to put me into his chaff bag; I was terrified not being with my mother. That can tell you something about her.

Cited in Ann McCulloch, *A.D. Hope: The Dance of Language*, p. 13.

Instructing Mum

Some poets are both born and made. Hope remembers an intolerably long poem he wrote when he was eight years old.

I can remember about the age of eight, I wrote mother a long serious poem in ballad stanzas, so I must have been going a long time before that; I could manage it all right. The text of the bible was used for each stanza — 52 stanzas to teach her Christian duty through the year. I can still see poor mum trying not to laugh and she thanked me very much and said that perhaps if I paid more attention to my own Christian duties things would improve.

Cited in Ann McCulloch, *A.D. Hope: The Dance of Language*, p. 13.

Burn the lot

To every poet his or her muse, and for a teenage Alec Hope the painter Violet McKee arrived in provincial Bathurst, to set him on the right track.

The other event, momentous for me, was the arrival in Bathurst of a young painter. Violet McKee, a former student of Julian Ashton, set up her studio there. She was a friend of the Ennises, and one day as she left after visiting them I arrived from school and was introduced. She said, 'I hear you write poetry.' I admitted it and she went on. 'Would you like to come to tea with me in the studio next Wednesday afternoon, on your way back from school and let me see some of your poems?' I said I would, greatly excited to be meeting a real artist and a very attractive one, and I appeared at the appointed time with a large sheaf of my productions under my arm. She took them from me, saying, 'Come again next week at the same time and we'll talk about them when I've had time to read them properly. Today I'd just like to talk and find out a little about you.'

At that time I had just discovered Swinburne and was busy turning out second-hand Swinburne verse of intense passion and probably appalling imitation of his diction. I must have spent the days before I returned to the studio in a frenzy of anticipation but we had tea together and at last Vi took up the pile of verses and asked me to read some of them aloud. Then she said, 'I think you have a good deal of facility in handling words and metre but on the whole you are writing at second hand about things outside your own experience. If I were you I would burn all these', handing me back the whole lot, 'and set to work to write about things you really know something about. Why don't you begin with a description of the kitchen at home and bring it to me next week and I will suggest something else.'

It was of course a terrible blow, but I was already so much under her spell that next day I did exactly what she suggested, taking my precious work of genius up to the shed in the backyard of the house with a lighted candle, reading each poem through for the last time and then committing it to the flames. Then I set about the dreary business of describing a kitchen in minute detail. Actually I knew a good deal about kitchens because my mother had taught me to cook while my father was away at the war. I soon began to see what Vi McKee had had in mind, to enjoy finding things to write about in concrete terms instead of abstract and emotional ones.

A.D. Hope, *Chance Encounters*, pp. 41–2.

Slim Jim passes judgment

In this anecdote, mild-mannered Hope, adrift in the 1930s, meets his formidable junior, James McAuley (1916–), and is once again set right.

Among the graduates in the class who witnessed my downfall was the young poet James McAuley. A few days afterward he and several other poets knocked at my door saying, 'We have come to take you to drink some beer with us.' They led me to a very down-at-heels pub in a horrible slum which rejoiced in the name of Golden Grove but explained that it was the only pub in Sydney that sold the Tasmanian Cascade ale then favoured as the best brew in the country. During our potations McAuley said to me: 'I am told that you write poetry.' 'Yes,' I replied. 'Then you'd better show me some hadn't you and I'll tell you whether it's any good or not.' I wasn't too sure myself and he had an air of authority. So I said I would if he would come and collect some next day. This he did and we made a date to have dinner together on the following week. After dinner we retired to his room in a lodging-house. I sat in the only chair and McAuley perched on the bed and produced my sheaf of poems. As he went through them his most frequent comment was: 'That's crap and you should know it.' And he would throw the poem on the floor. But from time to time he would read all or part of a poem and say: 'Now that's a duck. You ought to carve that duck.' The pile of ducks was pitifully small when he handed them back to me and he made no detailed criticism, but when I compared the two piles, I saw what he meant and was forced to agree with him. Brief as it was, it was almost the only instruction I ever had in the art of poetry and the most decisive.

I may add that I told this story several times in Jim's hearing and he always denied that it had ever taken place.

A.D. Hope, *Chance Encounters*, p. 88.

Uncle Wiz

Always in awe of his greatest contemporary and Oxford predecessor, W.H. Auden, Hope records the shock of Auden's death in 1973. In conversation Hope once lamented the fact that, unlike Auden, he had little proficiency with verse forms.

Yesterday a newspaper reporter rang me up to tell me that W.H. Auden had died the day before. I was shocked but not grieved — mainly shocked. I suspect, because he was born in the same year as I (21-11-1907) and it was a sort of *memento mori* to know that he was dead.

The reporter, who was plainly not a reader of poetry, said he had been told that my own poetry was like Auden's and had been influenced by it. I remember that earlier, after I came back from Oxford, which he left before I arrived, I used to think so and to console myself with the fact that I had at any rate invented [my kind of verse] quite independently. I don't know why I bothered, since now I cannot see any likeness at all at my age. He was in any case much cleverer, more intellectually agile and verbally inventive than I could ever hope to be. I admired him a great deal and in many ways, but I never liked him much. I suppose I shall have to give up the idea of publishing my Housman piece in *Diamond-cut-diamond*, now he is dead. It would be poetic justice but would be as bad mannered as he was to the dead Housman.

In spite of the fact that I can see no likeness in our poetry, I have always felt in an odd sort of doppel-ganger relation to him as though we were opposite sides of the same coin so to speak. I feel as though my twin brother had died — no grief but a real gap in nature.

A.D. Hope, Notebooks, Book XV, pp. 87–8.

Who's to go Viking?

How many people, I wonder, have been led to decide between poetry and scholarship through the toss of a coin? Gabriel Turville-Petre won this toss and went on to become one of the world's leading Old Norse scholars. Hope settled for poetry.

Gabriel and I had decided to devote ourselves to Old Norse while we were both at Oxford and we had arranged to go to Iceland together after our finals. He had already been there once and had a good working knowledge of modern Icelandic. We met in a pub after our finals and before the results came out and discovered that we were both low in funds. In fact between us we had only enough money for one of us to go.

'All right,' said Gabriel, 'let's toss for it?' I agreed, we tossed, he won, and he went back to Iceland and ultimately to a chair in the subject at Oxford, having won a brilliant first, and I went back to Australia with my miserable third. It was a decisive turning point, but one which looking back, I now think to have been almost providential.

A.D. Hope, *Chance Encounters*, p. 99.

A bum steer

Prime Minister R.G. Menzies was a weighty man, as Hope found to his cost on one formal occasion.

My other memory of contact with a prime minister is of a quite literal and very physical bump. I had been selected to attend on behalf of the University College one of the innumerable celebrations of a National Day — then as now occasions that come round annually. They were then very crowded affairs usually held at the old Hotel Canberra involving drinks, speeches, performances of the national anthem of the country concerned, further drinks and gradual dispersal. On this occasion the room was so crowded that it was very hard to move at all. I was industriously pushing my way through to escape when I came on Menzies standing just in front of the grand piano which had been used for the national anthem earlier. There was just room for me to edge through between it and the Prime Minister, which I proceeded to do. At that moment he was greeted by the wife of the ambassador of the country in question that day. Menzies had put on a very great deal of weight. He bowed gallantly to the lady, who put out her hand to be kissed. I was directly behind him. His massive behind rose up, caught me just below the stomach, raised me and hurled me back on to the keys of the piano behind me. There was a hideous and deafening crash and all eyes turned to see me sitting there. The Prime Minister was still out of sight and there seemed no reason for my extraordinary position; however, as he straightened up I slid to the floor. I was able to admire Menzies's presence of mind. He did not start or look around and behaved as though nothing had happened as he continued to chat with the lady. I followed his example by suppressing my first impulse to apologise, and made myself scarce.

A.D. Hope, *Chance Encounters*, pp. 107–8.

Lust rules, OK?

Modern cultural exchange means many things. In this case Hope's notebook entry is almost as enigmatic as the Japanese poet's greeting.

I have just, at her request, entertained the Japanese poet Kazuko Shiraishi to dinner. She presented me with a copy of translations of her poems into English with the title above. She used the title page to write an inscription which, incorporating the printed title, reads:

Dedicated to
A.D. HOPE
SEASONS OF SACRED LUST
which I dream to see you.

'Poetry is my country,
my passport.'

Kazuko Shiraishi

It left me wondering if it means what it seems to mean. Her English is odd but quite adequate, as she grew up in Vancouver. (If so, comes too late.)

A.D. Hope, Notebooks, Book XXI, p. 82.

The cicada

Barely an anecdote, this one, but at least the graphic record of one stage in a life's journey, and who could resist the force of Hope's concluding phrase?

Now that I have retired at last and feel thirty years of academic drudgery lift from me, it is surprising how quickly what I thought ingrained habits of mind dissolve and leave me in a pleasantly indeterminate attitude to things and books and writing. It is the way a cicada must feel, wet and weak after climbing out of its carapace and 14 years below ground. I think of it as the end of a sort of long constipation — getting the professional shit out of my system.

Cited in Ann McCulloch, *A.D. Hope: The Dance of Language*, p. 21.

Going for the wooden spoon

Many poets revel in the fact that they cannot drive a car at all. Alec Hope bought a car with the proceeds of the Britannica Australia award in 1965 and drove with a kind of negative distinction, throwing in the sponge at 85.

The financial rewards that came with this award enabled Hope to buy a car which he drove in a fashion that was of some concern to residents of Canberra. Manning Clark and A.D. Hope both referred to each other as 'the worst driver in Canberra'. Hope was persuaded at the age of eighty-five that his driving days were over.

Ann McCulloch, *A.D. Hope: The Dance of Language*, p. 20.

Mending fences

Stephen Spender (1909–96) was the longest-lived of the 1930s 'Pylon Poets'. Here he debates his attitude to a biography of Auden with expatriate poet Peter Porter (1929–). Porter and Charles Osborne were Brisbane contemporaries who both finished up in London.

Two nights ago I mended fences with Peter Porter, poet and reviewer. In the *Evening Standard* he wrote how delighted Auden would have been with Charles Osborne's biography of him. As the book was totally against A's expressed wish that no biography should be written and his still more vehement wish that nothing confidential and private about the poet's life should be published, I said something to the feeble effect that I had a bone to pick with him and explained (very mildly) why. He said he felt Charles had been attacked by other reviewers, and he wanted to defend him. Even as I spoke, I began wondering what right I had to think that Auden would stick to his declared objections. He would probably have forgiven Charles, whom he was fond of, straight away (as he did me for passages about him in *World within World*) having wagged a finger at him and said, 'Naughty, naughty' …

Stephen Spender, *Journals 1939–1983*, pp. 432–3.

Domino theory at I Tatti

Alan Moorehead (1910–83) was a stylish war correspondent and travel writer. In his time he met Bernard Berenson, the aged Brahmin who ruled over artistic taste from I Tatti, his villa in Tuscany.

I do not even appear to have been much impressed by Berenson at the beginning. Early in the diary there is a tart note: 'When the old man says, "So you believe that the mass of the people can be educated," and laughs; when he says, "Universal suffrage is rubbish. Why then not give domestic animals the vote? Only those who have political education should vote," I find I have nothing to bring against such Edwardian quaintness. It's not worth answering.'

Berenson talked a great deal about politics in those days, and among his *obiter dicta* I remember him saying that no people ever feel secure until they have succeeded in persecuting somebody else; thus in America the Spaniards demolished the Incas and the Puritans the Red Indians, and so it would go with the state of Israel which was just then coming into being; the Israelis were bound to assert themselves against the Arabs until they could stand on their own feet. But the great aim of politics should always be, he thought, to establish a balance of power. Whenever that balance was lost war and anarchy supervened.

For myself I wanted to know nothing of these things, for the time being I had had enough of wars and politics. I wanted to drink my wine, to talk of the past and to be free to spend long silent hours in the library at I Tatti. I read Symonds' volumes on the Italian renaissance, and then went on to make a study of Angelo Poliziano, the poet and friend of Lorenzo the Magnificent. It was Poliziano's old house, built at San Domenico da Fiesole four hundred years before, that I had rented.

Berenson was amused at this. 'Why are you bothering about him?' he asked.

'Because he fascinates me.'

'Well, he fascinates me too. He was an interesting chap but with no real intellect. You might dip him into what I call the sauce of the epoch, but then the little shrimp would disappear.'

Alan Moorehead, *A Late Education: Episodes in a Life*, pp. 151–2.

The duck hunter

Also in Italy, but in the mountains, Moorehead found that his path had already crossed that of Ernest Hemingway, here encountered as a hunter in elaborate self-parody.

To make a break we went up to stay for a few days with Ernest Hemingway and his fourth wife, Mary, who happened to be an old friend of ours; they had taken a chalet at Cortina in the Italian Dolomites. We arrived in heavy snow, and Hemingway was out shooting duck, a gruelling business in that weather since it involved standing by the hour in a barrel in a frozen marsh waiting for the dawn to break. When he came in at last he was the walking myth of himself. Cartridge belts and strings of teal and mallard hung in festoons from his shoulders, powdered snow clung to his beard and woolly cap, and when his gun was laid aside in the corner he had to be helped off with his clothes — layer after layer of sweaters, leather jerkins and a coloured shirt. At the end of it all he fished a cable out of his pocket and held it out to me.

It read: 'Nothing could be better than a piece on Venice by you but it so happens we have got someone called Alan Moorehead who may be doing it one day so I am sorry ...' It was signed Harold Ross.

This was both embarrassing and ridiculous, and it also helps to explain why Harold Ross was more loved than any other editor of his time. Two years before in New York he had suggested to me over lunch that I should write for the *New Yorker* an article on Venice, and I had demurred, saying that I disliked Venice, that the place gave me claustrophobia, that unpleasant things always happened to me when I went there, I got a cold, I lost my passport, I had rows with my friends. Ross answered simply, 'Oh well, one day you may do it.' That was all that passed between us, there was nothing more. And now after two years Hemingway, the most sought-after writer of his generation, had cabled Ross saying he had been in Venice for a month and would like to write an article about it, and had had this reply.

Alan Moorehead, *A Late Education: Episodes in a Life*, pp. 156–7.

For whom the dog rolls

At Cortina d'Ampezzo, Hemingway deals briskly with a large dog.

Hemingway at that time was still very robust, and not drinking much except red wine. One night in the piazza at Cortina an Alsatian and another big dog began to fight in the snow, surrounded by screaming women, and Hemingway, throwing his coat over the Alsatian, picked it up in his arms and threw it bodily over the wall, a masterful bit of business in his true *genre*. Yet there was a certain gloom overhanging the chalet — the gloom of his not being able to work I think — and we were a little sad about them as we came away.

Alan Moorehead, *A Late Education: Episodes in a Life*, p. 160.

Yevgeny's caf

Hal Porter recalls having sought a definition of Australia from the bombastic Russian poet, Yevgeny Yevtushenko.

You recall a nocturnal garden party at Colonel Something's where, for a reason you can't define, but perhaps because you're politically conservative and an ardent anti-communist, you break through the circle of idolators around Yevtushenko to ask:

'And what do you think of Australia, young man?'

Yevtushenko, whose English you've been led to believe consists of about six hundred words, makes an instant and interesting choice.

'It is,' he says, very clearly, 'a cafeteria built on a graveyard.'

You've got your answer. You go back to drinking.

Hal Porter, *The Extra*, p. 113.

A Scotch breakfast?

Porter had his idiosyncratic way with many aspects of life, from choice of a kimono to how he took his Weeties for breakfast.

On one occasion when he was staying with us he had been up late drinking and, as usual, slept in, not emerging from his room until about 10.30 a.m. Margaret Howell, a neighbour and friend who had not met Hal, had dropped in for morning coffee. We were amiably chatting when Hal, looking a little less than radiant, appeared in a lurid green and gold kimono. He rallied a little when he saw I had company, acknowledged the introduction with excessive courtesy and urged me not to disturb myself, he would look after himself.

I offered him coffee, which he declined vehemently as though I'd offered him arsenic and said: 'No stimulants for me, dear girl, I'll fix myself breakfast. Something simple for this old gentleman, I think.' He paused as though considering. 'Perhaps just a little whisky and Weeties.' Margaret, fascinated, watched him get a bowl from the cupboard, shake a goodly portion of Weeties into it which he followed with an even goodlier portion of whisky.

'Would you like a little milk with that?' asked Margaret, more out of disbelief at the evidence of her eyes and ears than concern for Hal's insides.

'I don't think so, dear,' replied Hal with the air of one politely considering a fatuous suggestion. 'But thank you for asking.' Had Margaret not been there he would simply had the whisky and skipped the Weeties.

Mary Lord, Hal Porter: Man of Many Parts, p. 119.

The rose bush

Snooty art patrons John and Sunday Reed found their old farmhouse, Heide, used as a staging post by Porter and a couple of his lady friends. The Reeds' adoptive son, Sweeney, had to do the Good Samaritan act, come morning. The story is told by Barrett Reid, friend and follower of the Reeds, but no relation.

They were supposed to be on their way to Warrandyte and had called in, I think, on the pretext that one of the women needed to use the lavatory. They were all very happy and I welcomed them. I was in bed; it must have been well after midnight. And I ushered them into the sunroom wearing my pyjamas and showed Hal: 'Look, Hal. There's the whisky and there are glasses. And God bless you all and I'm going back to bed because I've got to get up in the morning.' Hal was very annoyed with that and never quite forgave me for it.

[…] Later one of the women, staggering out into the garden in the dark, got caught in a big rose bush.

She ... flailed about and the more she flailed about the more she was caught. Hal went out to rescue her and he too got caught. I think I heard a few faint cries for help but sternly turned my face to the wall and thought 'Let them kill each other — bastards all!' and promptly went back to sleep.

Early in the morning, Sweeney came up from the new house and found them caught in the rose bush. He delicately unpicked them, soothed them, bathed their wounds and gave them hot coffee before sending them on their way with Sun and John none the wiser.

Mary Lord, *Hal Porter: Man of Many Parts*, pp. 214–15.

The pleasures of simile

Clem Christesen (1911–), founding editor of the long-lived journal, Meanjin, *can turn a vivid phrase or two when his ire is up.*

In August 1971 the *Australian* published an interview with Brian Kiernan, who dared suggest that Clem might no longer be at the forefront of literary trends. Clem snorted that he was even more anti-establishment than he had been in 1940. His detractors, he suggested, were themselves failing to keep abreast of world literary movements; they had 'their eyes on the drought-stricken gibber-plains like a mob of bloody emus'.

Judith Armstrong, *The Christesen Romance*, p. 135.

A bit of a larrikin

Famous for his autobiographical novel, My Brother Jack, *George Johnston (1912–70) was full of irreverent high spirits, as his East St Kilda neighbour Fred Kneale recalled later.*

George loved to 'take the mickey' out of people, especially if it involved deflating their pomposity. Kneale recalls 'one dull gent, the quintessence of suburban man, was much put out when George, from sheer exuberance, greeted him with "H'ya, Fred, old ram! Getting any?" Fred, plainly unamused, made no reply.' On another occasion the Johnstons and the Kneales were invited to a 'musical evening' at the home of an *Argus* correspondent who liked to maintain a high tone in such matters, insisting that the men wear black tie and dinner jacket. Johnston and Kneale turned up in lounge suits. When their host greeted them at the door he was wearing a dicky (a false shirt-front); in a flash Johnston produced a lipstick and inscribed on the dicky 'we love you Rupe'. The host was furious. 'Damn you,' he said. 'You've buggered my dicky and I wanted to wear it tomorrow night!' Johnston further blotted his copy-book by escaping with Kneale to the kitchen to burst into laughter at the dismal incompetence of the musicians. Neither he nor Kneale was invited again.

Garry Kinnane, George Johnston: A Biography, p. 32.

Fancy dress in the jungle

'Wally' Crabbe, who was serving in the RAF, kept coming upon Johnston, bobbing up in the strangest places in Asia. The war against the Japanese moved people around arbitrarily and gave them strange uniforms to wear.

[It was] at a place called Maymyo, about one third of the way up the Burma Road to the Chinese border of Wanting …

The night before, our location had been severely bombed in an attempt by the Japanese to 'collect' either Generalissimo Kai-shek or the U.S. General 'vinegar Joe' Stillwell. In our partly wrecked building, and the few remaining bungalows in the smashed courtyard, we were a strange, mixed collection. Suddenly a superbly uniformed U.S. war correspondent intruded. To my surprise it was George Johnston. He said he had come by air from Chungking, and had with him a staggering collection of watercolours he had painted in different war areas of China.

K.E.I. Wallace-Crabbe, 'Pens and Yarns, Wings and Wheels'.

A spider!

The first days on the Australian continent could be very strange for a Pommy migrant. Memoirist Graham McInnes (1912–70) had his first spider as a boy, newly landed in Fremantle.

The sky and the beach and the sea shimmered and shook in an intense blue-white light and induced a powerful thirst. I whined for a drink until our English nurse, Mabel, dispensed a grudging penny. Across the blazing sand and over the bubbling tar road among the scrubby bushes stood a wooden shed with its front hooked up. In its somnolent depths lurked a sun-yellowed female face.

'Whatcher want, sonny?'

'A drink please.'

'Well, what about a spider?'

First sharks, now spiders; perhaps other demons lurked in the olive-grey scrub. The woman gave a laconic glance.

'New around here ain't you? Thought so. Pommy eh?' I shook my head. ·

'Course you're a Pommy! Straight off the boat from Home. "Coom out on the Arse-over; bin out a month all but three weeks." I can tell. You just try a spider. You'll love it.'

She swivelled on her seat in the heated gloom, yanked from the icebox a bottle of ginger beer and unscrewed the rubber top with a magnificent pop and a small cloud of smoke. She reached for a thick yellow glass and poured in the ginger beer. While the foam sizzled she pulled a wooden scoop from a pail of water and dipped it below the counter with a twist and a grunt. It came up with an enormous dollop of ice-cream which she dropped into the ginger beer.

'There's your spider.' She shoved a straw into the sulphurous bubbling mess. I drank with the ecstasy of revelation and forgot at once about sharks and heat and tiresome Mabel; and also about payment.

'That'll be tuppence,' the woman said sharply.

'A penny's all I've got.'

She nodded with a tired air. 'Then I'll have to be satisfied with that, won't I sonny?' She swept the penny into her apron. 'Pay me next time you come back.'

'But we're not coming back; we're going on to Melbourne.'

'Off with you now!' and her laughter pursued my puzzled steps back across the boiling tar and the blistering sand to the warm waters of the Indian Ocean into whose shallows I flopped exclaiming 'I've just drunk a spider, Maybie.'

Graham McInnes, *The Road to Gundagai*, p. 14.

Dickens versus the footy

McInnes was the son of the vivacious English novelist Angela Thirkell (1890–1961), who endured this country for some years after her marriage to an Australian officer. She was determined that her sons should be well educated. She succeeded: both Graham and his brother Colin became writers, and both left Australia.

One afternoon I brought home from school a boy named Nelson, destined to be the most long suffering of mates. Just as we rose from the supper table to dash from the room for a game of twilight football among Dad's citrus trees in the back garden, Mother said: 'You have five minutes before Reading Aloud.' This stopped me in my tracks, while Nelson stood his ground and tried to mask his mistrustfulness with a nonchalant neutrality.

'Reading aloud?' I said.

'Yes, stupid,' said Mother. 'You know perfectly well we have it every night.'

'But what about Jim Nelson?'

'Jim Nelson can listen to *Little Dorrit* if he wants to,' said Mother. I slouched moodily into the back yard with my hands in my pockets followed by the perplexed and wondering schoolfriend.

'What does your Mum mean?' he asked. 'And who's Little Dorrit?'

With a strangled grunt, I threw him a ball. 'Catch.' He caught the ball but, 'I wouldn't mind hearing about this Little Dorrit,' he said. Deserted, even by my friend.

Graham McInnes, *The Road to Gundagai*, p. 284.

When the Rudyards cease from Kipling

Here the young McInnes meets his formidable cousin, Rudyard Kipling. As it turned out, Kipling was well aware of his antipodean counterpart in verse, 'Banjo' Paterson (1864–1941).

As the door of Elsie Bambridge's house opened to us, the raw dampness of a London February recoiled before a warm wall of sherry-scented conversation. We walked through the door and the tide ebbed, sucking us in with it. Our hostess greeted us with an amiable smile and led us to where the sea of people broke like surf upon a tiny island whose centre I could not see. I was taken to the edge of the island, still craning my neck to get a view of the guest of honour, when I heard my mother say, 'Cousin Ruddy this is Graham.'

'Well, young man,' said a deep, slightly harsh but pleasant voice.

I jerked my head down. I had of course expected him to have a stature worthy of the magnificent domed forehead which I remembered so well. But now this same domed forehead confronted me at the level of my own shoulder. Beneath the forehead two dark, penetrating eyes shone from great caves whose entrance was partly masked by the thatchwork of those terrible eyebrows.

'Good evening, sir,' I heard myself say. A firm, dry handshake; then, 'I hear you've just come from Australia?'

The buzz of scented conversation receded. The bobbing heads and gesticulating arms of the guests grew blurred, and the great head loomed even larger. I found myself examining the terrible eyebrows almost hair by hair; noting how they greyed at the edges and how the skin between the eyebrows and the temples was drawn tight and sallow, giving the eyes and the great brows themselves an expression of ferocious kindliness. I saw that the eyes had started to wander, so I barked out.

'Yes, sir.'

He nodded and brought his eyes back to mine.

'You're rather young, of course,' he said, 'but I wonder if you ever came across my friend "Banjo" Paterson?'

I explained at once that I had indeed been too young to meet the great 'Banjo', but that I was a firm admirer of his work. I essayed, a little nervously, to praise 'The Man from Snowy River'; but he cut me short.

'Yes, yes. Tell me, how is he? Do you know?'

Anxious to impress, I plunged into the gap.

'Well, sir, I think he's dead.'

Cousin Ruddy's eyebrows shot up almost a full inch, and quivered violently.

'Dead?' he said, with such vehemence that several people near us stopped talking and turned their heads with glasses half raised to their lips. 'Dead?' he repeated. 'That's very curious. I had a letter from him just recently. Is this true?'

I swallowed the last of my sherry. A vision arose before me of an oval portrait in a collection of Australian verse: a sad-eyed man in a tall Hoover collar, with hair carefully parted and plastered down at the side; a portrait in a school prize book; a fusty, dusty portrait that spoke of a century dead and gone these thirty-odd years. Surely that portrait was conclusive evidence? Besides, no one was writing poetry like the 'Banjo's' in Australia today. I blundered on.

'Well, sir, I certainly thought he was dead.'

Cousin Ruddy looked at me in some perplexity. Finally he gave a faint snort, and the eyebrows twitched in what seemed to me a horribly threatening murmur.

'Thought!' he said abruptly. Then, catching Mother's eye, 'Your son seems to think my old friend "Banjo" Paterson is dead.'

The noise of conversation became as the roaring of a freight train in a tunnel. I fiddled with my empty glass and waited for the blow to fall, but Mother took refuge in an enamelled smile and a sip of her sherry. The great head turned back to me for the last time, and in the deep-set eyes a small light was kindled, like a candle at the end of a very long corridor. He reached up with a firm brown hand, and put it lightly on my shoulder.

'After all,' he said, 'why should you know? He isn't read nowadays.' He shook his head and smiled the faintest of friendly smiles, as if perhaps to say, 'No more am I.'

'Good luck my boy.'

He turned and was swallowed up in a group of impatient admirers. In a few moments Mother bid her adieus, and we left. During the long ride home in the taxi, we talked of many things, but not of Cousin Ruddy.

A month later I left England for Canada. I never saw Cousin Ruddy again, but a copy of the portrait with the terrible eyebrows still hangs in my home; and beside it is Burne-Jones' portrait of Kipling's sister, Alice Fleming, 'Aunt Trix'. As for Andrew Barton Paterson — the 'Banjo' — he died in February 1941; and, as this tale reveals only too clearly, I never saw him at all.

Graham McInnes, *Goodbye Melbourne Town*, pp. 207–9.

A cool dude on campus

A glimpse of the quick-witted Cyril Pearl, whose beautiful wife we have already glimpsed in Ian Mair's anecdote.

Pearl was a swart thickset fellow with a sallow complexion, a pendulous lower lip, an untidy Chaplinesque moustache and a great shock of long black hair. Assuming wrongly that his appearance connoted inarticulate decadence, the bully boys — the rowers, the footballers and the Toorak socialites — attempted to engage him in heavy-handed witticisms. He sliced them off at the ankles before they knew what hit them. The Gurkha with his kukri on the Western Front and the Scimitar of Saladin were as nothing compared to the ease with which Cyril Pearl vanquished his attackers.

His effortless superiority was perhaps easily come by since most of us were five or six years his junior. He was also bad for us to be exposed to; for we sought to ape him, and, being neither as quick witted nor as ruthless, failed lamentably. Cyril had a tough punning humour developed to a fine-honed edge. His appearance, usually without a hat and often accompanied by Irma, was to us more intoxicating than a lecture by Professor Scott, a visit to the Bijou or an evening at 9 Darling Street.

Graham McInnes, *Humping My Bluey*, p. 216.

The mouse

Irish-born Roland Robinson (1912–92) worked at every imaginable job from ballet dancer to boundary rider. While gardening at a convent he met the popular poet, 'John O'Brien', author of that immortal ballad, 'Said Hanrahan'.

The Resident Chaplain at the Convent was Father Hartigan. I can't remember how we got to know one another, but I learned that Father Hartigan was 'John O'Brien' the Australian poet who wrote 'Around the Boree Log'. Father Hartigan and I became great friends. I remember him with deep affection. As I have said, I am not a Catholic, but, if Father Hartigan was a Catholic, then so am I. I mean by this that we were natural mates, in the true Australian sense. The above may sound 'Irish' but then Father was of Irish extract and, after all, I am 'Irish bred an' born'.

I was cutting back a hedge when Father came along in his black robes from a chapel mass or service. A little poem of mine had appeared in the *Sydney Morning Herald*. Father had seen it and expressed surprise that they had another poet working for them. Father said that he liked the poem a great deal. 'Ah, Father' I said, 'it's only a little thing. You see, I thought I had a great poem when I started. You know, there's a story about some peasants who had their homes and vineyards on the side of a mountain. One day the mountain began to give signs that it was a volcano and was going to erupt. All the people ran away from the mountain and stood watching to see what was going to happen. After a while the mountain became quiet. Then the people saw that a crack had appeared in the mountain. And out of this crack crept a little mouse. Well, I was like that mountain when I started to write that poem, and when the mountain had quietened down, out crept that little poem. That's my curse, Father, but that's how I am.'

Roland Robinson, *The Drift of Things: An Autobiography 1914–52*, p. 321.

Accepted by the SMH

Robinson storms the Bastille.

I wrote verse for years and years before I had anything published. The first verse I had published was in a little newspaper edited by Henry Boote. But I considered that the *Sydney Morning Herald* was the real test. My verse always came back from this main newspaper. Then I resolved to write a poem so good that no editor would reject it. My poem was a sonnet. It made references to Aucassin and Nicolette, to Palomides and Launcelot from Malory. It began 'Now would I speak of love that does not die.' This was the weapon with which I meant to assault 'The Bastille' as I called the *Sydney Morning Herald*. I had submitted a poem to this newspaper, with a self-addressed envelope, and it had not been returned. I decided that this was my excuse to gain entry to 'The Bastille'. The *Sydney Morning Herald* then occupied a large stone building on the corner of Pitt and Hunter Streets. One afternoon when I was on night shift I began my assault. I went up the marble stairway inside the building to the Inquiries on the first floor. At the Inquiries window I asked the girl if it was possible for me see the editor. The girl said I could and directed me to the editor's room. I braced myself, and knocked on the door. I heard a cultured voice say 'Come in.' The first thing I saw was a furled umbrella, a hat and a pair of gloves on a table near the entrance. At a large desk by the window overlooking Hunter street, sat the editor. I told the editor my name, and he asked me to take a seat and then asked what he could do for me. I explained that some verse I had submitted had not been returned. 'Ah, yes' said the editor. 'It has probably gone astray. I suggest that you submit it again.' 'Well' I said, 'as a matter of fact, I'm glad it's gone astray — you see, since then, I've produced something much better.' 'You have?' the editor politely asked. 'Do you happen to have it with you?' 'Well — it so happens …'

I opened my brief case. 'I did bring it with me, I …' I handed the sonnet to him.

The editor sat studying the sonnet. 'The last line' he queried, 'I see you have two beats, stresses, coming together.' I leapt into the breach. 'Oh yes, that's a spondee. Tennyson often used spondees.' Ah, what a knowledge of versification I had. 'Hmm, I see' the editor murmured. He put the sonnet on his desk and began writing something on it. 'Yes' he said. 'I think we would like this. I suggest that, from time to time, you might submit other examples of your verse.' I could have dropped, pole-axed, through the floor. The editor stood up. He extended his hand across the desk to me. 'Foster's my name' he said. I don't know what I mumbled. I thanked him, not too profusely, I hope. I took my leave. I trotted down the marble staircase and out into the sunlight of Pitt street. I was dazed. I had stormed 'The Bastille'.

Roland Robinson, *The Drift of Things: An Autobiography 1914–52*, pp. 149–50.

Art and pain

Being an artists' model was another of Robinson's occupations. He sought inspiration from the bush muses while he posed. One of the artists in the studio was the wife of that dashingly unreliable poet, Kenneth ('Seaforth') Mackenzie, who was to drown in a creek near Goulburn in 1955.

I had to keep an engagement book, a dated diary. The teachers booked me right through the term. A six-hour posing day was common to me. One day I posed eight hours. Models were always failing to turn up. I would be leaving the Tech. in the afternoon when one of the teachers would come running after me. His model could not come for the evening class. Could I pose for him? He would give me an easy, sitting pose. I made good friends with the teachers, Mr

Gunther, Mr Harvey, Mr Lyndon Dadswell, the sculptor, Mr Dundas, the painter. Often, while I was posing, I would be going over a poem I was struggling with in composition. I was sitting by the campfire, one arm resting on the knee of my angled leg. When I got down from the pose, one of the students asked me what I was thinking about when I was posing. I said that I was away in the bush, composing a poem.

If the students observed me, I often observed the students. I was doing a term long pose for Mr Dadswell, the teacher of modelling and sculpture. The face of one of the students, a woman, absorbed me. There was grief in her face. Her face looked as though she had been weeping all night. I learnt that this student was the wife of a poet and novelist called Kenneth Mackenzie. I had never read his poetry, but through his wife's face I read the whole range of mental pain and agony which, whether he wished it or not, the poet inflicted on her.

Roland Robinson, *The Drift of Things: An Autobiography 1914–52*, p. 216.

In the Blitz

Patrick White (1912–90) was a different kind of expatriate writer from those of the postwar years. He was largely educated in England, then lived the arty life in Belgravia's Ebury Street before returning to settle in Australia in 1948.

Brought up to believe in the maxim: Only the British can be right, I did accept this during the earlier part of my life. Ironed out in an English public school, and finished off at King's, Cambridge, it was not until 1939, after wandering by myself through most of Western Europe, and finally most of the United States, that I began to grow up and think my own thoughts. The War did the rest. What had seemed a brilliant, intellectual, highly desirable existence, became distressingly parasitic and pointless. There is nothing like a rain of bombs to start one trying to assess one's own achievement. Sitting at night in his London bed-sitting room during the first months of the Blitz, this chromium-plated Australian with two fairly successful novels to his credit came to the conclusion that his achievement was practically nil. Perhaps significantly, he was reading at that time Eyre's *Journal*. Perhaps also he had the wind up; certainly he reached rather often for the bottle of Calvados in the wardrobe. Anyway, he experienced those first sensations of rootlessness which Alister Kershaw has deplored and explained as the 'desire to nuzzle once more at the benevolent teats of the mother country'.

Patrick White, 'The Prodigal Son', in *The Vital Decade: Ten Years of Australian Arts and Letters* (ed. Geoffrey Dutton and Max Harris), p. 156.

Steamy ladies

Service with the RAF in Africa yielded one of White's few positive accounts of female sexuality.

22-i-1941

To L. by air. More swamps, more bananas, more of the brown mud houses, the little toy houses of Africa. From the air, surf is motionless, frozen. The Royal Hotel, L. Brothel-cum-*bal musette*: the vases of dirty paper flowers, the bead curtains. We are given a bare dormitory for six. Outside the window negroes scuffle and fight. All the usual African smells, the smell of burning wood and black bodies ... the negresses of L. dance on the hotel roof. The beginnings of European coquetry. The husky dusky laughter of the dancing negresses, twined and twirling to a gramophone. *De jeunes negresses en fleur* ...

Patrick White, *Patrick White: Letters* (ed. David Marr), p. 37.

Coping with Alec

One of the most striking events in the history of Australian letters was the review by A.D. Hope (1907–) of White's Tree of Man, *which he saw as vitiated by passages of 'illiterate verbal sludge'. White never forgave him. Despite the novelist's disclaimer, Hope was a professor at the ANU.*

30-vi-1956

As most of the Australian reception of *The Tree of Man* is now over, I can write and tell you what happened. Eyre & Spottiswoode drew it out and drew it out, until everyone was thoroughly exasperated, booksellers thought they were being imposed upon, reviews came out too soon, and the public was bewildered. Finally, the book was released last week.

But let us return to the reviews. Melbourne was the first, with a very grudging one in the *Age* by somebody who must once have written a novel, I think. His line was: 'This is quite unlike anything by any other Australian novelist, therefore it cannot be good.' The fact that it was not a naturalistic novel seemed to get him down more than anything, and he finished up accusing me of copying Faulkner, Carson McCullers and Capote. This review was bad enough, but there was worse to come.

After a very sympathetic one by a man called John K. Ewers in the *West Australian*, the *Sydney Morning Herald* sprang upon us. I am enclosing it to show. Admittedly the *Herald* has jumped upon everything I have written, but they excelled themselves this time. A.D. Hope is an embittered school-master and poet of a <u>certain</u> distinction. During the War he was Professor of English at the Teachers' College Sydney, I am told, and now he is at some College (not the University) at Canberra.

Somebody I know on the staff of the *Herald* says they have been flooded with letters of protest since the review appeared. Only two of these letters were published, while the Editor was away. The latter, an importation from England, called Pringle, replied in this vein to one man who had written: 'A.D. Hope is the best critic in Australia, one of the four best poets, and a Professor of English Literature — '

Patrick White, *Patrick White: Letters* (ed. David Marr), pp. 105–6.

The soul of suburbia

White's letters briskly caricatured people he met on social occasions. False teeth and hats were among his more horrible interests.

27-i-1958

We went to a terrible party the other evening at Warrawee at the House Beautiful of my stockbroker cousin. Why we were asked, I don't know, as we always feel that his wife, who is the soul of suburbia, hates us. Anyway, one looked at all the people and wondered to whom, out of about 50, one might possibly talk. They were all middle-aged, or elderly, North Shore business and the men all similar — they could have been wearing *papier mâché* masks for an expressionist play — , the women all in false teeth, and little hats made of flowers, either pink or blue. We stood under a crepe myrtle and drank about a gallon, but nothing happened. I was introduced to a Mr Horn who announced with pride that he had been made to read *Dombey and Son* at school, and as a result had not opened another book since. Finally, in desperation, we took to urging the daughter of the house, who was dressed in what looked like a Bebarfald curtain, and who will probably become a permanent spinster, to run away to Italy or France and live by her wits.

Patrick White, *Patrick White: Letters* (ed. David Marr), p. 128.

Can bloomers be knickers?

One can add nothing to the exquisite story told by Barry Humphries (1934–) about Miss Firbank's knickers.

In 1960 the wardrobe of Heather Firbank, sister of the novelist Ronald Firbank, was sold and dispersed. Gowns by Worth, Mme Vionnet and Patou, some never worn, others worn no more than once and all in storage, were snapped up by the Victoria and Albert Museum, and the remnant knocked down to the public. From this, on some absurd caprice, I bought a pair of fine cambric bloomers trimmed with lace and blue ribbon, and bearing Miss Firbank's embroidered monogram.

Once, as Patrick White and I talked about our mutual attraction to the author of *Valmouth* and *The Flower Beneath the Foot*, I showed him the Firbankian knickers. Never before or since have I seen him so excited, but as he tremulously fingered the fabric, his delight changed to an expression of regret. At the evanescence of this flimsy text? Or perhaps also at the size of the garment — impossibly slighter than his own substantial loins.

Barry Humphries, *More Please*, p. 227.

Mr Porter and Mr White

The good looks of young actor Jack Thompson help to set off a celebrated tiff between novelists Patrick White and Hal Porter.

I was invited to the party that Beatrice Davis gave in Hal's honour during that week. She invited, as well, those librarian friends of Hal's who were also writers, Barrett Reid, Frank Kellaway and Peter Stansfield. She was continuing to promote Hal in Sydney's literary society and to this end had invited Thea Astley, John and Patricia Thompson, Rosemary

Dobson, Alec Bolton and many others, but her most important guest was Patrick White, who came with his friend, Manoly Lascaris. Many conflicting stories have been told about this party, which became the source of legend, little of it with much basis in fact. It is true, though, that this was the party where Porter and White met for the first time and where they had a falling out which made it impossible for them ever to have friendly relations.

Patrick White was the towering figure in the landscape of Australian fiction at that time. He had published the major novels *The Aunt's Story*, *The Tree of Man* and *Voss* which, whether they attracted praise or scorn, had made him the most discussed writer in the country. He was a year younger than Porter and the antithesis of him in all the ways that mattered to Hal. Born of wealthy parents from a prominent pastoral family, he was wealthy in his own right, Cambridge educated and aristocratic by temperament.

Hal was an appalling snob and exceptionally class conscious, making absolute judgements on trivial signs and treating people accordingly. The person who used 'mirror' for 'looking-glass', for example, would be subject to his obvious disdain. The subject of social class came up so often in his conversation that I once asked him directly what class he would put himself in. He thought for a bit and then said that, as an artist, he belonged to all classes and no class, which was his clever way of dodging the question.

Hal was jealous of everything about Patrick White, including his elevated position on the social scale, but most especially was he jealous of White's literary success. Although Beatrice had the best of intentions when she invited White to the party, she was not to know that Hal would not have appreciated the appearance of a genuinely famous author at what was, after all, *his* party. He saw himself as the star of the show; it was not in his nature to share the limelight with others except if they acted as foils for him.

I was chatting to Frank Kellaway and missed what was for many the highlight of the evening. The bare bones of the story, as far as I can determine, are that there was a very good-looking young man present, the son of the poet, writer and broadcaster, John Thompson, a man who had been both friend and patron to Hal, and who, with his wife, Patricia, was on friendly terms with White. White was homosexual but out of the closet. Porter, at this stage, was well and truly in it. White, according to all reports, was attempting to make conversation in the way one does with strangers at parties. He was disposed to be pleasant and said some flattering things about Hal's books. Then he jokingly remarked on the handsomeness of the good-looking young man and the fact that he was engaged to be married. Did Porter think he was being married off by Patricia in order to prevent him from being or becoming homosexual? Porter reacted to this badly, probably suspecting an implied assumption behind the question that he, too, was homosexual. He replied icily and dismissively that he had no idea, and suggested White should ask Patricia himself if he really wanted to know. This was a supercilious rebuff to a friendly overture and White was both embarrassed and offended. Porter, he concluded, was 'a detestable man'.

Porter later developed the incident into one of his humorous dinner-party stories, one which he would perform rather than relate whenever White's name came up, miming White's gestures with his asthma spray, his slight stutter and Manoly's facial expressions.

Mary Lord, *Hal Porter: Many of Many Parts*, pp. 128–30.

Hares in winter

Maie Casey (1892–1983) was an original, versatile writer. Her husband, Baron Casey of Berwick, was among other things Governor of Bengal and Governor-General of Australia, so the Caseys got about a good deal, with or without garlic breath.

30-vii-1966

The reason I am writing so soon is that Maie Casey was here yesterday … The lunch turned out very well. The hares arrived two days in advance. After I had cut them up our kitchen was a horrific sight; Duncan's chamber can't have looked bloodier. And the twelve lemons and twenty-four cloves of garlic gave spectacular results. We had chlorophyll for Maie, but she refused to take it. I'm sure those she met later in the day must have suspected the lunch of being a republican plot.

Patrick White, *Patrick White: Letters* (ed. David Marr), p. 299.

Australian misanthropy

The American film star Anne Baxter (1923–85) depicts in memorable detail a lunch at White's house, along with novelist Thea Astley (1925–). Baxter's 'Adjustment' refers to her new life in the Australian bush.

It was hell deciding what to wear. I can't remember what I did pick. Patrick would. His memory is disturbingly keen.

I'd arranged a Hughes Hire car from the Sweetapples' phone and was driven to Parramatta.

The old-fashioned house was all but obscured by a remarkable tangle of growth. Vines and roses and nasturtiums fought the tiny weathered gate as I pushed it open and hesitantly searched for a path and a door. The place reminded me of Miss Hare's Xanadu in Patrick White's latest novel, *Riders in the Chariot*. His ascetic countenance appeared suddenly, its body hidden by the disheveled garden.

'Here you are,' said his dreamy, haunting voice.

'Yes!' I cried breathless with excitement. 'Here I am!'

He was even taller and a bit younger than I remembered, and I was even more in awe of him. He leaned halfway out from behind the shrubs. 'Come in. It's this way.' What was there about him that made me robe him in a monk's habit as he moved soundlessly away? I wound my way, picking away the twigs and rose thorns as they plucked at my skirt. I looked up. He was standing in the doorway, smiling slightly with amusement. His almost colorless eyes bored through me like augers, without meaning to. They just did.

A dark-eyed, vibrant young woman rose from the couch as I entered.

'Hello,' she said intensely, stretching out her hand. 'I'm Thea Astley.'

Ah, I thought, here's another eager beaver like myself.

'How nice to meet you,' I replied, answering her nervous warmth. 'I loved your book,' I enthused.

'Good!' She laughed. 'I want to hear!'

A foreign voice sounded richly from the next room. 'You must have needed a cane knife — the garden is so wildly overgrown from summer.'

And a handsome young man walked in with the lithest of steps. He must be the Greek friend Thea had described to me in the letter that came with her book. Small-boned, graceful as a dancer, with skin the colour of olive oil.

I do not have the temerity to report our luncheon conversation. I do not have Patrick White's elephantine accuracy. We drank cold, rather too sweet, white wine; and ate some delicious cold eggplant dish and salad which the beautiful Greek had made. Two things I do remember vividly: first that our conversation was rife with theatrical possibilities. A film of *Descant for Gossips*, Patrick's new short plays, a trip to Greece, Patrick's novel in progress, Thea's novel in progress, exotic food, London, and my Adjustment. As for the last-mentioned, I not only didn't mind it being discussed, we found it worth a laugh. Which is a lot.

The second thing I remember is as alive in time as if he'd just spoken. I was about to leave. I haltingly tried to voice some of my vague apprehensions about the hostile presence of the Australian bush. Patrick looked down at me, his eyes the same opalescent augers that first dismayed me, and spoke in his peculiar, faintly acrid voice. 'But didn't you know? Australia doesn't like people.'

I left in the wake of that remark and roused my driver who was cooking in the car, and went back to Sydney in a daze.

Anne Baxter, Intermission: A True Tale, pp. 259–60.

Gone West

Labor politician and quiz whiz Barry Jones reports on a confusion of White with novelist and former Christian Brother Morris West (1916–), a horse of a very different colour.

I first met Patrick White in January 1974. He had been named Australian of the Year for 1973 after the award of his Nobel Prize. Somebody from the Australia Day Committee telephoned me. He said, 'We have been told that you are good at handling difficult people and that Patrick White is a very difficult person; would you be prepared to look after him when he flies down from Sydney to Melbourne for the award, pick him up at the airport, entertain him before and after the lunch and put him on his plane?' I was happy to do it and agreed that he had a legendary reputation for being difficult. But, I asked, should not somebody from the committee do it? I was told, 'The problem is that nobody on the committee has read any of his books except *The Shoes of the Fisherman*.' I commented, 'You had better not tell him that.'

That *Shoes of the Fisherman* story was a running joke between us until Patrick White's death.

Barry Jones, in *Patrick White: A Tribute*, compiled by Clayton Joyce, p. 45.

Aargh!

To epitomise the laconic note of Australian wit, novelist Nancy Phelan (1913–) tells a joke against herself.

One result of education by television seems to be a decline in real wit. Australians used to be known for their dry laconic way with words but now that television has lowered our standards this is growing rather scarce. Wittiness has been replaced by clumsy farce imported from or inspired by the Land of the Tin Ear, by shrill wisecracks and simple-minded clowning, helped along by gales of canned laughter and described in advance as hil*air*ious. It reminds me of my German acquaintance who always preceded a 'joke' with 'This is funny … you will laugh'. In fact with a few marvellous exceptions, television 'comedies' are rather like German jokes, which as Mark Twain said are no laughing matter.

It is over twenty years since I came face to face with real Australian wit. I was alone in the house, convalescing from an operation. It was winter and I had to go downstairs to tell the delivery men where to put the anthracite for the slow-combustion stove. I was not looking my best. My hair, which was long, was still lank from the anaesthetic, my face was a ghastly pallor, I was wearing a dressing-gown of blue-black quilted satin.

There was a large man at the door and at the far end of the garden another man with the anthracite. He couldn't see me and as I shut the door after giving directions I heard him say, 'Who was that?' Without hesitation his mate replied, 'Dracula'.

Nancy Phelan, 'Messing about with Words', p. 33.

Some of David's pranks

Manning Clark (1915–91), the most famous — or, in some quarters, notorious — of our historians, spins yarns about his old mate, the squatter–poet David Campbell (1915–79). Canberra must have been a pretty lively place back in the 1950s.

I knew many David Campbells. He came down our drive in Tasmania Circle at all times of the day and the night. He came once at three in the morning, knocked loudly on the glass in our gallery, woke us up and asked whether we could lend him a jemmy. He wanted to prise open a window in the old Riverside Art Gallery, remove a picture painted by Sir Alan McNicoll, then a rear-admiral in the Australian Navy, to win a bet with the latter that its absence would not be noticed. Mr Handyman and his wife did not have a jemmy. So they offered him a chisel which Mr Campbell said would do. He won his bet. That was the daredevil Mr Campbell.

There was also David Campbell, the swashbuckler. One day he came down the drive to tell me he had had a gay time at a dance in a ballroom in Forrest. His hostess told me later that while David and his partner were swirling together, he fell into the big bass drum. They helped him to his feet. Next day his hostess had a phone call. 'Oh hello, it's Dave.' My God, she thought, David Campbell is going to apologise. But no, the voice on the phone was not that of a contrite heart. 'I want to thank you for last night,' he said, 'I found it very therapeutic.'

There was the man of delightful fancies. One day he walked down our drive to tell me he had just called on Tom Inglis Moore, the man who introduced a course in Australian literature at the Canberra University College in 1955. David asked Tom, 'Is there a gum tree in the house?' Somewhat startled, Tom asked him why he, David, wanted a gum tree. David replied that he had a great desire to hang his hat on a gum tree.

Manning Clark, *The Quest for Grace*, p. 215.

A monosyllabist

The communist poet and musician, John Manifold (1915–85), was at Cambridge with his coeval, David Campbell. They engaged in serious flyting together.

Another of his friends at Cambridge, by coincidence, was a Campbell also, this was the Australian poet David Campbell, a man of extraordinary charm and panache. On at least one occasion they both attended a meeting of the Spenser Society: 'After we'd sat through a really appalling exhibition of ultra-modernity we went to the pub and bought ourselves a couple of bottles and went back to my rooms where we invented a totally new school, absolutely contemporary, up-to-the-instant, the Monosyllabist School.' The theory they cooked up was that the point of a poem was not necessarily its relevance to contemporary subjects or indeed to subjects at all, but the existence of a scheme of perfect rhymes. The important element in a line was the rhyming syllable; so in its purest form the poem should be this and this only, nothing else could be allowed to stand. The ideal poem would consist of monosyllables, all rhyming according to some formal pattern and arranged down the middle of the page.

'As I recall, David borrowed his girlfriend's lipstick and prepared to write the opening cantos of a monosyllabist epic on the walls of my room. Yet it must be confessed that I was the only member of the school who ever actually produced a complete poem …'

Rodney Hall, *J.S. Manifold: An Introduction to the Man and His Work*, p. 37.

A scholarly burden

Manning Clark calls back a family story from the scientist Julian Huxley.

Humphrey Sumner invited Dymphna and me to tea to meet his friend Dr Julian Huxley. On meeting him I was so nervous I gave him a mini-lecture on the habits of the platypus, before realising I was speaking to a world authority. When I paused for breath he said one icy word: 'Quite.' I was silent for the rest of the afternoon. He told us why the novels of his brother Aldous were sprinkled with knowledge well off the beaten track. One winter the Huxley family holiday was spent high up on the Pyrenees. As the members of their party sipped their tea on the balcony he, Julian, noticed some mules struggling up the path to the chalet. He asked, 'What on earth is this?' Brother Aldous sheepishly confessed not to worry, it was his special rice paper edition of the *Encyclopaedia Britannica*. So no wonder the pages of his novels were sprinkled with the learning of the ages.

Manning Clark, *The Quest for Grace*, p. 93.

High jinks in the ACT

Patrick White was not at all amused by the satyrs of Canberra. The reaction of novelist Kylie Tennant (1912–88) to all this attention is fortunately not recorded.

3-i-71

DEAR CYNTHIA AND SID,

The night you rang was rather a hectic one and no doubt you thought I sounded vague. We were having a dinner for Manning Clark, arranged weeks ahead, and which became a snowball over the weeks till we were finally ten at table. Both Manning and David Campbell became exceedingly amorous, David embarrassingly so at one stage with the wife of a senator (the husband sitting at the other end at dinner). Manning kept asking Kylie if she was promiscuous, and as he tried to pull her on to his lap in the middle of the meal I heard him tell her she reminded him of his father. The Canberrans certainly behaved like canecutters from the north, as Manoly said afterwards, but you would have to do something to make up for an existence in Canberra.

Patrick White, *Patrick White: Letters* (ed. David Marr), p. 372.

Red Ted's retrospect

That omnivorous writer Humphrey McQueen retails — at third hand — an encounter between a naturalist and a once-famous politician, in order to give us a first-hand insight into a historian's mind.

We arranged to meet at the La Trobe Library in Melbourne. How should a tutor talk with the professor who had not only given him a job but had established Australian History as a subject? As my then wife, who had studied his books of documents at both school and university, put it: 'Manning Clark *is* Australian History.' As we were strolling down Swanston Street I made an effort to impress him with a mention of E.G. Theodore, the sometime Queensland premier who was forced to step aside as Federal Treasurer during the depression of the 1930s because of allegations about his corrupt dealings regarding the sale of mining leases around Mungana. Professor Clark took up my theme with an anecdote from Alec Chisholm, editor of the *Australian Encyclopaedia*, who had been at school with Theodore and who in the late 1940s had stood beside the by-then millionaire on Bondi Beach and asked if he might put a question.

'There's nothing you couldn't ask me,' came Theodore's reply.

'What's the truth of this Mungana business, Ted?'

Without diverting his gaze from the glare on the horizon, Theodore replied: 'You know Alec, there are many pleasures in life but none half so grand as Sydney on a fine day.'

By now we were at Flinders Street, where Professor Clark farewelled me to shop for a wedding present for a member of his staff. As I took the train home to South Yarra I turned over the lesson I had been given in historiography: some truths a historian can never know, not even by attending to the silences.

Humphrey McQueen, *Suspect History*, pp. 112–13.

Over the border

John Manifold tells of his politico-musical escape from Germany at the beginning of World War II.

It turned out that the English consul had bolted without warning nationals in the neighbourhood about their danger and war seemed to be breaking out, so I put Katie on board what turned out to be the last train out of the Rhineland for foreigners, and finished the chapter, and sent the chapter to Berlin, and discovered no more trains were running. So I went down to the riverbank — this just shows how things pay off — I'd spent a long time on the riverbank one time and another trying to fish, getting to know the names of the skippers on the barges. And presently a Dutch barge came past and the skipper said: 'I expect you want to clear out, I'll take you to the Dutch border but I can't guarantee getting you across.'

The fare I paid was ten pounds sterling down.

I had the unalterable pleasure of watching a nervy German anti-aircraft battery open fire on the rising moon, it convinced me really that everybody was amateur at this stage of the war. We were about two hundred yards short of the

Dutch frontier at the time and I just hoped they wouldn't stop us. Home Guard, I expect. And very early in the morning we inched our way into the dock just on the frontier, and a Dutch customs officer came on board. The skipper had told me to go below and sit on the coal but I didn't really fancy being hauled up ignominiously from sitting on the coal so I sat in my cabin. The Dutch customs officer and a couple of rather brawny border police came in. He said: 'Passport — visiting Holland — shall I put you down as a tourist?' I said: 'If you don't mind, yes.' He said: 'Ah but can you guarantee you won't stay?' I said: 'No, not really.' He said: 'What are you carrying?' I said: 'Rucksack.' He: 'Open it.' The first thing that stuck out was the mouthpiece of my treble recorder which he fished up and looked at, rather lovingly I thought. Then he groped inside the bag where there was a clean shirt and a pair of pyjamas, a pair of socks and a lot of music. He pulled the music out and said: 'Those late seventeenth-century English are fun aren't they — I rather like Blow, what do you think of Blow?' I said: 'I don't really know much about Blow except *Venus and Adonis* and it's a fine opera, the flute parts are trickier than they look.' He said: 'I'm thinking of taking up singing. I'm interested in the madrigals you know.' I said: 'I know something about Morley.' He said: 'Ah yes, Morley, the four-part balletti!' I said: 'Well look, what about the two-part ones!'

And there we sat side by side looking through the stuff I had. Finally he sighed and said: 'I'd better get back to duty, you won't be with us long, will you? I'll give you a tourist visa.' *Bang* with the rubber stamp. (Roar of laughter.) It doesn't happen twice; they'd been turning back an awful lot of people.

Rodney Hall, *J.S. Manifold: An Introduction to the Man and His Work*, pp. 51–2.

Baggy cords and the 'Tribune'

Cultured scion of a famous pastoral family, Manifold was an unlikely revolutionary, as writer Rodney Hall (1935–) recalls.

To me, he was full of surprises. Once, in the winter of 1954, I was visiting a friend at Raby Bay, a tiny fishing village some ten kilometres south of Wynnum. We had been roaring round on a BSA motorcycle for an hour or so and came back to my friend's place, smarting with the cold, looking forward to hot coffee and something to eat. As we parked and the motor cut, I heard a familiar voice, calmly announcing to the empty street, '*Tribune*, Communist Newspaper ... *Tribune* ...' The voice bearing those years of military authority managed to project the length and breadth of Raby Bay without the least hint of being raised. And there was John, large and faintly shambly in an old houndstooth sportscoat over a khaki flannelette shirt and baggy corduroys, apparently indifferent to the piercing gritty wind. He was standing holding up a fistful of *Tribunes*, the briefcase at his feet fat with further supplies. Occasionally the street would be filled (as only the wide street of a tiny place can be) by one or two men, generally heading for the pub. Some shunned him; some spoke briefly, almost covertly, as if from a sense of duty to some hazy promise of socialist plenty. A few stopped and exchanged greetings, chatted about the weather and bought their papers which they folded small and stuffed in coat pockets for reading later. When my surprise had been mastered and my interest satisfied I stepped out into the street and walked towards him. He smiled and raised a hand as if I were the most expected person in the world. Yet inside myself I felt a terrible weight of conspiracy, almost of guilt, in declaring my friendship. I was eighteen, and yet I was trembling slightly, actually trembling, under the scrutiny of all those faces I imagined watching me from the public bar. Although I had known him for three years, this was the first inkling I had that he himself might have had to master nervousness and even fear in learning to live his life as a public communist.

Rodney Hall, *J.S. Manifold: An Introduction to the Man and His Work*,
p. 116.

We who with songs beguile your pilgrimage

Like many a schoolboy, Manifold had learned Flecker's poem about the golden journey to Samarkand. On the road back from that imperial city he is told a folktale about Tamburlaine the Great, whose lovely tomb is one of the sights of Samarkand.

Another entertaining narrative ballad is 'The Saint and the Sepoy'. This is one of those cases of a poem being written for a specific audience — during a visit to the USSR.

'I'd been taken to Samarkand and Samarkand really is lovely, even Flecker wasn't over-stating it. Along the Golden Road, it was all irresistible. I have a weakness for Mahommedan architecture — it was a tremendous experience. And on the way back to Tashkent in the car, an Uzbek poet with us, Samig Abdukakhar, told me the original story of Hussein Ibn Abbas. Well it's a good story, but it's got tied up with another one that comes in Tolstoy, and probably Grimm, Perrault and all the fairytales in Europe … the sepoy *was* sent down the well by Tamburlaine and when he got to the bottom of it he found the saint still alive sitting in a kind of phosphorescent fairyland at the bottom, meditating; the saint was a bit put out and threatened him with blindness. When the sepoy got to the top, Tamburlaine wanted to know what he'd seen, bribed him: "If you tell me I'll make you a Prince with as much land as you can ride round between sun-up and sun-down." This becomes tremendously dramatic because in the last few yards of his

wild ride around the land, the curse of blindness falls, he
goes arse over tit over the horse's head and kills himself
against a rock. But feeling so happy about Samarkand I
couldn't take tragedy at that stage of the journey and said:
you know, I suspect that isn't what happened ... and literally began versifying on the spot in a sturdy but rather shabby
Intourist car, lurching along the golden road, borrowing bits
of paper from everybody, scribbling verses on them and
passing them round. Samig was doing a fluent verse transla-
tion back into Uzbek and everybody was laughing their
heads off.' Manifold has the story ending:

> But I believe it's incomplete,
>> Distorted, barely true.
> I wouldn't have climbed back again
>> To face Timur.
>>>> Would you?

> I think the sepoy and the saint
>> In harmony divine
> Sit playing chess in paradise
>> And drinking Uzbek wine.

Rodney Hall, J.S. Manifold: An Introduction to the Man and His Work,
pp. 200–1.

Notches

*Bernard Smith (1916–) is the doyen of Australian art histori-
ans and the author of the deeply influential* European Vision
and the South Pacific. *His arresting autobiography is told in
the third person, here focusing on his foster mother and Tennyson.*

His wide reading gave him renewed self-confidence; and it
was encouraged by the brilliance of Jeffrey's dialectical
method of teaching. At the age of eight, with his Bible-
reading to support him, he had developed into a little
religious prig; at the age of sixteen he was in danger of

becoming an intellectual prig. But they were all living at that time through a severe social crisis, and they knew it. A high proportion of their fathers and brothers were out of work. So after ten minutes with Walker and Madgwick the discussion might range over socialism, Douglas Credit, religion, communism, fascism, the New Guard, almost anything that the papers, or some boy in the class, might start up. It became a kind of recognised class game to see whether it was possible to defeat old Jeffrey in an argument. One day he caught Ben cutting a small notch in the protruding ledge of his desk.

'What in the devil are you up to, Smith?' he said.

'You see those six little notches there,' Ben replied, 'each one marks a time when you've lost an argument to one of us.' Jeffrey was always a bit reluctant to agree that he had lost an argument. But decided to be generous.

'Okay, okay, I can't be expected to win all the time can I? But that's no reason why you should start destroying the furniture.'

There was so much to read; so little time. The world of English poetry suddenly opened out before him in its immensity. There were books of poetry in odd places at Burwood, but only Mum Keen herself had been touched by that world. She had given him a little book of Tennyson's poems for his twelfth birthday. He had 'The Brook' off by heart and would recite it round the kitchen table. So later she had given him her own treasured copy of Tennyson. It was that strange poem 'Maud', she said, that she liked best. But he would not understand it until he grew up. Not that she ever read much poetry; there was always too much to do at Braeside. But the memory of Tennyson had lingered on from her girlhood. In his fourth year, with Palgrave's *Golden Treasury* as a guide to further reading, Ben now began to read as widely as he could.

Bernard Smith, *The Boy Adeodatus*, p. 164.

Hospitality

The playwright Sumner Locke Elliott (1917–91) was the 1977 winner of the Patrick White Award. In time he joined that host of people who fell out with White.

After their first meeting in New York in 1968, Patrick White and Sumner corresponded for several years, and became reacquainted when Sumner made a return visit to Sydney in 1974 for the Adelaide Writers' Week, an invitation White had encouraged him to accept. Four years later, after winning the Patrick White Literary Award, Sumner returned to Sydney again and White and Manoly Lascaris gave a special dinner for him at their Centennial Park home. The dinner was a great success, but when Sumner was leaving the party he fell prey to a touch of White's acidity.

> After saying our goodbyes, with Patrick standing at the top of the stairs, I began walking down and I heard him cry out behind me: 'Come back! Come back!' As I was returning to New York within the following days, I thought he meant to Australia, and perhaps even to visit with him and Manoly again. So, with my back still to him, and wanting to immediately reassure him, I also called out my reply. 'I will! I will!' I exclaimed most delightedly, glad I'd made a good impression. 'Not *you*,' I heard Patrick say, caustically, behind me. 'I was talking to the dogs.' Apparently his schnauzer dogs had begun to follow me down the stairs.

In the years since this dinner, this story has been widely circulated in Australian literary circles — told so often in fact that some have declared it fiction. Sumner, however, endorsed its authenticity. But his interpretation of 'that' comment — which could have been merely an insensitive joke on White's part — reveals Sumner's own hypersensitive need and longing for approval from 'home'. No doubt,

Sumner's telling of this story was also coloured by the later rift in the friendship between White and himself.

Sharon Clarke, *Sumner Locke Elliott: Writing Life*, p. 239.

This here bulldust

Storyteller, communist, and Fitzroy barracker, Frank Hardy (1917–96) gave rise to a great many stories, but the most exciting were those surrounding the publication of his novel, Power Without Glory. *Hardy, also a cartoonist, began his writing while serving in the second AIF. He goes here by the name 'Ross Franklyn'.*

One Sunday afternoon in 1943, a sergeant named Frank Ryland, who had been a professional writer and journalist, walked into an igloo-style hut. A sign nailed above the entrance announced: *The Kremlin. Enter at your own risk*.

The Editor of the *Troppo Tribune* was keeping the Sabbath holy — playing blind poker with three of his mates.

'Excuse me,' Bluey Ryland said. He was a nervous freckled man. 'Who writes the stories and verse in the *Troppo*?'

'I write all the unsigned stuff, including the editorials,' Ross Franklyn answered, vexed at the interruption because he was buying two to a pair of aces and a swinger.

'You should become a writer,' the sergeant said.

'Me, a writer?' Ross Franklyn asked, accepting two cards from the dealer.

'Yes, you have a natural flair for it.'

'Turn it up,' Ross Franklyn replied, using the conversation as a screen for the full hand he now held. 'I tried to be a writer and an artist some years ago. Haven't got a clue.'

'It's really very simple,' Bluey Ryland insisted, launching into a lecture about the literary forms, the short story, the play, the novel, the essay.

That set Franklyn thinking. P'raps the stuff in the *Troppo* was good. Just because you published a thing yourself, didn't mean it was crook. But it wasn't literature, and to be a writer you had to have an education, know all about grammar and the sort of stuff they taught in the universities. An ignorant man could learn to draw a little, but he couldn't learn to write literature.

Next day, he met the sergeant crossing the parade ground.

'Listen, Bluey, this here bulldust of my becoming a writer. I wondered, well, what would I write about?'

'If you would write down some of the stories you tell on beer nights, you'd make a fortune.'

'What? Those! But that's not literature.'

'Literature is life,' the sergeant replied.

Frank Hardy, *The Hard Way: The Story Behind Power Without Glory*, pp. 32–3.

Mysterious labours

Power Without Glory, *based in such detail on recent Melbourne politics, was hard going to write — and the very devil to get published, when the time came.*

All through that winter and until *Power Without Glory* was finished he burned the candle at both ends. Joan Clarke, a Sydney writer, stayed at Hillard Street for a few days and was amazed to find him writing when she left for the city in the morning, still writing when she returned for the evening meal, still writing when she returned home from a meeting at midnight, and still writing when she got up again next morning.

But he couldn't keep that up for long. He hadn't the physical strength, the inspiration or the self-discipline. But he worked till the early hours every morning quite often. The all-night radio announcers were his nightly companions and he would crawl to bed near daylight frozen, having allowed the fire to burn out to conserve fuel.

He was obsessed with *Power Without Glory*, gave no thought to anything else even to how it could be published.

Once his wife said: 'Will there ever be a time when we shan't have to live with it?'

And his son, aged three, asked one day: 'What are you writing, Daddy?'

'A book.'

'Still the same book?' was the reply.

Frank Hardy, *The Hard Way: The Story Behind Power Without Glory*, p. 121.

With help from Lilibet

Hardy also had to do much of the distribution of the big novel himself. Soon he would have to undergo a nine-month trial for criminal libel, but was finally acquitted.

Ross Franklyn walked with tentative strides into a leading bookshop with two books under his arm. One was a profusely illustrated sample of the English *Woman's Annual*, the other was *Power Without Glory*.

'Have you had Mr Waters' circular about the English *Woman's Annual*?' he asked the buyer.

'Have you got a sample?'

'Yes, here it is.'

The buyer gazed admiringly and patriotically at the coloured photograph on the front cover of the Princess in evening dress stepping into a luxurious motor-car outside a theatre. He seemed on the verge of curtseying. Recovering his composure, he thumbed through the pages of fashions, recipes, advice to the lovelorn, and advertisements.

'I'll take fifty for a start,' he said.

Nervously, Ross Franklyn handed him *Power Without Glory*: 'Um — an Australian novel Waters is handling; asked me to show it to you.'

The bookseller took it with the lack of interest of his kind in Australian books and an added air of suspicion. He perused the dust jacket, looked at each drawing on it, then began to read the front inside flap.

'If he looks at my photo on the back flap, I'm goosed!'

He didn't — but began to 'read' the book in the manner considered sufficient by bookseller's buyers and daily press literary critics: he thumbed through it stopping occasionally to read a few paragraphs. He accompanied this remarkable performance with ominous 'ums' and 'ahs'.

This fellow is being difficult. According to the plan he should have been so pleased with the Princess that he would order a few of *Power* without even looking at it.

'Ah, well — send me two copies and we'll see how it goes. I'll post the orders to Melbourne in the usual way.'

Mumbling thanks, Ross Franklyn gathered up the books and left hurriedly. At the corner of the street he found himself outside a hotel, entered and forced himself to sip a glass of Toohey's beer. Should he take off the dust jacket for future interviews? Don't know which is worse: the photo on the dust jacket or the crook binding. Anyway, the Princess would solve the problem — must be the first time Royalty ever helped a battler.

Frank Hardy, *The Hard Way: The Story Behind Power Without Glory*, pp. 140–1.

Carn the Blues!

It is often believed that the literati barrack for Carlton Football Club. Manning Clark's first meeting with poet James McAuley (1917–76) took place at a Carlton match.

The historian Manning Clark was standing among the crowd at the Carlton Football Ground in Melbourne one Saturday afternoon in the winter of 1943. He was distracted from the game by a stranger dressed in khaki standing near by. Clark remembered he was 'timid with people in uniform', even though he was 'used to handling fast bowlers and so on'. This chap was edging closer and seemed to want to speak with him, or worse, pick a fight. Clark had not gone to the war, and soldiers could get aggressive about it. He was 'obviously drunk, this chap in the sergeant's uniform'. He had 'craggy cheeks' and a 'ravaged' face: he looked 'quite old, though his body was young'. By now he had moved so close his voice could be heard above the hum of the crowd. 'When he spoke he spoke very clearly and he uttered the most astonishing sentence.' 'I am', the drunk man in the uniform said to Manning Clark, 'a disappointed radical.' It was James McAuley.

Michael Heyward, *The Ern Malley Affair*, p. 42.

Ethel writes

The avant-garde journal Angry Penguins *was edited from Adelaide by the young poet Max Harris (1921–96), once described by Hal Porter as looking like 'a beautiful young Levantine sweetmeat-seller'. One day he received a simple letter, accompanied by some poems of apparent genius.*

At the end of October 1943, Max Harris sat down at his desk with the day's mail. There was a letter with a Sydney postmark from some woman he'd never heard of.

> DEAR SIR,
>
> When I was going through my brother's things after his death, I found some poetry he had written. I am no judge of it myself, but a friend who I showed it to thinks it is very good and told me it should be published. On his advice I am sending you some of the poems for an opinion.
>
> It would be a kindness if you could let me know whether you think there is anything in them. I am not a literary person myself and I do not feel I understand what he wrote, but I feel that I ought to do something about them. Ern kept himself very much to himself and lived on his own of late years and he never said anything about writing poetry. He was very ill in the months before his death last July and it may have affected his outlook.
>
> I enclose a 2½d stamp for reply, and oblige,
>
> Yours sincerely,
>
> ETHEL MALLEY

Michael Heyward, *The Ern Malley Affair*, p. 55.

A gumshoe on the job

Ah, but did the wonderful, mysterious, late poet Ern Malley really exist? Harris was determined to find out.

Harris hired a private detective in Sydney named Bannister to watch Ethel Malley's address. Bannister ran his business out of an office on the ground floor of Newlands House, in Elizabeth Street in the City. Find out if Ern Malley ever lived in Dalmar Street, Harris told him. Bannister was not terribly sure of his brief. In the beginning he cased the wrong joint and in the early afternoon of 15 June wired Harris to tell him that someone called Millard lived at number 14, and had been living there for the past ten years. He asked people walking up and down the street, and knocked on doors, but no one had heard of Ethel Malley. Bannister searched the electoral roll and found there was no E. Malley listed living in Croydon. He concluded she must have another address, and wired Harris to this effect, who wired back telling him to find out who lived at number 40. Harris was worried by now and telegrammed Reed on the morning of 16 June: 'STRONG CHANCE MALLEY FRAUD HAVE DETECTIVE AGENCY INVESTIGATING'. Bannister meantime, in thorough confusion, assumed this must be just another divorce job. He staked out the little house with the rose bush in the front yard, and kept Harris on tenterhooks, letting him know who came and went from the house, and how many times the lights were turned on and off. But who lived there? Bannister finally knocked on the door that night. There was no answer. He went next door, and discovered the family at number 40 was called Stewart. At eight the next morning he paid another visit. A middle-aged woman answered the door. The only person, she said, who could tell him anything about Ern Malley was in hospital and could not be contacted. This information was sent to Harris.

Michael Heyward, *The Ern Malley Affair*, pp. 70–1.

Lenin's emotions

In fact Ern Malley's poems had been concocted at Victoria Barracks in Melbourne by James McAuley and his fellow poet, Harold Stewart — allegedly in a single afternoon.

We produced the whole of Ern Malley's tragic life-work in one afternoon, with the aid of a chance collection of books which happened to be on our desk: the Concise Oxford Dictionary, a Collected Shakespeare, Dictionary of Quotations &c.

We opened books at random, choosing a word or phrase haphazardly. We made lists of these and wove them into non-sensical sentences.

We misquoted and made false allusions. We deliberately perpetrated bad verse, and selected awkward rhymes from a Ripman's Rhyming Dictionary.

The alleged quotation from Lenin in one of the poems, *'The emotions are not skilled workers'*, is quite phoney.

The first three lines of the poem *Culture as Exhibit* were lifted, as a quotation, straight from an American report on the drainage of breeding-grounds of mosquitoes.

The last line in the last poem (printed in *Angry Penguins* as: *'I have split the infinite …'* &c.) read in the manuscript: *'I have split the infinitive. Beyond is anything.'*

Our rules of composition were not difficult:

1. There must be no coherent theme, at most, only confused and inconsistent hints at a meaning held out as a bait to the reader.

2. No care was taken with verse technique, except occasionally to accentuate its general sloppiness by deliberate crudities.

3. In style, the poems were to imitate, not Mr Harris in particular, but the whole literary fashion as we knew it from the works of Dylan Thomas, Henry Treece and others.

Having completed the poems, we wrote a very preten-tious and meaningless *Preface and Statement* which purported to explain the aesthetic theory on which they were based. Then we elaborated the details of the alleged poet's life. This took more time than the composition of his *Works*.

James McAuley and Harold Stewart, cited in Michael Heyward, *The Ern Malley Affair*, p. 93.

Detective Vogelesang arrives

The Ern Malley hoax leapt into prominence when Harris was charged with publishing obscene matter in Angry Penguins, *that is to say, several of the elusive Malley's poems. Detective Vogelesang's pretty name added colour to the court proceedings.*

The Crown then called its major witness, Detective Vogelesang, whose name translates into English as 'birdsong' but who was known around town as 'Dutchie'. Vogelesang was Nordic in appearance: he was a tall, well-built man with an open face, square jaw, fair hair and blue eyes. He stood up straight in his uniform and obtained the court's permission to recount from notes his questioning of the defendant on 1 August. That afternoon, the court learned, Jacobus Andries Vogelesang, Detective stationed at Adelaide, armed with a copy of *Angry Penguins* (Autumn number, 1944), had visited Maxwell Henley Harris, Student, of 20 Churchill Avenue, Glandore, in his office at Room 83, Second Floor, Brookman Buildings, Grenfell Street, Adelaide and for the attention of the defendant had opened the magazine to page 11, where Ern Malley's poem 'Sweet William' was printed.

'Are you acquainted with all the poems in the Ern Malley section?' asked Vogelesang.

'Yes,' said Harris.

Vogelesang waved a hand at the magazine where the poem was fully visible.

'What is the theme of that poem?' he asked, like a teacher prodding a student.

'I don't know what the author intended by that poem,' Harris replied. 'You had better ask him what he meant.'

Vogelesang was not about to tolerate any sophistry about literary intention. He had his own ideas about the theme of the poem and they had nothing to do with who wrote it. There was another thing too — if the gossip was true, finding the author might prove a slippery task. Harris was the man he wanted. 'What do *you* think it means?'

'I am not going to express an opinion.'

Vogelesang saw straight through this. 'That means you have an opinion but you are not prepared to express it.'

Harris paused. 'I would have to give it two or three hours consideration before I could determine what it means,' he said.

Detective Vogelesang did not have that long. The kind of meaning he had in mind was easier to find. It was time to drop a hint. The magazine was spread open on its spine. 'Do you think it is suggestive of indecency?'

'I haven't got an opinion,' said Harris.

The suspect was being difficult. Detective Vogelesang turned the page and pointed with his policeman's finger at 'Boult to Marina'. He renewed the exegetical pressure. 'What do you think this poem is about?'

Harris looked at him. 'Do you know anything about the classical characters?' he asked.

A bluff, best ignored. 'What I want to know is what it means,' said Detective Vogelesang in a gruff voice. The scene of the crime lay still on the page.

'Pericles and Boult are both classical characters and, when you know what they stand for, you can understand the poem.'

'Do you think the poem is suggestive of indecency?' inquired Detective Vogelesang, sticking to his task.

'No more than Shakespeare or Chaucer or others.'

Vogelesang thrust into this opening. 'You admit then that there is a suggestion of indecency about the poem?'

'No I don't,' said Harris. 'If you are looking for that sort of thing, I can refer you to plenty of books and cheaper publications that you can fill your department with. Our publication is intended for cultured minds, who understand these things, and place ordinary thoughts on a higher level.'

Vogelesang was not about to place ordinary thoughts on a higher level. 'What does it mean when it says "Part of me remains, wench, Boult-upright/the rest of me drops off into the night"?'

'I can't help the interpretation that some people might place on it.'

'Do you think that some people could place an indecent interpretation on it?' Vogelesang could, but didn't want to say so.

'Some people could place an indecent interpretation on anything,' said Harris.

'Well, what is your opinion of the poem?'

'I haven't got one,' said Max Harris, learning fast.

They stumbled through 'Night Piece' and its alternative version. When Harris confessed he didn't have an opinion on either poem, Vogelesang thought it time for some straight talk and told the court he informed the defendant, 'I think they suggest sexual matters, and I consider they are immoral.' Harris had no opinion either about 'Perspective Lovesong' and 'Egyptian Register'. Detective Vogelesang did and fixated on the word 'genitals': 'The genitals refer to the sexual parts,' he remarked brightly. 'I think it unusual for the sexual parts to be referred to in poetry.'

Michael Heyward, *The Ern Malley Affair*, pp. 186–8.

The black swan of trespass

The vanished Sydney garage mechanic, Rimbaud-like author of 'The Darkening Ecliptic', had left one elegiac lyric, which petered away on a preposition, to mark his passing.

Ethel was nothing if not thorough. What was this extra sheet on which Ern doodled, in bed of all places? The wan title 'So Long' had been scored through and a smudgy 'No' etched in above. The pen fumbled its inconsolable way through the lines before sputtering to an inky silence:

> The wind masters the waves
> As the waves the sea
> And all of it entire
> And none of it to me
>
> I had thought it was finished
> And now it is useless
> Like the writing on grave
> Empty of future
>
> Renew
>   the sign
> At the moment of

Michael Heyward, The Ern Malley Affair, pp. 186–8.

In vino veritas?

The Melbourne poet and academic Vincent Buckley (1925–88) maintained a lively sparring relationship with McAuley, who was also a chivvying good mate of Alec Hope.

Our meetings, however, were prolonged, immensely friendly, and insatiably boozy. 'Alec told me you were a sot', he said, grinning, during one of these sessions. Same here, I thought.

Vincent Buckley, Cutting Green Hay, p. 150.

Little Gwendoline

Surely the greatest joker among Australian poets was Gwen Harwood (1920–95). The letters in Blessed City *merrily recall wartime days in a public service department in Brisbane. 'Mafeking' is the nickname she gave to her boss.*

My dear Tony,

In a way I envy you your wilderness; I could do with a wilderness myself after a day's brawling with Mafeking. You know, it's just like trying to fight a large ball of dough — your hands sink into the dough and there you are! What a mind the man has! He doesn't even know what I'm talking about unless I speak in words of one syllable. He has also that strange habit, that public servants acquire after long years, of reading his mail over to himself in a mumbling voice, with slight inflections at the paragraphs. This makes me laugh so much that he looks up, and because he doesn't know what I'm laughing at he gets frantically annoyed and then goes on reading and mumbling with suppressed rage. Today he asked me why I didn't behave in a normal manner, and I replied 'Little Gwendoline was never quite like other girls.' The look of blank amazement on his face was worth recording ...

Gwen Harwood, *Blessed City: Letters to Thomas Riddell 1943* (ed. Alison Hoddinott), p. 125.

Interpretations

Harwood could take a person's outlines and turn her into sheer caricature.

Pears is wonderful! I was once staying with an appalling woman who used to push back the chairs against the wall after you had sat on them and who owned a hideous red carpet that gave me a headache every time I walked through the house. She knitted incessantly and made horrible biscuits out of wheatmeal flour that tasted like sawdust. I should have gone mad had it not been for Pears, which became my companion day and night ...

The woman ... also used to tell character from handwriting (with the aid of a large book wonderfully illustrated). It was a strange thing that her and her best friends' writing revealed them to be generous, loving, trustworthy, clean-living, kind to animals, and possessed of amazing brain, while her enemies revealed themselves to be mean, low, base, ignoble, dissolute, cruel and full of unsuspected vices. I pointed out to her that you could change your handwriting, but not your character, at will, whereupon she examined mine more closely and found that I was unbalanced. Since then I have maintained correspondence on a typewriter.

Gwen Harwood, *Blessed City: Letters to Thomas Riddell*
(ed. Alison Hoddinott), p. 58.

Crabbed age and youth

Here the impudent young Harwood engages in poetic scholarship with the pie man. She has the upper hand, but it may well be that she failed to recognise 'The Phoenix and the Turtle' at the time. Case not proven.

I am still sitting in glory in Mafeking's chair. The chief clerk came in yesterday and saw me here, and looked absolutely horrified — as a Father Superior would look if he found a novice occupying the abbot's chair in chapel. However he said nothing.

Weitemeyer (the pie man) came in a few moments ago with several sheets of paper and said, 'The other day you were talking to me about poetry.' I said, 'That is so.' He went on, 'You said that Alice Duer Miller was not much good.' I replied, 'That is definitely so.' He handed me the papers and said, 'I have written out a few poems here. Just see if you can identify them. Ha-ha. A test for a highbrow.' He departed. I found written on the paper:

(1) Under the greenwood tree.
(2) Crabbed age and youth Cannot live together.
(3) Prologue to the masque in *Midsummer Night's Dream*.
(4) Wordsworth's Daffodils (one verse)
and (5) a strange poem which I couldn't make out at all.

It sounded like one of the very minor Elizabethans at his worst and was full of laments for 'the turtle and the phoenix', and yet it had some most un-Elizabethan phrases in it. It referred to 'married chastity' and said 'Now to earth let those repair, Who were either true or fair.' So I took the papers back to the pie man and impressed him with my recognition of the poems above; then I said, 'I cannot identify this at all.' Mr Roland Weitemeyer drew himself up proudly and said, 'I wrote it!' 'Good Lord,' I said. 'Well,' he acknowledged, 'not exactly all of it. Mother helped me.'

Gwen Harwood, *Blessed City: Letters to Thomas Riddell* (ed. Alison Hoddinott), pp. 104–5.

In the wake of 'Fantasia'

Who but Gwen Harwood would have spoken of eidetic visualisation?

'Fantasia' is to be shown here this week. Father is taking us on Friday; I'm sorry you are not here to come too. I can't remember whether you have seen it or not. I wonder what the intellectuals of the gramophone society will have to say about it! They make me sick, with their 'theories' about the ideology of this, that and the other. One young lady asked me if I thought drama ought to be 'sociological', so I said 'I have devoted the whole of my life to a study of the eidetic

visualisation of St Bonaventure, and do not feel competent to
speak upon any other subject.'

Gwen Harwood, *Blessed City: Letters to Thomas Riddell* (ed. Alison
Hoddinott), p. 177.

The vampire

*It was not until she was well settled in Tasmania that Harwood
got cracking as a poet. There she met Hal Porter and got on
remarkably well with him, their kinds of wit chiming or crackling
together.*

Porter was not merely writing poetry in the Jennings' house,
he was taking the rare step, for him, of sending it off to the
Bulletin where it was being published. It was through Ann
Jennings that Hal met her close friend, the poet Gwen
Harwood, who was at the beginning of her poetic career and
had not yet begun to publish. Gwen had seen him about
when she was living at Fern Tree and he was boarding there
several years earlier but they had not met. She recalled that
he 'was immaculate in his dress; fingernails, shoes, cuffs,
moustache all perfect. There was a kind of military air about
him (he might have been a colonel in civvies).' She noticed
that 'he was a favourite with the old ladies who went to the
Fern Tree Post Office: probably their outing for the day.
"Such a witty man!" or "So entertaining to talk to,"
they would say. "He takes such an *interest* in what you tell
him!" '

Gwen had read and much admired Porter's poems in the
Bulletin while he, delighted to have a fan, set out to charm
her, exclaiming as Ann introduced them: 'Ah, look, it's only
a dear little woman!' When Gwen asked what he had expected, he responded: 'A bead-hung vampire!'

Mary Lord, *Hal Porter 1911–1984*, p. 56.

Not all editors, surely?

Not only did Harwood employ a gaggle of noms de plume but also she had more tricks up her sleeve. The two acrostic sonnets of 1961 were, perhaps, the highlight of her joking. Read downward, they spelt out SO LONG BULLETIN and FUCK ALL EDITORS.

It was under the name of Walter Lehmann that she published in *The Bulletin* in August 1961 a pair of sonnets, 'Eloisa to Abclard' and 'Abelard to Eloisa', which contained an acrostic that some people found aggravating and others titillating. Copies of the journal sold for ten or twenty times their normal price; Australia is a *very* parochial society, and poetry is something to be sniggered over behind the school shelter-shed. Donald Horne was the (new?) editor of *The Bulletin* and he was furious: was this some malicious conspiracy? Was it political? I was in Sydney at the time, knowing nothing about Gwen's jape, and was questioned closely; many poets and others knew the identity of Lehmann, and it had been easy for Horne to learn it. Nothing more, *nothing*, was to be published in *The Bulletin* from this woman. 'I'll do my best,' I said, barely able to restrain my laughter. I passed the message on to Gwen. 'Ho, ho,' she said, for she recovered quickly from the shock of other people's shock; 'keep your eyes open; I have friends everywhere.'

Vincent Buckley, *Cutting Green Hay*, p. 170.

The sentry entry

And then there was a teamwork prank, by way of which a Buckley poem appeared, unsignalled, in one of Harwood's collections of poetry.

Meanwhile, a poem called 'The Sentry' was being published in journals and chosen for anthologies. This was written, but not by Gwen, at the same time as the two offending sonnets, which in their earlier versions were to have been signed by me. In both cases, the poems were to be examples of undeliberated, immediate, if not automatic writing. 'The Sentry' took a few minutes. In August 1962, Gwen wrote on a postcard:

> Remember a poem, *The Sentry*? —
> distinguished in content and style.
> Through the gates of Aust. Lit. it made entry
> then sank to oblivion a while.
>
> Some heads are no bigger than buttons,
> but yours, though of usual size,
> may swell: an anthology (Dutton's)
> has captured the poem as a prize.
>
> Is it yours? Is it mine? or the Muse's?
> Whose hand drove the talented pen?
> With the right hand that never refuses
> a guinea, I signed it.
>
> Yours,
> Gwen.

Vincent Buckley, *Cutting Green Hay*, p. 171.

Napoletana

Gwen Harwood read at a provincial festival with the present editor, late in her life. At the final session she concocted a brand-new story about the circumstances of her childhood.

In 1994 Gwen and I were guests of a weekend literary conference in Shepparton, an apricot and pear town in central Victoria. Our panels and workshops were quite demanding, our audiences enthusiastic. On the Saturday Gwen had talked about her life in the standard reading: Brisbane childhood, organist at All Saints', married life in Hobart, geese, Tasmanian foreshores and so on. When she stood up in a Sunday panel, however, Gwen cast all this to the winds. She declared that she had been abandoned as an infant in the slums of Naples; left in a basket on a stony doorstep; nameless and nourished only by a bag of sweet biscuits and a packet of dry spaghetti. Then, she said, her basket had been discovered by a couple of Australian tourists who took pity on this motherless babe, adopted her and brought her home to Queensland. 'And this,' she concluded, 'is why my maiden name was Foster.'

Chris Wallace-Crabbe, 'Character Isolated by a Deed', p. vi.

A picaresque villanelle

Three poets, Barbara Giles, Joyce Lee, and Connie Barber, drove off together to the Warrnambool Festival in 1986. Their inability to agree about opening windows in the car produced this villanelle from Connie Barber.

> We're heading for the coast: no time to stop.
> The morning air sweetens the old car.
> 'It's cold' she says and winds the window up.

'The draught across my back is cold and sharp.'
'Then I'll shut mine. You open yours for air.'
'My hair' she cries, and winds the window up.

I think my passengers should do a swap.
The heater warms the front seat passenger.
We're running late and there's no time to stop.

The back seat passenger has ears that pop
in pressure. As she's cold she does not care
to fuss about the window's being up.

I stop and extricate her from the crop
of bags and bundles, put the front seat lady there.
Though heading for the coast we had to stop.

Now with warm feet and cool air from the top
of her side window, the front revolved to stare
at her replacement. 'I am cold. Please wind the
            window up.'

Now overheated and enclosed we hope
the lady in the back will like her lair.
We're running later still; no time to stop.

'I'm hot' she says. 'Then let your window drop.
Just wind the handle. You will get some air.'
We're heading for the coast; no time to stop.
'My hair' she cries and winds the window up.

Connie Barber, published in the menu for Poets' Lunch and Wine Tasting
International PEN and Centre for Studies in Australian Literature 1987.

Subversive literature

Oriel Gray (1920–) was a member of the Communist Party until 1950. Long associated with the New Theatre in Sydney, she has written many plays, of which The Torrents *is probably the best known.*

Police raids were made on a number of well-known communists, or suspected communists. Stories circulated about policemen confiscating what they took to be *The Political Works of Shelley* and leaving behind Engels's *The Origin of the Family*, believing it to be a book on family planning. I fear these stories were apocryphal, though looking back on the evidence given in later obscenity trials, I'm not so sure.

Oriel Gray, *Exit Left: Memoirs of a Scarlet Woman*, p. 52.

In time of war

Betty Roland (1903–), playwright, bohemian, and sometime communist, recalls the end of a love affair with 'Diamond Jim' McClelland, later a senator and judge. Guido Baracchi (1887–1975), mentioned in passing, was a charismatic figure of the Melbourne Left and formerly Roland's lover.

It was during this cosy period that Leading Aircraftsman James McClelland came back on leave from Melville Island. We had corresponded more or less regularly during the time he had been away and I was unreservedly glad to see him. His time in Sydney was brief, as he had spent the greater part of his leave in Melbourne, visiting his family and, I gathered, renewing past friendships and an old romance, though who the lady was I did not know. Nor did I enquire, but it was undoubtedly she who accounted for a certain coolness on Jim's part, which I had not anticipated. He also showed a preference for conducting a polemic with Guido on the theories of Karl Marx when he should have been paying attention to me.

At the time I was friendly with a girl called Claire who was living in the so-called castle on Bungen Head, overlooking Newport Beach. It was an untidy heap of stone and had been unoccupied for years and how Claire came to be there all by herself was a mystery. She had a husband somewhere in New Guinea and took his absence very lightly, as she had an American captain staying with her on this occasion, no doubt to scare away the ghosts that undoubtedly haunted the place.

I told her about the resistance I had met with from Jim, and she suggested that both of us should come and have a few preliminary drinks before taking him down to the beach and letting nature take its course.

'He'll make love to me tonight if I have to rape him,' I said.

The place was dimly lit by a kerosene lamp, the wind howled round the crumbling walls and the four of us sat consuming gin, or bourbon, while the American captain sat at Claire's feet and stroked her leg and grew more and more amorous with every drink. It soon became clear that we were no longer welcome, so Jim and I got up to go and by the time we reached the beach it was clear that his resistance to me had been considerably reduced. It was one of those nights that linger in the memory and I was surprised when he made no mention of it in his book, *Stirring the Possum*.

My feelings for him had undergone a change — perhaps that night on the beach had lit the fire that had been missing before — and he was no longer just one of the men who had made love to me, but a man I began to dream about and yearn for much in the same way I had yearned for Nick. It had also appeared to have made an impression on him, as he wrote more frequently and ardently, and I lost all wish to resume the promiscuous way of life that I had found so futile. Therefore I was totally unprepared for a remark he made in one of his letters to me.

'I think I am in love with you and if you were ten years younger I would ask you to marry me.'

Of course, he was right. I was then forty-one years old and he was twenty-nine, but it was a horrible awakening. Though totally unaware of it he had told me I was finished, and consigned me to the scrap heap. Good enough to go to bed with but not to marry.

Betty Roland, *The Devious Being*, pp. 97–8.

An ex-rover

Geoffrey Dutton (1922–) weaves two versions of Max Harris into this brief pen portrait. Harris's criticism is well known, but his football years are generally forgotten.

Max Harris, at the other end of the intellectual spectrum, faces rebellious youth as an ageing rebellious youth. Ruefully surveying his waistline he reminds his readers that he was once (actually about the time that Murdoch was writing 'Nihilism in Literature') written up in the *Advertiser* football notes as 'Harris, a neat little rover with a strong left-foot kick, who gave a most courageous exhibition'. Harris gets stuck into contemporary youth (no eighteenth-century elegance for him) not for reading something like *Slaughterhouse Five*, which Harris hails as a masterpiece which may help to explain the hazards of youth, but for self-indulgence, laziness, mindlessness, arrogance. Writing in the 1960s of a new batch of films, he singles out 'an incredible feature called *Bucke Shotte* by some ex-Commonwealth Film Unit character called Peter Weir. For extravagant boredom, infantile surrealism and disjointed continuity, this simplistic creation will take a lot of stacking in the twenty-seven self-expressive films that threaten to follow on our late-night telly box'.

Geoffrey Dutton, *Snow on the Saltbush: The Australian Literary Experience*, p. 138.

A passing murderer

Ruth Park (1922–) remembers the rough days of life in Sydney's Surry Hills and one dented noggin.

One boiling day I was writing in my garret when the murderer knocked at the door below. I knew it was the murderer because I looked from the bedroom window of our landlady, Mrs Cardy. Her window surveyed Devonshire Street and the rowdy world, whereas mine was slapbang up against the sweating wall of the Chinese grocery next door.

As Mrs Cardy was at church, I went downstairs to see what he wanted. But it was merely to inquire if my landlady could put a few stitches in the torn lining of his coat pocket. His demeanour was as circumspect as his knock had been modest.

'Leave the coat with me, Mr Green,' I said, and we parted civilly. As he turned I observed on the back of his head the rubbly dent where some friend had once cracked him with a hatchet.

In Devonshire Street, Surry Hills, we were not short of murderers, no. We had Sweetpea, a child strangler, a musty old rapist who had inexplicably slid by on a manslaughter charge, served his time and been freed, but still had bottles and hard words thrown at him. We had rabbity women who had done in their newborns but got off on a plea of insanity. In those days of the second World War it was still widely believed that women who had just delivered could reasonably be expected to be off their heads.

Ruth Park, *Fishing in the Styx*, p. 3.

Glamour

*A beautiful young woman on the lookout for thrills, Charmian
Clift (1923–69) wins a beach girl contest, which puts some wind
in her sails and gets her to the Big Smoke.*

What happened next in my life — oh, I went back to my
small hometown where my mother, of course, received me
back as sweetly and reasonably as ever, and patched up my
bruises and said, 'Well, never mind, think again what you
really want to do.' Well, at this time a rather odd thing happened. My sister had taken a photograph of me on the beach
and she had sent it, without my knowledge, to a magazine
which was running a Beach Girl Quest, and I won it, which
gave me a little bit of money, enough money to come to
Sydney, and so with £20 — £25, I think it was — in my
pocket, I came to Sydney on the search for glamour. This is
a country girl's search. I think country girls always dream of
the big bad city and glamour in that sense.

Charmian Clift in *Self Portraits* (ed. David Foster), p. 59.

After the ack-ack batteries

*Military service is inherently boring, most of the time. Charmian
Clift was lucky during World War II. She joined the AWAS and
there found the opportunity to write.*

Now, that is it, here is my big stage, set for adventure, and
what I will do is to join up. And I did, and I spent a total of
1110 days in the army, first as a gunner on anti-aircraft bat-
teries, which I loved actually, because that was dramatic
enough for me and I felt very important. Later on I was trans-
ferred to Melbourne to LHQ and I had a commission and was
allowed to live out, so one of my ambitions was achieved. I
had a little flat of my own, and in a strange way the army gave

me my chance to write, because someone discovered that I liked writing, and the Ordnance Corps were running their own little magazine at this stage, and they asked me to write it for them, which I did, and found that I could do it very well, and I loved doing it. Then I began having short stories published, so the strange thing of joining the army actually brought about all sorts of wonderful things for me.

Charmian Clift in *Self Portraits* (ed. David Foster), p. 158.

Under the table

In London in the 1950s, Clift met the poets: a supercilious Mac-Neice and a polite Eliot, the latter caught in a slapstick position.

Charmian wrote home to Toni Burgess that she had met Louis MacNeice and T.S. Eliot. MacNeice, whose poetry she had always enjoyed, was a bitter disappointment, after he sneered something superior to her about 'awful colonials'. The Eliot meeting was comic. As head of Faber & Faber, Eliot liked to meet his authors socially at least once, usually for afternoon tea, and this he did with Johnston and Clift. They turned up at his office a bit panicky, Charmian hastily pulling on a fresh pair of white gloves she had kept in her handbag especially. They knocked, and a voice said 'Come in'. They saw, at one end of the room, a lectern, from which Eliot apparently read his verse, but no poet. A movement from under a desk drew their attention, and there, greeting them, was Eliot's posterior — their first glimpse of the great man. 'I beg your pardon,' he said from the floor, 'I dropped my pencil.'

Garry Kinnane, *George Johnston: A Biography*, p. 113.

Frauendienst

The hyperbolic autobiography of Dorothy Hewett (1923–) gives us a glimpse of life in the CPA after the 1948 coal strike.

Since the coal strike and the lockout, the Communist Party isn't too popular in the mills. It's put them too far behind. Besides, the older hands remember the war years when waves of strikers were sold out by the Commos — patriots who were more interested in keeping up production levels for the war against Fascism than fighting for the mill workers' wages.

I have become the delegate on the job for a vicious, right-wing union who meet only once a year and if the rank and file are seen at the union meeting, immediately report them back to the boss.

I spend five days out of every week with the female lumpenproletariat of Sydney, a group of workers unorganized and unknown to the cadres of the Communist Party. I roughen my accent ('Are you a Pommy or somethin'?'), disguise my handwriting ('You're very handy with the pen there, luv'), and discuss Bing Crosby, Frankie Sinatra, *True Love Stories*, sex, husbands, men, dirty postcards, comics, contraception, pregnancy, kids, dirty jokes, false teeth, the latest song hits, the ills of the flesh (female), and the old maid in Marrickville with the big Alsatian dog who gave birth to triplets with dog heads but it was all hushed up and they had to be quietly destroyed. Not much chance of masterminding the Revolution in the Alexandria Spinning Mills, nor of selling the *Tribune*, but I learn to know them all — old Bet, old Lil and Jessie, Julie, Shirl, Dawnie, Al, Beryl, Pattie, Jeannie, Gwennie, Val, Bonus Happy Maise, Curly the Horse, Greenie the leading hand, Dick the pannikin boss, Kenny his off-sider and Creeky the right-wing union organizer.

It is our fabulous year and I don't even recognize it.

'What do you and hubby do on the weekends, Skin?'

'Oh, we go walking.'

'Walking! Christ, you'll soon get over that caper when the first kid comes along.'

Dorothy Hewett, *Wild Card: An Autobiography*, p. 169.

The other woman

In the Cold War years, ASIO took an unusual degree of interest in Australian literature. Some of its interventions could be described as cack-handed.

Soon after the *Orcades* berthed at Melbourne at 8am on Tuesday 2 September 1952, Dorothy Coade Flood (née Hewett) was seen leaning over the rails for some time 'as if expecting to be met on arrival'. But no one came. During the voyage she had behaved in a quiet, unobtrusive manner and did not fraternise with other 'suspect' travellers. According to her file, Hewett was returning to Australia after a five-month European tour which began with the International Conference for the Defence of Children held in Vienna the previous April.

It is a poignant image — a woman standing alone on the deck of a liner looking for a familiar face in the crowd on the dock. Standing forlornly until the crowd disperses, still waiting. It is a picture that provokes speculation about whom she was expecting and why they did not arrive. Already a story that might go under the title of 'The Broken Appointment' has been spawned and with it, a series of questions that cannot be answered. Was she too waiting for the delivery of a brown zipper briefcase? All that is known is that she will disembark at Sydney three days later. There she will again be watched and her luggage searched. For a Royal Commission concerned with identifying and interrogating individuals named in incriminating documents, this episode holds great significance.

Dorothy Hewett had been the subject of a Security file for three years when this report was filed. She was a known Communist and was on record as being five foot three or four, of medium to stocky build with blonde wavy hair, fair complexion, blue eyes and thick legs and ankles. She had a 'big mouth' and a 'round chin'. In spite of this Identikit image, Security failed to register that the woman on the deck of the *Orcades* did not meet this description. Hewett returned from the Vienna Conference by plane, not by ship. The woman leaning on the rails was Hewett's sister-in-law, Dorothy Clare Williams, née Flood, who had also been to the conference in Vienna. (According to Hewett they were not similar in appearance.)

While apparently unconnected with the workings of the Commission, this incident prefigured, and set the pattern for, events leading up to the two women's appearance at the hearing three years later. More generally, this vignette of mistaken identity was a very literal example of the file's pursuit of the illusory subversive — of surveillance creating its own reality according to a set of pre-existing assumptions about what was occurring.

Ironically, Security had spent the previous two years ascertaining Hewett's legal name. Although she was known as Dorothy Flood when she left Perth with Les Flood in 1949, it was discovered two years later that there was no record of her divorce from Lester Lloyd Davies, whom she had married during the war. In the intervening period the files had referred to her as Davies, née Hewett, known as (or alias) Mrs Flood. After a series of inquiries by the NSW Regional Director of ASIO it was discovered that Davies was granted a decree nisi in December 1951 on the grounds of Hewett's adultery with Les Flood. The unstable nature of any identity built on the shifting sands of a proper name was further accentuated by Les Flood's statutory declaration submitted as part of his passport application. At birth Flood had been registered as Les Blood. After his father's death when Les was eight, his mother changed her name by deed poll to Flood.

Fiona Capp, *Writers Defiled: Security Surveillance of Australian Authors and Intellectuals 1920–1960*, pp. 144–5.

Boys

The humour of Elizabeth Jolley (1923–) is too cunning to be easily classified; she is a chameleon of possible selves.

We had spotted frocks, matching each other, frocks with lines and squares on them, embroidered rosebud frocks with reversible ribbons at the waist, frocks with frills and puffed sleeves, and one summer, our mother had our hair shingled and we each had a pair of shorts. No one else in the street had shorts. An old lady passing our front garden looked through a gap in the hedge. Are you two boys or girls, she wanted to know.

'I'm Monica Elizabeth,' I explained, 'and she's Madelaine Winifred, we're boys.'

Later on, being too old for Shirley Temple frocks, we each had a Deanna Durbin dress.

Elizabeth Jolley, 'My Sister Dancing', in *Sisters* (ed. Drusilla Modjeska), p. 171.

The mystique of reason

Franta (Frank) Knopfelmacher (1923–95) was a leading anti-communist figure in Melbourne for many years. A psychologist, he was a great exponent of the comic wit for which the Czechs are famous.

What most people most value in him is his marvellous clownishness, his clown's demeanour and tone and self-presentation, partly self-aware and self-mocking, partly the habit of a man who had been soldier, prisoner, and psychologist. He was delighted when I said that the good soldier Schweik was the best commentary ever written on war. Schweik was one of his heroes; Karl Kraus was another: both extreme ironists and ironists of extremity, both, I suppose, lacking in shame. Once when I had been giving him a pessimistic prognosis for Australia, he said seriously, 'Do you think I should leave the country?' I burst out laughing. Many of his associates, Irish-Australians among them, were regular and heavy drinkers; he was most abstemious, and never needed alcohol to relieve depression or strain. One evening, in quite a state, he stalked into the staff club, University House, and said, 'It is awful. I am going to get scientifically drunk.' 'All right', I said, 'what will you have.' 'A slivovitz, double.' This was brought, he clicked his heels (or some part of his anatomy), knocked the drink back in one swallow, and banged the glass on the table. 'Another', he said, 'A double.' It all sounded very unscientific to me, but after all he was an experimental psychologist, and he had the right to his research material. The second drink went the way of the first; by this time he was saying, 'Scientifically drunk. I am a psychologist. I know how these things work.' 'Another, Franta?' I asked. A benevolent inclination of the head. I went to the bar and said to the barman, a fellow countryman of his, 'These are not for me. They are for Dr Knopfelmacher. He's getting scientifically drunk.' 'Ah yes,' he said, laughing.

The third drink left Knopfelmacher as reasonable as before, if somewhat less vigorous, and it was not followed by others. He was, as we all knew, incapable of willing himself to be drunk. A kind of rationalism, a mystique of reason, was built into his most intuitive and emotional dealings. Further, if he accepted that one had good will towards him, he could usually be talked out of absurdity. He was late in learning to drive, and shortly after he did so he gave me a lift downtown. 'I was the worst pupil my instructor ever had', he said, 'I couldn't learn to back. Even at the end I backed into a wall. My instructor closed his eyes and said, "Oh you're a fucking idiot, chief." ' Knopfelmacher was laughing at the memory. I shouted, 'Look out, Franta. Christ!' We had committed some unbelievable folly that nearly had us pulverised by two cars, whose drivers were mouthing and fisting at us. It was all very Mack Sennett. 'I had better see that we get to the meeting', said Franta, gripping the wheel fondly. The likelihood is that, like myself, he was 'not mechanical'.

Vincent Buckley, *Cutting Green Hay*, pp. 227–8.

Sitting on a chair of gold

For many a writer-to-be there is that moment of epiphany in which the doors of literature swing open, revealing the wonderland ahead. Autobiographer and social historian Patsy Adam-Smith (1924–) was no exception.

Dad came in laughing, 'Look what I've got!' It was the *Sun* newspaper, opened at a remarkable almost-too-good-to-be-true advertisement for a book, *A Children's Treasure House* it was called. All you had to do to get it was save the coupons each day for a certain time, and for a sum of money small enough that even we bushwhackers in those hungry days could afford, the book would be sent to us. It was, the advertisement said, a treasure house of marvellous things like

Aladdin's Cave, or the wondrous hoard of gems behind a rock where old Ali Baba cried, 'Open Sesame' and became rich beyond his dreams.

The book was slow in coming; a week passed and another and another and then, 'It's here! Quick!' It was a 768-page tome. It was beautiful. The cover a deep rich red impressed with the Dream Piper surrounded by laughing children. Dad said, 'Open Sesame!' and turned back the cover and there were the beautiful colour plates and line drawings and decorations and — stories.

For some time I jumped about all over the place, from poems to fables, stories to sagas and excerpts from books such as *Coral Island* or *The Bishop's Candlesticks*. Dad said, 'Why don't you start from the beginning?' So I did.

First there was Jonathan Swift's story of 'Gulliver in Giant Land', followed by 'The Goose Girl' from *Grimms' Fairy Tales*. I read every word carefully, knowing the speech to be different from any I had heard from any man or woman I knew. I didn't talk about it to the few people who passed our way, I believed it to be the most unique literature in the world and because I believed it, it was. Little of it I disliked, although I was surprised at what I took to be a blunder when I came on 'The Pixies' of Edith E. Millard. Miss Millard for my money 'could go he'. How could this silly verse rattle on immediately before the story from *The Mabinogion*: 'when he beheld the castle of Carnarvon he saw the maiden sitting on a chair of gold, and the Emperor threw his arms about her neck, and that night she became his bride.'

Patsy Adam-Smith, in *Birth, Death and Taxes* (ed. D. O'Hearn), pp. 31–2.

Grand Canal mangroves

A novelist with great powers of invention, Thea Astley was not going to be snowed by her introduction to the glories of Venice.

And Thea Astley, travelling overseas for the first time, came initially to Venice. My wife and I met her as she got off a vaporetto at the Riva degli Schiavoni, and helped her with her bags. We asked her what she thought of Venice, as an opening impression. In a very broad accent she replied, 'Geez, it looks just like the mangroves at the mouth of the Brisbane River.'

Chris Wallace-Crabbe, 'Character Isolated by a Deed', p. ii.

Asking for Sean

If book censorship was a mid-century issue in Australia, then it was doubly, trebly, so in Ireland, as Vincent Buckley discovered on his first two visits to ancestral Ireland.

On the first or second trip, in the mid fifties, coming from Liverpool, we had a lot of luggage roped under tarpaulin on the open deck. All promises delivered in England about how and when it could be got off were obviously null and void. No uniformed person knew or would say. It was time to turn to the non-uniformed ones, the men of no property, the hawkers and spitters. On Dublin docks I approached a group of idlers, who considered my case most politely, indeed with a deference mounting to pity, before deciding whether they would release the secret. 'Go down there, turn left, then left again, and ask for Sean.' Sean! the most common name in Ireland. Still, I did it, and there was a Sean, or someone pretending for the moment, and he did get it off for me: as a favour, using brazenly uninstitutional methods, and refusing a tip. He had seen my daughter Brigid's five-year-old face, and was captivated.

On that or the next visit, we faced the customs men. Book censorship at that time in Ireland was a wonder of generalized bigotry; but I had forgotten that, and when the customs man tapped the brown paper carrier bag in my hand and demanded, 'What's in that?' I answered; 'Books!' he half-shouted, looking up sharply. 'Not banned books!' 'I've no idea,' I said. 'What books are banned here?' He was a large ageing man with a fire-red face, like the parish priest of some child's nightmare. 'Give us a look. Give us a look,' he yelled. The top exhibit was a copy of *Masses Ouvrière*, a French left-wing Catholic journal. 'What's this? What's this?' he carolled, scenting a winner. 'Well, it's a French …' I began, but he had already thrown it on the counter and was facing the next. This said in firm gold capitals on a black ground *Holy Roman Missal*, and I could see his mind clicking from disappointment to renewed suspicion to resignation; but he knew when he was licked. Into Ireland, fly as you please, with the help of Sean and of some unlikely Providence.

Vincent Buckley, *Memory Ireland: Insights into the Contemporary Irish Condition*, p. 27.

Village poets

The Yeats Summer School in Sligo is a great Irish literary event, a poets' jamboree. But like all cultural festivals it has its ups and downs, something that Buckley found out.

When a number of writers, particularly poets, is together, the complexities of the poetry-game become incomprehensible. Not that there is anything which does not have its national version elsewhere, in Australia and Canada, for example; but in Ireland the contradictions are remarkable for drama and pace. Nowhere is this more obvious than at the Yeats summer school at Sligo, which I have attended twice, and where I have taken part in two public poetry readings.

The school is held in August, when you may get marvellous weather (one year people were fainting in the heat), or you may be faced by late-summer rain-storms from the Atlantic. This oddity in the weather adds to the uncertainty generated by the poets; they may come early, they may leave tomorrow, they may read, they may not, they can't be certain, they are waiting for Godot to create an effect of secretiveness and slow tension. In 1973, the reading was in the Sligo townhall, and among the readers were Seamus Heaney, Michael Longley, and the famous English poet Basil Bunting. We had been given our places in the reading-order beforehand, and I had chanced one of the two most favoured positions. I arrived on time, as did Bunting; but with the crowd growing restive, two readers had still not arrived, and the usual apologetic requests were made, 'Would you mind going first?' and so on. I agreed, just as the slowcoaches ambled in, to be told that they would now be reading in different positions. All very well but Bunting, who had originally had a position of a sort which few poets like, overheard these rearrangements, and demanded testily if he too could have a better place. At one stage, it looked as if I might have to read both first and in the middle, to prevent anyone else having so discommodious a place in the poetry universe.

Heaney read with his usual perfect pacing; but Bunting, reading several of his lesser poems, was struggling in unfamiliar going. At one point, just as he had announced that he was about to read a poem written for the birthday of a young girl, a local woman rose in the audience and cut across him loudly. It was a great thing to commemorate birthdays, but we should acknowledge all and not only some birthdays; Mrs So-and-So, of Sligo, had her birthday this very day, and the speaker would like Bunting to present the poem not just for his own friend but also for the Sligo woman. This was marvellous stuff, but Bunting seemed not to understand a word

of it. 'What? I beg your pardon?' he said carefully in his flat
Geordie accent. This was a mistake; for the woman, who had
got some applause for her first effort, struck once more, rising to commend a poet of the village genius type who, so she
said, had come all the way from Kilkenny to be present. The
reasons for celebration were getting more and more odd,
and Bunting more and more bewildered. 'Oah,' he said slowly and detachedly, and read on as if nothing had happened.

Vincent Buckley, *Memory Ireland: Insights into the Contemporary Irish
Condition*, p. 27.

Poor old horse

*Francis Webb (1925–73) was a deeply troubled poet. The
strength of his feelings was apparent from childhood on.*

One episode from this period stands out vividly as an illustration of the young Webb's extreme sensitivity to injustice in
the world and of the power of his language. His sister Claudia
recalls how the children had a strong affection for the baker's
cart-horse which they used to feed on the way to and from
school. One day on their way home they were shocked to see
the horse lying dead by the side of the road. Worse than this,
the carcase was overrun with older children, who were abus-
ing the dead horse by pulling its mane and tail. The diminu-
tive Frank, horrified by what he saw, gave way to such a
torrent of withering invective that the desecrators slunk away
in shame, cruelly muttering threats of reprisals. When the
children got home Ma warned young Frank against the dan-
gers of displaying his feeling so openly in public.

Michael Griffith, *God's Fool: The Life and Poetry of Francis Webb*, p. 18.

A short sprint

Sporting competition is often a mateship ritual, as this account of Webb and Buckley attempting to race inside a university pub makes clear. Webb, a poet of genius, did not remain a student for long.

I knew quite well that Sydney was where the strong poets were, and so to Sydney I was delighted to go. It was, of course, Francis Webb's city, insofar as he had a city; and I had met Webb the previous year, or earlier that year, in Melbourne. He had enrolled as a freshman English student after a freshman year at Sydney, and Bob Brissenden was his tutor. He had with defiant shyness revealed that he was a poet of some standing to Brissenden, who asked me about him. 'Oh', I said, 'you mean "A Drum for Ben Boyd?"' 'The very man. I had read him, and of him, in the Red Page, and was excited to meet him. We spent an hilarious afternoon drinking in Naughton's in Royal Parade, at one stage getting down on our marks in the back bar to compare our starting techniques as middle distance runners (Webb being a successful and I a failed performer in that game); Webb was wearing hobnailed boots, and at the shout of 'Go' got off his mark too quickly, so that he hurtled clear across the bar into the opposite wall. He was declared the winner, and neither of us mentioned the fact that middle distance runners do not normally get down on their marks; what was being demonstrated, after all, was not running but some more primitive rite of passage. Webb and I remained friends for life.

Vincent Buckley, *Cutting Green Hay*, p. 147.

Lost in the terrible city

Hal Porter's delineation of a meeting with Webb is impressionistic, neurasthenic, elaborately detached.

Someone else, somewhere else, also with a faintly stuttering hand, lifts a drink towards lips you'll not ever, now, see it reach. He's turned his marble head farewelling in your direction, and a smile with something sombre behind it. He's that haunted poet, Francis Webb. The drink's milky coffee, instant; the cup's Woolworth.

Place: fourth floor, editorial office, Angus and Robertson, 221 George Street, Sydney. You've popped in briefly. Francis Webb, you learn, has escaped — no, that's not the word, because he's in the institution of his own choice, and's free to come and go — not escaped, wandered away from the sanctuary he commits himself to when the world frightens him, when he feels naked as a worm, and other men seem enlarged agricultural pests. He's been adrift in Sydney for two or three days, doing who knows what, sleeping who knows where. Like a lost animal whose sense of direction's suddenly back, he's stumbled in from the threatening and tarnished fields of Sydney. He's jaded, sullied and crumpled, but in a way that suggests haystack dossing, Gerard Manley Hopkins starlight, and a spiritual scrimmage with himself, rather than alleys, the glint of broken bottles, a brawl with dead-beats. Now, safe at a wayside inn he knows, he's being ministered to. John Abernethy, editor, and Douglas Stewart, poet/editor, are talking to him. An office girl's out buying a razor-blade, a tooth-brush, chicken sandwiches, éclairs. In the office-kitchen, somewhere beyond the cubby-holes Nan McDonald and Elisabeth Hughes work in, coffee's being made. Practical affection surrounds him and his convoluted distresses. Passing by only, you think you can't afford time to be entertained by his gentleness lined with intensity, his charm scorched by fires too intense for you to risk your placidity near. You and he get no further than complimenting each other with the most skilfully lucid politeness on his recent this, your recent that.

You've a sudden urge to linger, and an inexplicable one to tell him that, under the grey flannel skies of High Street, Kensington, London skies seared by jet-liners from Rome, Orly, Zürich, there, in the sky-scraper-top garden of Derry and Tom's department store, are now flamingoes. You'd like to ask him if …

A motherly young woman appears with a tray: the sandwiches, éclairs, the coffee. They're his. There's also a polite cup for you.

'You shouldn't've bothered, love,' you say. 'Thanks, but I shan't have time. I must away.'

Must.

You're nearly sorry to be rushing madly off from this powerful weak man out of whose depths comes the tantalising whiff of chasuble and asylum, pain and … and … the Nature Boy wiliness of a jungle creature.

You edit what you say:

'Sorry to be rushing off …'

Hands are proffered and accepted. His hand's damp, hot, charged with wincing Jesuitical nerves. Before you've reached the door, and turned to say (for God's sake why?):

'Auf wiedersehen!'

that hand's taken up the cup of coffee. Over it he unlooses a strange (and, for you, final) smile, which well may hint/ warn/ protest/ wearily accept that your unease hasn't passed unnoticed; or it may be merely the smile of a fatigued and hungry man who needs a shave.

Hal Porter, *The Extra*, pp. 179–80.

Foulness and hogwash

David Ireland (1927–), a businessman-turned-novelist, discon-
certed the conservative critic Colin Roderick with the sexual sur-
realism of A Woman of the Future. *Roderick's comments*
display their own kind of surrealist invention.

A Woman of the Future has been selling well in Australia and in
America and has attracted many new readers to Ireland's
work, particularly young readers. Ironically, the Macmillan
Company of Australia refused to publish it, believing it
would be damaging to Ireland's reputation; and one of their
readers considered it too pornographic. It won the Miles
Franklin Award for 1979, considered Australia's top literary
honour, and Ireland became the first writer to win the award
outright three times (in 1971, 1976 and 1979). The judges
stated that *A Woman of the Future* is about Australian society 'as
it may develop in the years immediately ahead': 'Its vision of
our future is not always pleasant. In many ways, indeed, it is
both ugly and disturbing. At the same time, however, it is
powerful, convincing and coherent.' The judges also commented on its 'marked frankness' as 'a necessary part of the
novel's style which blends grotesquerie, fantasy, black
humour and biting satire in equal measure'. However,
Professor Colin Roderick, a member of the panel, publicly
dissented from the panel decision and published the following review of the novel:

'Psst! Mister! Wanter buy some feelthy pictures?'
'No. Certainly not. Not while this book's about.'
The jacket tells us it's a novel. To the pure, Paul said, all
things are pure. The reader finding purity in this sewage would
smell eau-de-cologne in the privy.
It purports to be jottings from the journal of a superior,
calculating, 18-year-old, nymphomaniac, incestuous-minded
schoolgirl who passes her coeducational high school days in a

sty of sex-obsessed, promiscuous, self-indulgent schoolmates. Her bizarre imagination oscillates between flights of fantasy and phantasmagoria. Her language is a compound of gutter-snipe foulness and blasphemous hogwash.

The pseudo-entries in her private journal are short and sour. No newspaper in this country would risk its circulation with the obscenities in them. If you want to wallow in a pubescent compound of putrescent Freudianism and picaresque chop-logic, you'll find it in the dirty extracts from this young genius's journal.

The rest of it won't save you from the boredom that sends her to limbo in some sort of mental Simpson Desert, that is, if, having paid the price for the book, you feel you must keep at it as persistently as the dogs did when licking the sores of beggars on the Balata Bridge.

Sounds disgusting, doesn't it? Well, it is.

Seemingly, Professor Roderick had some minor reservations about the panel's commendation of the novel.

Helen Daniel, *Double Agent: David Ireland and His Work*, pp. 11–12.

Ouch!

From the expatriate playwright Alan Seymour (1927–) comes this Max Harris quip about one of Australia's best-known poems.

In '60 or '61, but certainly not long after my play 'The One Day of the Year' had been launched in Adelaide and then professionally in Sydney, my friend Ron Baddeley and I were invited to Castle Hill for lunch with Patrick White and Manoli. It was to be five or so years before the inevitable falling-out with Patrick and this occasion was festive, jolly and very warm. The other guests were all from the Adelaide literary mafia: Geoffrey Dutton, Max Harris and (a young) Peter Ward.

Australian poetry was being discussed and someone, Peter, I think, began to intone, in the usual caricature of an Oz accent, the only one, as he said, that everybody in Australia knows — because we all learned it at school: 'I love a sunburnt country, a land of sweeping plains …' etcetera. Patrick proclaimed (in that high patrician voice, so reminiscent of Dame Edith Evans playing Oscar Wilde) that, though we all laughed at the poem's simplicities, its author Dorothea Mackellar, was in fact a quite sophisticated person and not at all as conventional as one might expect. For instance, in the '20s (or '30s?) she lived in a Palm Beach house she'd had built around a courtyard so that, when it was more shocking than it would be now, she could sunbathe every day in the nude. Instantly — in probably the quickest response I have ever heard — Max Harris cried: 'Oh, then we've had it wrong all these years, what she really wrote was "I love a sunburnt cunt."'

Alan Seymour, letter to the editor, 24 May 1996.

Half-a-pound of butter

Young writers in the making often acquire the gift of phrase-making early in life. Poet Bruce Beaver (1928–) reveals this in recalling the aftermath of his grandfather's death.

So I'd come back to a house of hushed mourning and grand-father's body quiet and sheeted over. When I looked at him the only difference seemed his hands and legs were still and his mouth and eyes closed. I was told to go to the grocer's and buy a half pound of butter. When I was snapped at for something or other by one of the smart alec assistants I said 'My grandfather's dead. I'm not in the mood for argument' and left them with that lethal flea in several ears. True, I must have been insufferable, but so were they. I was full of a very special kind of self-importance: I carried news of death like a white-paper wrapped slab of cold, hard butter straight from the freezer.

Bruce Beaver, *As It Was*, p. 31.

The melted rocket ship and the flying comic

In this remarkable tale, Beaver reveals the ways in which family life can have all the vividness of a comic-book.

Early on one particular mid-week evening I was sprawling on my kitchen bed which served also as a couch, placed beneath the big window. The procedure on all weekends was simple, my mother and I took flight on Saturday afternoons to my aunt's house a mile away at Balgowlah. We'd return the next morning but my father would spend the day in bed and not get up until Monday. Perhaps this night he'd skipped the evening meal. For some reason he'd begun to harangue my mother and me, but this time I refused to listen, burrowing my nose into a Buck Rogers comic in which something rather horrible had just occurred. Buck had investigated a melted rocket ship and looked down in horror and pity upon the luckless pilot whose slumped back was facing the inventive reader. I could imagine without much effort the pilot's face resembling a Christmas ham overlaid with glazed crackling, or maybe a distorted charcoal mask, the ship's instruments had dripped into stalagmites of steel and bubble shapes. I was really consciously ignoring my father's berating but was hypnotically drawn to the comic's happenings.

My father strode across the room to my bed and seizing the comic book from me, hurled it through the open window into the night outside. Without a thought I leaped after it through the window and onto the lavatory roof a foot or two below then jumped about another eight feet into the back-yard, rolling on grass and clay and grabbing at my comic.

Almost immediately my father had launched himself out of the window and bounced off the roof to land beside me and inspect me for breaks or bruises, the while warning me never to do such a thing again while he, the rentpayer, was talking to me.

I wept and groaned a bit and he accompanied me up the wooden stairs and back into the kitchen where my mother made a pot of tea for us all, shaking bewilderedly her dark head at the peculiar misfortune that had landed her with a brace of aerobatic madmen.

Bruce Beaver, *As It Was*, p. 31.

Sweet Thames, run softly

Poet Peter Porter (1929–) and novelist Jill Neville (1932–97) would appear to have had a stormy romance during their early days in London. It is quite a poetic gesture, throwing somebody into the Thames.

Pessimism and party-going are an explosive mix. A favourite spot for parties among young Australian expatriates and their friends was the boat colony on the Thames near the Lots Road Power Station in Chelsea. Jill Neville, who shared a houseboat with a friend, was a focal point at these gatherings. *Fall-Girl* gives a vivid account of a party which became legendary among Australian expatriates, in which the twenty three year old Porter's pent-up frustration, combined with jealousy, suddenly erupted. Australian journalist, Murray Sayle, had invited along a young man called Ralph Howard, who worked in advertising. Jill Neville began to dance with Howard, and to demonstrate her affection for him. In the novel, the narrator's dancing partner, Reg, puts on a Stan Kenton record while Seth lurks behind the *Evening*

Standard. She feels as if her joints have been 'oiled by an Esso bottle'. Although she has been having an affair with an older man, she is inclined to follow this 'young and callous man's mating-call'. Seeing this happening, Seth's repressed feelings of 'dismay and wrath and jealousy' burst forth. A fight starts on the houseboat and he throws her in the Thames. Recalling the incident later, in an interview, Jill Neville's account differs little from the episode in her novel:

> I swam out of the Thames and saw Peter and Ralph struggling in the houseboat ... Ralph got away from Peter ... And I ran away from Peter with Ralph running with me up that Chelsea embankment. Peter was running after me with all his friends, who thought I was a bitch. But we caught a taxi, and I escaped to my life of crime.

Bruce Bennett, *Spirit in Exile: Peter Porter and His Poetry*, pp. 16–17.

Quick as a flash

The meticulously sardonic humour of Evan Jones (1931–) has often been regarded as deeply Melburnian. He is even a long-standing Collingwood supporter, a guarantee of his dinkumness.

The most superior flash of on-the-spot wit in my memory comes from Evan Jones. Back in the late fifties we had been invited out to the poet Alex Craig's 'red intrusive house' in Box Hill for afternoon tea. Not long before this, Evan had finished a long, plaintive poem in *terza rima*, which resoundingly concluded, 'Life echoes in the falling of the leaves / And light plays on the face of history.' Alex said that he greatly admired the poem, but that Evan had not completed the final triad of rhymes required for formal perfection. 'Give me a pencil,' replied Evan. Without a moment's hesitation he wrote, 'I pinched it all. I am the prince of thieves.' 'Evan,' protested Alex, 'you're not serious, are you?' He seemingly was, and there the matter lay.

Chris Wallace-Crabbe, 'Character Isolated by a Deed', p. v.

Pot luck

Tasmanian novelist C.J. Koch (1932–) had, like Evan Jones, a creative writing fellowship to Stanford University in California. There Koch encountered pot culture, as personified by Ken Kesey, author of One Flew over the Cuckoo's Nest.

We are formed by our grandparents as well as our parents, and mine were Victorians. As well as that, I came from a country where many Victorian values were still preserved in amber. This made Ken Kesey not just startling to me, but disturbing.

It was during one of the parties in our Nob Hill apartment that Kesey introduced my wife and me to pot smoking. Marijuana was still dangerous then, police surveillance being seriously carried out — so it was with a thrill of risk as well as unease that we passed through the door into the maze.

It must have been good-quality stuff. At one stage, Ken sat me down at a table and spread out handfuls of peppermints in even amounts in front of himself and me. These were little men, he said, and he and I were going to fight a battle. After a time, in spite of my ability to retain some grip on reality, I began actually to believe in the campaign and these little men, and grew hilarious about them, aware that much of it had to do with Ken's power of suggestion. Later we went to a night-time fun fair and rode the roller coaster: we were truly flying, and our bodies roared with delight and terror. But eventually I became somewhat alarmed at being inside a bubble I couldn't escape, and I began to understand the term 'spaced out'. There was a space at the front of my brain, and I found this an alarming phenomenon.

Christopher Koch, *Crossing the Gap: A Novelist's Essay*, p. 57.

A man of action

Here Koch reveals powers not often displayed by our writers, in briskly getting rid of a trouble-maker from the office of a federal MP.

For a brief time the novelist Christopher Koch, then resident in Launceston while in the process of writing *The Year of Living Dangerously*, worked in Newman's Launceston office. Chris was a far better novelist than political operator. Still he did offer one piece of useful advice as to how to administer applied anger for the benefit of personkind.

For quite some time the office had been under siege from a most unusual Tasmanian family — consisting of a mother (aged about seventy), her son (aged around forty) and her daughter (aged around thirty-five). It was alleged that the son (who could not speak, but who could grunt with conviction) had had his eyes on both his mother's welfare cheque and his sister's favours for a considerable time — apparently with some success on both counts. Welfare workers told stories of how, from time to time, the daughter would feel compelled to go up on the roof of the family house and throw tiles at her (advancing) brother.

The problem was that the X family had got into the habit of conducting some of their rows inside Newman's office — the practice had commenced when Newman's predecessor Lance Barnard was the Federal member for Bass. In between these family get-togethers son X used to turn up at the office and threaten the female staff by walking up behind them and placing the scribbled note 'I kill you' on their typewriters and demonstrating same by quickly moving a finger across his neck as in 'I will cut your throat'.

What to do? Before the arrival of Koch, son X was tolerated. But Koch convinced the staff that anger should be met with anger. And he demonstrated how a bit of applied anger could go a long way. The next time son X's homicide-threatening grunts were heard Koch grabbed him by the shoulder, tightly held one of his arms behind his back, frog-marched him to the glass door and literally threw him out on to the street. It worked — and staff morale increased exponentially. The next time son X returned he got the same treatment. He soon disappeared from our lives.

Gerard Henderson, 'Anger', in *The Eleven Deadly Sins* (ed. Ross Fitzgerald), pp. 73–4.

The Frisco view of history

Former Senator John Button (1933–) records the literate knowledge of Australia displayed by a San Francisco cabbie.

New York, for all its sophistication, must be one of the most self-absorbed cities on earth. San Francisco, on the other hand, is a good place for Australians to start if they want to be recognised and feel at home. More than any other city in America, San Francisco looks west across the Pacific. Thirty per cent of the population is Asian. It has a mild Pacific climate. Eating out at an Italian or Chinese restaurant, the people seem familiar. You could be in Carlton or Double Bay.

In a cab on the way to Fishermen's Wharf, the black driver asked, 'You're from Australia, aren't you?'

'Yes,' I said.

'I thought you were. Tell me,' he asked, 'have you read Manning Clark?' He seemed pleased that I had. 'Manning Clark wasn't the best of students at Oxford,' he said. 'But he went on to become an interesting historian. I've read his

History of Australia. That Robert Hughes … he's more of an amateur, but he writes well. I liked *The Fatal Shore*.'

I asked the driver where he came from. He said he was born in Ethiopia, and went to school in Malta. His father had studied at Oxford at the same time as Manning Clark. He himself was a part-time student of international relations. Really he was a citizen of the world. San Francisco seemed a natural place for him to be.

John Button, *On the Loose*, p. 194.

Sea legs

Bary Dowling's (1933–) exchange with a psychiatrist unearths the fact that he was meant to be a girl, which must have been disconcerting for him, by and large.

The next time is a week later, and very different 'UHFF-HUH UHFF-HUH!' The tape begins with Greek music of dubious quality. The physical effects start as before with tingling in the limbs and face, but I grow rapidly cold. The muscles that quivered on the first occasion now bunch themselves like fists and stay hard. I feel that I am lying on stones. I also feel flayed, as though my musculature is displayed on a gruesome medical chart. I consult with the tiny observer and we agree not to tolerate this horror. I ease my breathing and open my eyes. I say to the psychologist, 'It's not good. It's not working. It's bad.'

'Breathe into the badness. Close your eyes. UHFF-HUH!'

'I mean, it's *very* bad.'

'UHFF-HUH! UHFF-HUH!' So I stay with it, and huhff. The Greek music has stopped, but what is playing I do not know. My body feels vile, and strange things begin in my mind. A great flood of information, none of which I can process, streams through at incredible speed. Yet I recognise material for poetry, and it is important to capture this in iambic pentameters. The palm of my hand beats pentameters into my chest da-dah da-dah, but the words will not arrange themselves — vital, visionary material streams by and will not be caught, there is language everywhere, the world is made of void and words, my mind and body twist, the music stops.

I open my eyes, unrewarded and desolate. He is lying down beside me, propped on his elbow, smiling.

He says, 'We find with this technique that the first session can be momentous and the second the least rewarding, inde-terminate, travelling simultaneously in many directions, often confused by language.' He is describing my experience exactly.

Then he says, 'I kept getting a name. But I'm not sure that I caught it properly. Martha Louise? Marie-Louise?'

'Did I say that name?' I ask this question very carefully, and watch him.

'No. Things fly around.'

I wonder whether I can entirely believe him, and know that I can, that we are in an area outside lies from either side. Martha? Mary? Mother? Marie?

'My mother's name was Marie. Marie Leonore. They called her Lorris. Louise was going to be my name.'

'Your name?'

'Yes. My mother wanted me to be a girl — she said to me: "You were meant to be a girl. Louise! You were going to be Louise." I was very small, and I looked up at her — she was doing something to her brown hair, had both hands above her head as she looked down at me, and we were the only two people in the house. The grandfather clock filled the silence, TOCK! She never let me forget — until I left home she introduced me to people: "This is our baby, he was meant to be a girl, but-we-love-him-all-the-same," with an arm around me, while I smiled. She very much wanted a second girl. Both of them did, but Dad was happy for me to be a boy — he liked me whatever I was.'

'Hmmm.' The psychologist is very mild. 'It seems she laid it on you. But now you can put that aside. A girl was what she wanted, you are the disappointment she got. She's dead, which does not mean she cannot continue to influence you, but you understand it now, and you can let the situation serve you. *You no longer have to serve it.*' He goes away to get tea. As we sip he asks, 'Have you got your sea legs yet, old man?'

Bary Dowling, *Mudeye: An Australian Boyhood and Beyond*, pp. 259–61.

A Technicolor yawn

The stories about comedian Barry Humphries (1934–) are legion and have been so from early in his life: even from his days as a rebellious Melbourne Grammar boy and certainly from his undergraduate years. Graeme Hughes was a fellow thespian.

In Adelaide I was billeted with a nice suburban family, but to be away from home and beyond parental control for the first time in my life was a heady experience, and I was out every night at riotous student parties with Hughes, my mentor in the novelties of intoxication.

One evening, after the Adelaide Dramatic society had given us Shelley's *The Cenci*, a production which did much to explain why this work is so rarely performed, we went to a party with a large bottle of the liqueur Parfait d'Amour, a viscid purple beverage scented with violets. The effects of this drink, quaffed by the tumbler, were disastrous, and I was volcanically sick in the middle of the Union lawn. The violet stain was still there several days later and inspired the song 'Mauve Chunder', which Hughes and I sang with great success at parties. Thereafter we drank more conventional beverages, but I had discovered Mandrake's secret; a simple and accessible substance that made everything disappear.

Barry Humphries, *More Please*, p. 123.

My Russian salad days

A master of Schadenfreude, Humphries became famous for public tricks and practical jokes.

The firm of H.J. Heinz had an excellent product called Russian Salad. It consisted largely of diced potato in mayonnaise with a few peas and carrot chips. Surreptitiously spilt and splashed in large quantities on the pavement of a city block, it closely resembled human vomit. It was a simple and delightful recreation of mine to approach a recent deposit of salad in the guise, once again, of a tramp. Disgusted pedestrians were already giving it a very wide berth, holding their breaths and looking away with watering eyes. Not I, as I knelt beside one of the larger puddles, curdled and carrot-flecked. Drawing a spoon from my top pocket I devoured several mouthfuls, noticing out of the corner of my eye, and with some satisfaction, several people actually being sick at the spectacle. I have done this in many parts of the world and only in Fleet Street in the 1960s did I come close to being apprehended by a policeman. He, however, was too profoundly nauseated to take my name, and as he stood gagging on the salad-splattered pavement I made my escape.

Barry Humphries, *More Please*, p. 118.

Passport problems

Life in London did nothing to abate Humphries' manic performances and improvisations.

Wells got involved in abetting Humphries in some of his capers. 'I socialised a lot with Barry, very happily,' he says. 'Once he decided he wanted to go to Paris. He hadn't got an updated passport. So I said rather pathetically and helpfully, "I think we should see if there's an emergency service at the

Foreign Office." We went down to the Foreign Office, which was naturally closed. Barry walked under the gateway into the yard. There was some Foreign Office man who was just driving his girlfriend home and had got out of his car to talk to the porter. Barry went up to him and asked in a rather odd way if he could direct him to where he could get a passport. While the man was pointing to some remote corner, Barry got into the car and started making advances to the girl. The man was furious. So we were chased out of there. We were then told that Barry could get a temporary passport if he had a photograph of himself. We went to some all-night photography place in Piccadilly. Barry got into a booth upstairs, took his own photograph, and went downstairs to collect the photo where it was being developed. It wasn't a machine, it was an actual laboratory. A hatch went up. It was a West Indian man behind the counter who was about to produce the photograph. And Barry said, "Now I understand why it's called the dark room." He finally got to Paris by saying his mother was dying of cancer in a Paris hospital and bursting into tears at the barrier. They let him through.'

John Lahr, *Dame Edna Everage and the Rise of Western Civilization*, p. 181.

A question of diplomatic strategy

Here Humphries and Patrick White invite the painter Sidney Nolan (1917–92) to dinner, despite Cynthia Nolan's attempt to head them off at the pass.

A visitor of this period was Patrick White, whose early novels I hugely admired. Patrick and his companion, Manoly Lascaris, had loyally come to see *The Bedsitting Room* but were politely non-committal in the dressing-room afterwards. Patrick's aged mother still lived somewhere in

Kensington, perhaps in a mansion flat next door to Miss Amy Halford. He was very censorious, indeed toffee-nosed, about Australians living abroad, however temporarily, even though he had lived in London and Greece for large chunks of the thirties and forties. After one of these chauvinistic outbursts, Manoly interjected: 'But Patrick, you know you hate Australia!' Patrick shot him his cold dowager's stare.

He had dedicated a short story to me and we invited him to lunch with Sidney Nolan. Sidney's wife Cynthia, a complex and saturnine woman, was excessively protective of her husband's privacy and their unlisted number was always being changed.

Later on the day of White's visit, after several bottles of Madeira, Nolan suggested that I telephone Cynthia and invite her to join us for dinner in the West End, but I had no sooner announced myself than she barked: 'How did you get this number? You can't speak to Siddy anyway, he's busy in his studio and doesn't want to be disturbed!' The phone slammed down. Poor Cynthia never knew her busy husband was standing right beside me, or that Patrick White, the great Australian novelist, was anxious to dine with her. She would have been mortified had she known, avid lion-hunter that she was.

Barry Humphries, *More Please*, pp. 226–7.

The blue Danube

Political scientist James Walter describes an accidental mace attack on the present editor, who survived, more or less unscathed.

My next story takes place in Budapest, summer 1992. The bus routes in Budapest are difficult to work out. The subway — though clean and new — gives limited coverage of the city. Tourists like us take to the taxis, which are plentiful. The cabs are mostly old, their decrepitude advanced by the high speeds at which they are driven over cobbles and other appalling road surfaces. Drivers have limited competence in languages other than Hungarian, and their meters are extremely variable: some turning over at breathtaking speed to generate a fare three or four times that you paid in another taxi over the same route. Complaints are greeted with incomprehension or menace. One pays.

One evening in high summer, a group of us — Australians in Budapest for a conference — are travelling by taxi to the conference dinner. In town for a couple of days now, having had time for sightseeing, we feel like we're coming to terms with this city. As the taxi careers through downtown, we swap horror stories of taxi scams experienced around the world.

We turn into the Freedom Bridge, crossing the Danube towards the Gellert Hotel where the dinner is to take place. The hotel is an extravagance from the end of the Austro-Hungarian empire. The bridge is gently arched — from the middle, the crest, there are long outlooks on the city, the hills, and the grand hotel itself.

As we sweep down towards it, by now fully engaged in architectural critique, there is, suddenly, a loud explosion. The passenger in the front seat — a distinguished Australian poet — slumps, groans and clutches his face, muttering, 'My eyes! Christ, my eyes!' We, in the back, feel a stinging sensation across our faces; someone cries out. There is a thin mist on the window next to me. Was something thrown into the cab (the window in front is open)? Was it a shot? Was anyone on the pavement just there — it didn't look like it, but looking back and at this speed, it's hard to tell.

The driver pushes his rattling cab even harder over the last few hundred yards, through an intersection and into the hotel car park, then brakes vigorously. We fall out of the cab, the poet still kneading his eyes. The driver wrenches open the car's boot, pulls out a jerry can, and starts to douse our friend's face with water. It's apparent now that, whatever the cause, some corrosive liquid has been sprayed through the taxi — and that he has copped most of it in the face.

Our alarm and anxiety is given a focus (I can already imagine the headlines, 'Australian poet blinded in terrorist attack', 'Tragedy at ill-judged conference in Eastern Europe'). Someone runs into the hotel for help. Another passenger finds the remains of a small cannister on the floor in the taxi. We show it to the driver. We can't understand a word he says, but his meaning is unmistakable — he knows nothing.

One of the hotel staff walks unhurriedly out to the car and talks to the driver, then turns to us, saying, 'It is painful now, but it will pass'. 'But what is it? Where did it come from?' we ask. He shrugs, and walks away. Our anxiety is turning to anger. The driver can see what is coming. He hurls the jerry can back into the car, leaps in and accelerates away into the traffic. (It was our only free ride in Budapest.) It's dawned on us now that it's probably mace, that the cannister was in the cab all along, and almost certainly belonged to the driver. It was just one of the proliferating anti-personnel devices of urban life. Rolling around the floor, agitated by the vibration of fast travel over rough roads and high summer temperatures, it had reached critical point and exploded.

Two question now: should we get medical help? Should we call the police? Our friend is already coming around. Though his eyes remain alarmingly bloodshot and swollen, he can see again, and the pain is abating. He refuses medical help. As for the police, an Australian official — in the hotel for the dinner — advises us that there's no point calling them for a case like this. He tells us the story of an acquaintance who lives in a palatial house near the Australian Embassy in the Buda Hills, outside town. Someone had thrown a Molotov cocktail against this man's front door as a means of breaking in. He called the police immediately. Fortunately, the door and the house had withstood the fire-bomb (the party apparatchiks had known what they were doing when they originally built those villas). The police arrived twenty-four hours later. The lesson, the official says, is that effective policing disappeared with the downfall of the communist state. The service had been so implicated in the old regime that it was more or less abolished. But you can't build a new police force overnight. So there is only a skeletal service, too stretched to cope with anything but major catastrophe. People have to look after their own security. That's why taxi drivers carry mace.

James Walter, *Tunnel Vision*, pp. 9–11.

Manning upstaged — for once

Brian Matthews (1936–), author of Louisa, *records how he not only took the chair but also lost it, sabotaging Manning Clark's authority in the process.*

Ten years ago, almost to the day, I ascended this rostrum in this tent for the first time. I was not a member of the Writers Week Committee but had been co-opted by it to chair a session called 'A Critical Survey of Australian Writing'. Never having chaired a Writers Week session before in my entire life, I was silly enough to think that being chosen for this job was some kind of honour; especially that particular session because it was an all-day event, amazing as that may now seem to us. It began in the morning at about 10.30 with a talk on documentary writing and went through drama and fiction and ended with poetry.

The first speaker of the day was Manning Clark. He needed little introduction, so I managed that well enough and then effaced myself by retiring to a chair at the very back of the dais. Unfortunately, and all unknown to me, the chair I retired to was not just suitably at the back, it was poised on the edge. The merest backwards tremor and it was over. Manning Clark had scarcely got himself launched on his preamble when, being a restless fellow, I gave the chair a bit of a push and thus disappeared headfirst, feet up, bum gracefully spiralling, into the pit. (I was stunned, by the way, to find on p. 55 of David Tacey's book this incident clearly referred to, thus: '... he begins his downward slide into the matrix of earth ...') To this day I remain astonished at the speed with which I resurfaced, holding my chair and assuming an expression which was supposed to assure everybody that what they were witnessing was the very latest in radical chairpersonship and that only the most stodgy and conservative custodians of intellectual sessions would pass up the opportunity to plummet backwards off the dais just as the guest got started. The screams and gasps from the audience, however, suggested that I hadn't quite carried the episode off with the debonair suaveness I was seeking. I then compounded the confusion by grabbing the microphone from the astonished professor and, *meaning* to say something apologetic and self-critical about clumsy, ineffective attempts to upstage the great etc., *actually* ended up saying the reverse, thus giving the impression that I was a proud and dedicated upstager of the famous and that, with Manning Clark, I was awarding myself both ears and the tail. Even Manning Clark couldn't follow this act and the whole, misconceived affair began to lurch ineluctably towards total chaos.

Brian Matthews, *Oral Dreams*, pp. 109–10.

From the principality of Y

The saga of Helen Darville (Ukrainian pseudonym: Demidenko) and the hoax elements of her novel, The Hand that Signed the Paper, *are richly complicated and have generated many kinds of tale. Whole books have followed her trail. It seemed sufficient here to draw upon Brian Matthews' amusing piece of detection.*

While quietly holidaying recently near the small village of X in the Principality of Y (I've always wanted to start a story like that), I received a strange letter — or rather, I had it read to me while I fed about fifty pounds worth of unfamiliar currency through the gut of the only public phone in the village square at X.

The letter, faxed to my office in London and dated 16 August, was from someone called Helen Demidenko. The name was familiar and as I listened to the distant voice of my London interlocutor rising about the clatter of rhythmically dropping coins, I summoned up what I knew of her: she'd won the Vogel Award; the resultant novel was called *The Hand That Signed the Paper*, it had become the centre of much controversy because of, among other things, an alleged anti-semitism; it had gone on to win, controversially, the Miles Franklin Award and the Australian Literature Society Gold Medal. That was the state of my knowledge as I stood in the phone box in the sleepy square at X.

The gist of Helen Demidenko's letter was that she was publishing a story in *RePublica*. Because of the controversy surrounding her and her work, the *Sydney Morning Herald* wanted to syndicate the story. *RePublica*'s publishers, Harper Collins, thought this was a splendid idea but Demidenko was holding off because, as she explained in her letter, her friend Michelle, whose judgement she unreservedly trusted, had read her story (entitled 'Other Places') and commented that it reminded her of a story by Brian Matthews. Demidenko said that she had made unsuccessful efforts to find such a story and was now writing to me direct to check if the text of 'Other Places' included any unintentionally plagiarised passages. She added that she had had occasional trouble in the past with her intermittent capacity for uncontrollably photographic recall of unattributed material.

I received 'Other Places' in the post from London a couple of days later and saw immediately that it involved three anecdotes that I had published as part of a commissioned

piece called 'Pioneering' in Andrew Sant (ed.), *Toads —
Australian Writers: Other Work, Other Lives,* Allen and Unwin
1992. Not only had I published these anecdotes but they
were also my personal experiences; they were not fiction,
but part of my earlier 'other life' as a school teacher. Not
having my own original text with me, I couldn't be sure how
closely Demidenko's material approximated to mine but,
offhand, it sounded just like me — my voice, as they say.

I sent a polite reply (hand-written and dated 22 August),
showing that there was indeed a problem and that she should
drop the offending sections. I explained that the first incident (in the order she uses them) was my description of an
outer Melbourne high school where I worked in the 1960s;
the second recorded an event I personally witnessed in a
northern Victorian technical school where I had my first job;
and the third was how the professional demise of my immediate predecessor was described to me when I arrived to
take up a high school appointment in Melbourne.

I said that some of it *struck me* as 'pretty well identical to
my originals'; I agreed that she 'didn't need a plagiarism controversy, however unconsciously the whole thing happened';
I remarked that 'the whole business of recalling and owning
anecdotes has always interested me'; and I suggested that
it was sometimes deceptively easy to make inadvertent use
of another's ideas and even whole sentences. In fact, though,
some sort of unconscious 'lifting' of so *much* material
seemed to me extremely unlikely, but I was not prepared
to say so without being able to check my original. My letter
was, therefore, firm and unequivocal but also unaccusing. I
concluded by congratulating her on her recent successes.

An hour or so after I'd posted this reply to London
(where my secretary would type it out and send it on, as
Demidenko had requested, through the English Department
at the University of Queensland), I bought the only English
newspaper left in X to see what was happening in the world
and learnt that Helen Demidenko was really Helen Darville

and that accusations of plagiarism had now been added to the miasma of argument surrounding *The Hand That Signed the Paper*.

Brian Matthews, 'My Demidenko Story', *Age*, 1995.

Powhatan's daughter's heirs

This is hardly an anecdote, yet who could leave aside the claim that the sparkling poet and novelist Randolph Stow (1935–) is the descendant of a Native American princess?

On both sides of the family, Randolph Stow belongs to the fifth generation resident in Australia and the third generation born in Australia. The Stows came to Australia from Hadleigh in Suffolk, and the Sewells from the nearby Maplestead Hall in Essex. The Stow family is connected to the Randolphs of Virginia, to Thomas Jefferson and (allegedly) to Pocahontas.

Anthony J. Hassall, *Strange Country: A Study of Randolph Stow*, p. xiii.

A dirty book

It has been hard to nugget genuine anecdotes out of the writings of Frank Moorhouse (1938–), so devious are the links in his stories between fact and fiction. One thing is clear: that he is a famously sexy writer.

Frank Moorhouse, the new writer in residence at Melbourne University, does not mince words about one of the four novellas in his latest book, 'The Everlasting Secret Family'. It is 'classic pornography', he says cheerfully.

'It's sexually arousing: I have testimonials,' he explains. 'I'm getting more mail about it than any other book I've written.'

And almost in the same breath, he says that his books should be recommended reading for young people. Clearly, Mr Moorhouse has not been inhibited by the fact that his book *The Americans, Baby* was banned reading for people under 18 in Victoria five years ago.

When the book was included in a college course, the Chief Secretary put the book on the R restriction list, to the dismay of Melbourne literary establishment and to the delight of one latter writer who called it 'vile' and 'sewer-ridden'.

The State Advisory Board on Publications commented: 'Some of the episodes deal with sodomy, homosexuality, transvestism, bestiality, fellatio, cunnilingus and free love with co-habitation and adultery.'

'Sexuality has been dreadfully played down in Australia,' says Mr Moorhouse. 'I'm interested in emotional relationships and this inevitably takes me into sexual matters.

'It's not the only thing that I've written about. I've published about 100 stories now, and they're about politics, small town businessmen, American Coca-Cola salesmen, Dutch immigrants ... I've written two sets of stories based at a conference, but nobody accuses me of being conference-obsessed.'

Jane Sullivan, *Age*, 28 August 1980.

Caffè latte country

The rest of Australia is sometimes suspicious about trendiness, which Moorhouse locates in Balmain, Carlton, and, generously, Adelaide: the inhabitants of Fremantle, Fitzroy, and Paddington might well be aggrieved at having been left out.

We thought we should write and let you know how things are here in Le Ghetto de Balmain (as *Le Monde* calls us). Spirits are low. We have been getting a bad press.

Behind our cruel and clever front, we here in the Ghetto, despite the opiates upon which we depend, are underneath it all sensitive people.

But we have been accused of being bludgers because we get more Australia Council money than any other suburb (for godsake, we *do more*). We are grubby, says Professor James McAuley, editor of *Quadrant*. We are pederasts, says the *Sydney Morning Herald*. We all write in short sentences, says the *National Times*.

Well, all right some of us are pederasts. Though we wish to point out that, since we edged the working class out of Balmain, pederasty may have increased but poofter bashings are down.

Jon Cleary said in an interview that he didn't think there was much of a future for Balmain regionalist writing. An apologetic journalist from the *Australian* came to us after the Literature Board grants had been announced and showed us a memo written by the editor. Beneath the heading 'Balmain writers', the editor had scribbled 'Who are these bastards? How much do they rip off the government? What do they do with it? Are they audited?'

The hostility was not really against the physical suburb of Balmain (usually extended in journalistic commentary to include Carlton in Melbourne, and sometimes the whole of Adelaide). Balmain became short-hand for the fantasised (and sometimes real) way of life of some of the people in Balmain, Carlton, Adelaide. It was hostility against the new writing, especially young writing, sexual explicitness, experiment.

They also write about each other, the allegations said.

Frank Moorhouse, *Days of Wine and Rage*, p. 119.

Parliamentary porn

Moorhouse is capable of an extremely lofty irony, as well as of a royal plural.

We ourselves once published a pornographic novella entitled *The Everlasting Secret Family* set in part in the Commonwealth Parliament, which suffered badly in sales because, we are inclined to think, it came out at the time of the prorogation of Parliament. Or at least, that is what our publisher, Richard Walsh, said at the time in his pathetic attempt to explain its sale of 72 copies.

We impute no defect at all to the work.

Frank Moorhouse, 'The Path of Excess, the Palace of Wisdom', p. 16.

A vanilla slice or something

The Bunyah poet Les Murray (1938–) has become a national institution, not only for his grand poems but also for the promiscuous range of his learning. Even in student days he was something of a Character.

One afternoon that winter a burly man in a dark blue jumper and beret came into the office, sat down and talked with a group of us for a while, put some pages in the features editor's in tray and asked me if he could interest me in a cup of coffee at the Union. I sat drinking my ninepenny cup of hot water and chicory and listened to my new acquaintance. I'd never met anyone like him. His name was Les Murray: I'd heard people mention him and I'd read some of his poems in *Hermes* and *honi soit*. He told me that he came from Bunyah via Nabiac. I looked askance at that, but he assured me it was a genuine place, somewhere up between Forster and Gloucester. Did I have any idea where he meant? I said yes, I'd been to Forster.

'Well, then,' Les said.

I began quoting 'Dr Foster went to Gloucester', but Les interrupted to tell me the religious and political significance of that and three or four other nursery rhymes. I looked at his domed forehead with incredulity.

'Sorry. I get carried away with facts. Comes from learning to read from an encyclopedia,' he told me. We proceeded to discuss university's poets. 'I'm flattered that you count me one of them,' he protested, a little too much, I thought. I said that I would buy the next cup of coffee, and could I get him a vanilla slice or something. Yes to both. I walked to the coffee counter in a new mood. If not levitating, I was certainly elated.

Penelope Nelson, *Penny Dreadful*, pp. 151–2.

The naked bushwalker

In this anecdote, two sides of the young Les Murray meet: the bohemian student and the bushman.

In Jan 1961, while students at Sydney Univ, Les, Peter Barden and John Mulhall went hiking up the Woronora river. The others bet Les, who was boasting about the toughness of his feet, that he wouldn't go unshod for the whole weekend. By way of accepting the bet he removed his shoes, dropped the cigarette he was smoking, and slowly ground it out beneath one bare sole. He then offered to go naked for the entire hike if they doubled the bet. They did, he did. On this hike the three of them found a corpse near the Woronora Dam: male, badly decomposed, hands tied, stones in the pockets. They went to the nearest police to report the find, and as it was growing too dark to take the police back there that night, they were asked for their names and addresses. Les had been sleeping rough round Sydney, couldn't provide an address, and the suspicious constabulary locked him and

Barden into a cell for the night: his only night in jail. The corpse was never identified.

Peter Alexander, letter to the editor, 13 January 1997.

Excuse me, sir

Even in later life Murray has shown himself capable of hyperbolic behaviour: what is more, he can carry it off.

And another policeman story, from the days when Les was at his most depressed and crazy: Les is a terrible driver who's lost his licence several times for speeding. He also hates wearing a seatbelt, and for a while carried a letter from a psychiatrist, attesting that his patient Mr Murray 'has a tendency to become hysterical and violent if constrained by a seat-belt'. On one occasion Les was driving Jamie Grant, and doing over 100ks in a 60k area. He overtook a line of cars in a traffic jam by driving on the wrong side of the road, and not surprisingly was stopped by a traffic cop. 'Excuse me, sir, but do you realise that you've just overtaken a whole lot of cars on the left-hand-side travelling at a hundred k's an hour while you're in the sixty zone and you're not wearing a seatbelt?' And then the cop looked at Les and saw the crazed face on this vast man filling up the car. And Les reached into his pocket and got out the psychiatrist's note. The policeman read it, had another long look at Les, folded up the letter very carefully and returned it to him. 'Drive carefully from now on, sir.' He got off without a fine.

Peter Alexander, letter to the editor, 13 January 1997.

Strike me lucky, mate!

Murray's verbal wit is often enlisted in the cause of cultural nationalism, or, as he would put it, on behalf of the Vernacular Republic.

Les Murray is at the PEN American Center in New York where he is the guest of honor on a panel that consists of Joseph Brodsky (moderator), Derek Walcott (pre-Nobel), Richard Howard. Richard Howard, at one point, demands in exasperation that Murray's poetry books carry a glossary of Australian terms. Murray (well into the bottle of whiskey on the table) replies (in oracular tones), 'Well, they never glossed words for us!' End of discussion.

Paul Kane, e-mail to the editor, 7 February 1997.

Vipers

On the whole, Murray evinces strongly romantic readings of his Scots ancestry and of his Catholicism. He would have made a perfect Jacobite and has, indeed, dubbed his cat Fauna MacDonald.

Les Murray, as befits a bard, changed the style of performance. He gave a splendid reading of the bulk of the poems from *The People's Otherworld*, linked by explanatory remarks. He explained the mystery of the book's title. Jokingly, at the University of Stirling, he had referred to Australia as 'the people's otherworld'. Of the first poem in the book, 'For a Jacobite Lady', he said that he woke up from a dream with three of its lines. This was the only time in his life that this has happened.

'The New Moreton Bay', written on the conversion to Catholicism of the poet Kevin Hart, was first published in the *Age*. Hart was teaching at Geelong College, and some parents protested about having such a viper in their children's bosoms. When Hart phoned Murray about this, he was comforted with: 'Consider it your first martyrdom, Kevin.'

Don Anderson, *Hot Copy*, p. 19.

Seamus demurs a little

Both Germaine Greer (1939–) and Dinny O'Hearn (1938–93) were irremediable extroverts. O'Hearn, a longtime personality in and around the University of Melbourne, appeared to recognise no limit, nor any weariness.

Was there something in common between Germaine's Catholic education and Dinny O'Hearn's? Many things were very similar indeed about their personalities, but Dinny played up his long-distance Irishness, which was not a card in her pack. Seamus Heaney, very fond of Dinny, could also be extremely funny about him, claiming that no such surname as O'Hearn existed in Ireland and that someone had possibly misspelt Ahern. One convivial evening in Boston, when we had been talking about the larrikin Sub-Dean and his dangerous charms, Seamus leaned across suddenly to say, 'And the worst thing is, Chris, that they blame *us* for him.' I suppose that Irish-Australians are a whole sub-species, most obscurely related to any actual Ireland.

Chris Wallace-Crabbe, 'Character Isolated by a Deed', p. iv.

Indeterminate hue and texture

Professor Sussex's piece is not precisely anecdotal, belonging rather to the past continuous tense; but his evocation of O'Hearn is beyond comparison.

For several years I used to play squash with Dinny once a week. This was a lively and unpredictable appointment. Dinny on the squash court was a physical metaphor of his verbal self: by turns brilliant, enigmatic, irreverent, bull-like, delicate, apocalyptic, abusive, profound, spectacular. No ball was too far to chase. Dinny motored around the squash court like a pocket-sized Hereford in overdrive, cannoning into walls, roaring encouragement and frustration at himself, and executing shots which no mortal should have attempted, let alone accomplished. I feared for his well-being. He seemed to fear for nothing, red of face, short of breath, incorrigibly competitive.

When playing squash Dinny wore a hat. This was in its way a pagan ritual. The hat was — of course — Irish. It had once been knitted from homespun wool, but when I knew him, it was of indeterminate hue and texture. He never washed it, claiming that this would deprive it of its potency. He must have been right: he beat me more often than not. I often wonder if he would have been less invincible without the hat.

Roland Sussex, letter to the editor, 7 November 1994.

Sex in the sixties

Germaine Greer moved from Melbourne to find herself in the Sydney generation of Clive James, Bob Ellis, and their kind. Greer and James have differing memories of attempted dalliance.

There was a lot of stupidity about sex. I remember that Clive James decided one night — this is a ridiculous story — that he was going to make me. And he actually told Mungo or somebody. He said: 'Oh, I'll 'ave 'er tonight.' And Mungo, or whoever it was — it might even have been Ellis — said: 'Oh, yeah. Tell me about it.' So Clive then went into an extremely odd routine. He began leaping through trees like an ape, swinging around and showing his physical strength.

I remember walking all the way back to Newtown with Clive bounding and rolling alongside me. (I lived in a place in Newtown above a butcher's shop at that time, and every time I'd go to work in the morning after drinking, I'd stop by the dripping vat where they were boiling up lard and be sick.) Clive was tottering along the street, and I bought a jar of oysters for the cat, and generally staged this most extraordinary situation whereby, as soon as we got home, I began behaving like Edith Sitwell. I just went completely off, fed the cat cream and oysters.

I don't think the cat had ever seen an oyster before, didn't handle the oysters very well, kind of licked them and wondered how you got them into your mouth. I was living with Pootynose at the time — a girl called Valerie Payne — in this strange unfurnished — we had no money at all — flat. It was vast, and of course we had no furniture, and half the area we couldn't even use. We just didn't have anything to put into it, not even a mat or anything.

Clive's story was that he was coming down with the flu, and he couldn't get home to Kogarah or wherever he lived. (He lived with his mother in somewhere like Kogarah.) And so I took him terribly seriously about his cold; and put him in my bed and put all the covers on him so he lay underneath them like toad-in-the-hole and sweated feverishly. He had a shower at one stage, I remember, and kept calling us in to look at him under the shower.

We were all very young, I think, though I should've been a little more sensible. I just went up to bed in Pootynose's double bed upstairs, and we lay in bed and giggled all night about how silly Clive was, and how he thought he was going to bowl me over by such a series of fibs and expedients. When I got up the next morning he was gone.

Germaine Greer in *Ferretabilia: The Life and Times of Nation Review* (ed. Richard Walsh), p. 170.

The wilting of axe-handles

Some memories are laid down in our memories by way of the TV screen. Thus Hope recalls the sheer authority that Greer, an accomplished actress, could exert to quash a television interviewer.

I shall never forget this interview. It began with a nervous looking Germaine in a very simple dress sitting rather on the edge of a couch alone on the screen. After a pause, to her left entered a magnificent figure, six feet tall, in full evening dress, shoulders at least two axe-handles wide and with a slightly plummy but superbly confident voice. He introduced himself to the intended victim who nodded nervously as though she expected the worst. He proceeded to shoot a number of questions at her all designed to give rise to her views on women's rights. To all she replied with a simple 'yes' or 'no'. After this had gone on for some five minutes or so and he was obviously getting nowhere at all, he began to sweat a little. The interview appeared likely to break down. That would never do. So he altered his tone. In a more kindly way he appealed to her to answer another question about her views on the wrongs of women. She remained silent. The silence went on till he was forced to break it:

'Miss Greer, I just asked you a question.'

'Yes, you did.'

'But you didn't answer that question.'

'No, I didn't.'

'Well, why didn't you?' He was getting a bit desperate at this point. Ten minutes had gone by and he hadn't got anywhere.

'Because', she said firmly, 'you asked the wrong question. *This* is the question you should have asked ... and this is the question I am going to answer.'

He collapsed, if only for a moment. But from that moment on, she never left him a chance to recover. I have never seen a big bully boy so completely defeated. I have been on Germaine Greer's side ever since. Not that I was ever against it.

A.D. Hope, *Chance Encounters*, p. 135.

The end of the universe

One of the most audible figures in Australian cultural life is Phillip Adams (1939–). He has always had a great deal to say about the non-existence of God.

It's during the war. I'm living in my little sleepout, listening to Sankey's Sacred Songs on my crystal set (not that I liked them but they were the only thing I could get). The wind is soughing in the pine trees; the rain is falling on the galvo roof, surely the most exquisite sound in human experience. To me the war simply means an occasional aircraft caught on the fly-paper of a searchlight. But I guess it added to my levels of anxiety. I'd pick up the signal from others. My father would occasionally appear on leave, sort of saffroned with malaria or whatever it was that soldiers got. Or an occasional coconut would turn up at the letter-box with 'Master Phillip Adams' hacked into its hide. And I'd lie in bed at night, five or six years old, and terrified by the thought of death.

I knew intuitively that the universe is completely sense-less, meaningless — that there is no reason to it — that there's no paternal figure in the sky. I knew it, oddly enough, because of a curious sequence of logic. It occurred to me suddenly that infinite time and infinite space are the same thing. I make that fairly obvious connection. I find myself falling through the stars. I fall up through the roof of the sleepout, past the pine trees, up past the aeroplanes and the searchlight — falling outwards, which itself is an eerie expe-rience. I'd fall for millions of miles through the stars and I'd say: 'This can't be! There has to be an ending. Things have a beginning, they have to have an ending'. I'm really dealing with the euphemism for eternity, and in my mounting terror I used to switch on the bedlamp, sit up in bed and say: 'My name is Phillip Adams of 798 High Street, East Kew', trying to ward off these absolutely apocalyptic terrors with a bit of meaningless data.

One night I found the experience of falling upwards so intolerable that I invented a rocky vault around the universe. It did have an ending. It had a huge rocky vault all the way around. I bounced off it with a great sense of relief, because that seemed to me to mean that time and space both had some sort of ending somewhere. But that only lasted a few months, because one terrible night I fell through the crust and instantly realised that it couldn't have an end, that just as surely as there always had to be a bit more space on the other side of any arbitrary rocky vault, there couldn't be an end to time. In that second I realised that the notion of God was irrelevant. Christianity seemed to me to have a most lop-sided sort of diagram of existence. There had to be a cre-ation, so you invent an original cause. But there can't be an end, so you postulate eternal life, and that seems to me to be the most unbalanced sort of see-saw.

Phillip Adams in *As the Twig is Bent: The Childhood Recollections of Sixteen Prominent Australians* (ed. Terry Lane), pp. 113–14.

A schoolboy's hero

Many writers start out with a strong sense of sporting heroes; some also keep diaries. Graham Little's diary takes him back to the day he had an introduction to Dennis Compton and to a Test match at Lords.

1953 is black with the palest yellow pages, sewn so well that forty years later it still opens flat and not a page has come loose. It's about the size of the slim bar of Nestles you once bought from station vending machines. There's a lilac ribbon for marking the place — *that's* a little frayed at the bottom — and the cover has the year in silver on the top right-hand corner while in the middle, also in silver, is *M&D Biscuits*. Meredith and Drew, they were. My father would have been given it in the way of business.

There can't be many diaries with a Foreword. In Britain in those days we had the confused feeling that we'd won the war, hadn't we, and didn't we have everything to be proud of, then why were we scrimping and saving, dowdy, depressed, and being told by the world Britain was finished? So I'm grateful to *M&D* for the good news that plants (an American usage already?) are set 'to expand the manufacture of creams and fancy lines of which the public has been starved for so long'. There are people who make 'the public' sound beneath them, and 'the people out there' is the same, but this is kind, isn't it? I can't help feeling pleased for the men of *M&D* — we are shown twenty-four of them, head-and-shoulders, starting with the young Scottish division, who will work their way down as they work their way up, to the London division, older men, looking more in control. They boast about the continuing expansion of 'our now famous half-pound packets' — I hope they went well.

On the calendar inside the front cover every month is crossed off except June. I still do this, crossing off the months till I'm dead, as if they were chores it is a relief to get done. Suddenly there's June, completely untouched. As it happens, the entry for the last day reads, 'I did not go to school but went to the Test match with Dennis Compton. Had a lovely day.' Talk of blandness: 'Had a lovely day' — with Dennis Compton, only England's most exciting batsman ever, and he also played outside right for Arsenal! This immensely exciting arrangement was my father's, some return for a favour, and it nearly went very wrong. I duly arrived at Lords and went up to the man at the famous gate where the players arrive and was told to wait while he let Tom Graveney through in a taxi. Then I asked him to tell 'Mr Compton' I was there. You can imagine the reaction, not to mention the colour of my cheeks because I wasn't stupid and just hadn't been able to think of a better way to put it.

I had a longish wait, feeling foolish under the gatekeeper's gaze. But Compton did arrive at last, full of apologies, and the gatekeeper looked surprised. Compton walked me to a seat in the pavilion and then excused himself saying he had to pad up, then he went to the wicket where an over or two later he was LBW for 53, most of them made the day before. The rest of the day belonged to Trevor Bailey and Willie Watson who assured us a draw and I went home early, my mother wondering how I could be at home while Freddie Brown, the England captain, in the only bright play of the day, was hitting fours on the television.

Graham Little, 'Counting Myself', p. 19.

Crib Point Bandicoots

Novelist Gerald Murnane, another child of 1939, has found a miniature focus for his sporting interests in a verbal game of footy. It should be added that most people who remember the days of hot lead printing know the nonce-word, but spell it 'etaoin-shrdlu'.

Gerald Murnane is a writer of fiction who has had five novels and a book of short stories published. I happen to work where Gerald teaches the writing of fiction and, in the course of discussing his being the number one member of the Roxburgh Park Settlers fantasy team in the EAT-WARFLEMSD, we discovered that we both have coordinated the running of fantasy football games.

Gerald consented to show me his game and how it was played with his son, Martin. He brought in a collection of manila folders, each with the front cover equally divided into ten squares, and within each square was a pictorial representation of a team's guernsey, shorts and socks within that folder's fantasy football league. Gerald informed me that if he strongly disliked Martin's choices of team colours, he would change them to a combination he preferred. Notably, some of the guernseys look suspiciously like jockey silks.

Each team in their league was named after a town in rural Victoria. One league was Tasmanian. All the teams were intentionally given an Australian nickname, like the Crib Point Bandicoots, Devon Meadows Lizards, Rosebud Sharks. Later incarnations of the game involved two divisions.

The rules of the game, simply described, were that each side was to select one consonant and one vowel from within the team's name. These choices could not be duplicated by the opposing side. A consonant was worth a goal, the vowel was worth a behind. Scoring was provided by the front page of *The Age*. Each quarter would be a segment of eight to 10 words, with goals and behinds being registered for the appearance of each consonant and vowel. Final scores were totalled and a league ladder kept within the manila folder until a final series was contested.

Deciding which team had the right to select the consonant first developed over the year of playing the game (many seasons could fit into one full year) but there was no hard and fast rule. Gerald, and his son Martin, with whom he played this game, did invent a word which made it easy to remember the decreasing frequency with which consonants and vowels appeared in texts. That word is 'etaonshridlu'.

Herbert Schlegel, 'Etaonshridlu', in *This Game of Ours: Supporters' Tales of the People's Game* (eds Peter Burke and Leo Grogan), p. 143.

How I met Rommel

Clive James (1939–), the Kogarah Kid, recalls the hazy line between fact and fiction from his playground days, between clicking and flopping. It seems that he always had the gift of the gab.

The small boy is usually obliged to be amusing just as the fat boy is usually obliged to be amiable. I cultivated a knack of exaggeration. Lying outrageously, I inflated rumour and hearsay into saga and legend. The price of fame was small but decisive. I had to incur the accusation of being a bull artist — a charge that any Australian male of any age wants to avoid. But I wanted notoriety more. Rapidly I acquired it. From a small circle of listeners in class, I progressed to a large circle of listeners in the playground. Bigger boys came to mock and stayed to listen. Adapted from a recently seen film, my story of the Okinawa kamikazes lasted an entire lunchtime and drew an audience which, if it had not come equipped with its own sandwiches, would have had to be fed with loaves and fishes.

My new line in yarn-spinning was an expansion of the same trick that I had been working in Sunday School. All I had done was throw caution to the winds. I had also mastered the art of laughing at myself a fraction of a second before anybody else did. Climaxing a story of my close personal acquaintance with Rommel, I produced a pair of old sand-goggles from my pocket. This convinced the smaller boys, but the older boys were not fooled. Before they could laugh, I beat them to it. I ran with the hares, hunted with the hounds, and never left a swing except to step on to a roundabout. Gradually even the most scornful among my listeners came to accept that what Jamesie said wasn't *meant* to be true — only entertaining. If it wasn't that, key figures drifted away, and soon everyone else was gone along with them, leaving me alone with my uneaten sandwiches. It was my first experience of the difference between clicking and flopping.

Clive James, *Unreliable Memoirs*, p. 104.

A symphony in velvet

Outside every genuine artist there is the discarded husk of a poseur.

By this time my first poems were coming out in *honi soit*. They were, of course, the most abject pastiche, but my first appearance in print led me to an excess of posturing beside which Nerval walking his lobster would have been as inconspicuous as the Invisible Man. A symphony in corduroy velvet, smoking cigarettes the length of a blow-gun, I casually sprinted into Manning House, spread out a dozen copies of the paper, and read myself with ill-concealed approval.

Clive James, *Unreliable Memoirs*, p. 141.

Dingbats and dung beetles

James's year on the Sydney Morning Herald *can be condensed into a surreal page or so, with a solitary skate at the end of it.*

My year at the *Herald* can be briefly recounted. The editor of the Saturday magazine page was a veteran journalist called Leicester Cotton. He was a sweet man whose days of adventure were long behind. We shared a partitioned-off cubicle just big enough to hold two desks. While he got on with choosing the serials and book excerpts which would fill the main part of the page, it was my task to rewrite those unsolicited contributions which might just make a piece. All I had to do was change everything in them and they would be fine. Apart from the invaluable parsing lessons at school, these months doing rewrites were probably the best practical training I ever received. Characteristically I failed to realise it at first. But gradually the sheer weight of negative evidence began to convince me that writing is essentially a matter of saying things in the right order. It certainly has little to do with the creative urge *per se*. Invariably the most prolific contributors were the ones who could not write a sentence without saying the opposite of what they meant. One man, resident in Woy Woy, sent us a new novel every month. Each novel took the form of twenty thick exercise books held together in a bundle. Each exercise book was full to the brim with neat handwriting. The man must have written more compulsively than Enid Blyton, who at least stopped for the occasional meal. Unlike Enid Blyton, however, he could not write even a single phrase that made any sense at all.

But the contributors most to be dreaded were the ones who came to call. Down-at-heel, over-the-hill journalists would waste hours of Leicester's time discussing their plans to interview Ava Gardner. Any of them would have stood a better chance with Mary Queen of Scots. Even the most sprightly of them was too far gone to mind spoiling the effect of his wheeler-dealer dialogue by producing in mid-spiel a defeated sandwich from the pocket of his grimy tan gaberdine overcoat. One character used to drop in personally in order to press for the return of articles which he had never sent. Another was in charge of a pile of old newspapers so heavy that he had to drag it. He was like a dung beetle out of Karel Capek. Our office was a transit camp for dingbats. Every form of madness used to come through that door. It was my first, cruel exposure to the awkward fact that the arts attract the insane. They arrived in relays from daylight to dusk. For all the contact they had with reality, they might as well have been wearing flippers, rotating bow ties, and sombreros with model trains running around the brim.

No wonder Leicester was relieved when his old journalist friend Herb Grady dropped in. Herb Grady bored me stiff with his endless talk of old times but at least he looked normal. He used to come in every morning about an hour before lunch, which he took in the Botanical Gardens. He was retired by then, so I assumed that the small leather case he always carried contained sandwiches and a Thermos of tea. I could imagine the tea growing cold even with its silver shell as Herb reminisced interminably on. Leicester didn't seem to mind, however. Then one day, as Herb was getting up to leave, the hasp on the leather case snapped open and the sole contents fell clattering to the floor. It was a single ice-skate.

Clive James, *Unreliable Memoirs,* pp. 162–3.

Experiences of noted buccaneers

Writers are in love with language, not least with proper names. Thus the novelist Glenda Adams (1940–) remembers how she was seduced by the grandiloquent title of an old book.

Although my father had left school at twelve, he wrote short stories and poems, most of them unpublished, and bought books for threepence and sixpence from the second-hand bookshops that lined Hunter Street. He presented his special finds to my brother and me in little ceremonies, inscribing them formally with the date and the occasion. When I was exactly four years and six months old, I received several leather-bound volumes, including one of 785 pages published about 1875 called *The History of the Sea: a Description of Maritime Adventures, Achievements, Explorations, Discoveries and Inventions, including Hazards and Perils of Early Navigators, Cruelties and Experiences of Noted Buccaneers, Conquests and Prizes of the Great Pirates, Discoveries and Achievements of the Great Captains, Conflicts with Savages, Cannibals, Robbers, etc., Arctic Explorations and Attendant Sufferings, Growth of Commerce, Rise and Progress of Ship Building, Ocean Navigation, Naval Power, etc., etc., Covering the many Centuries of Development in Science and Civilization from the Ark to the present time, to which is added an Account of Adventures beneath the Sea; Diving, Dredging, Deep Sea Sounding, Latest Submarine Explorations, etc., etc.,* with 'over 250 spirited illustrations'. (No wonder we dreamed of places far away.) As I look through this book now, for the first time in forty years or so, I see that these spirited tales and illustrations include descriptions of the colonisation of the South Pacific and of the phenomenon of coral reefs, which happen to play a part in some of my recent fiction.

Glenda Adams in *Inner Cities: Australian Women's Memory of Place* (ed. Drusilla Modjeska), p. 19.

Maenads amid the Riesling

Poet Kevin Roberts (1940–) recalls the Adelaide Festival at which Ted Hughes was assailed by radical feminists. All festivals in that era had their share of Russian writers, complete with opaque minders.

The two Russian poets with their Russian minders lurking at their backs finish reciting their poems from the podium set up on the lawn at Southern Vales Winery. They thrust a silver samovar into the hands of the host and stride determinedly to the ice troughs of wine. Each poet pulls out a bottle of Riesling, throws back his head, and gulps the whole lot down. They reach into the troughs again for a new bottle, sit and swig with less eagerness. Adelaide Writers Festival. Late 1970s. Heat shimmers over the rows of limp green vines.

I'm introduced to Ted Hughes. We smile as the Russians get stuck into their fourth bottle. By now they are sprawled out, their backs propped up against the troughs. We just start talking about animals in England, when bursting out from the rows of green vines, three women appear, track pants, sandshoes, sweat shirts. The three rush towards us, feral and fierce eyed, chanting in nasal Australian, You killed Sylvia! You killed Sylvia!

Ted Hughes bolts for the buses that have brought us down here from Adelaide. He locks himself in. The three women parade about the bus, banging on the sides and windows shouting at him. Finally the three are restrained and escorted away. The afternoon falls into nervous tatters. The buses start up. The Russians stagger up onto their bus, carrying a pair of dripping Southern Vales Riesling bottles in each hand.

Kevin Roberts, letter to the editor, 7 February 1997.

Romantic heights

For story-writer and novelist Beverley Farmer (1941–) a sublime Mount Buffalo waterfall under a full moon brings back the sense of a lost, beloved friend.

I spent the summer after the second-year exams working at Mount Buffalo. (The summer before that we had worked together at a beach resort, sleeping in one single bed, and now where was she?) After work once, when the moon was full and the track clear, I walked along the path at the lip of the gorge and down to the creek in its cleft, sinking my feet on to the flat rocks where they quivered, and spread, icy, bright in the white light. A little further along out of sight the water rolled through a notch in the dark cliff face down to the valley spread out wide and pale. I fastened my cold hands round rocks at head height — not at the extreme edge, there was a still lower pool to go, rimmed with rocks, before the water plunged a thousand feet down in a ribbon of fall — I clung with both hands to the rock walls, my back to the edge, and sank naked under the surface. The hissing roar that battered me was the one thread of sound in all the luminous pit of silence. I felt, not heard, myself gasping in my frozen, stubborn terror — urgently wishing I could hurtle over the cliff and be a flung white shape flying, a moon-burnt Icarus — as I whipped one hand from its rock for a moment to pass it throbbing, wave-cuffed, over my breasts and thighs: they were rock themselves now, white crystal in the black crystal, icy and rough. I loved them and found them beautiful, splashing moonlit there, because she had loved them, and I hated them at the same time because she (why? and how was it possible to stop loving?) no longer found anything in them to love.

Beverley Farmer, *A Body of Water: A Year's Notebook*, p. 33.

End of the world in Sydney

Penelope Nelson helps Bob Ellis to escape from the end of the world.

The next day, Friday 26 October, found Bob beside himself with panic and urgency. 'We'll have to leave Sydney, there's nothing else for it,' he said.

He believed that within twenty-four hours, every city of more than a million or so inhabitants would have been targeted and attacked. An escalating nuclear war would engulf both hemispheres. We would have to leave before nightfall, but it mightn't be safe to use public transport because the government could put it under curfew at any moment.

I could see where this was heading.

'You've got the key to your mother's car, haven't you?'

'Yes, but that's more for when she's away. When she's here I can only use it with permission if she's not using it herself.'

'The only thing is, I promised Mrs Masters something …'

'What? Who?'

'I promised Olga Masters, Ian's mother, that I'd look after Ian. We'd better take him with us.'

Ian Masters was a handsome, boyish-looking seventeen year old with wide brown eyes and a pleasant grin. Like Bob, he came from Lismore. Knowing how Ian looked up to Bob, his mother had asked Bob to help him cope with the big city in his first year at university.

I can't remember what I packed, but it wasn't much. I can't remember what I said in the note I left Micky, but I suppose I mentioned the Cuban crisis and the risk of nuclear attack. I told her I'd borrowed the car.

I collected Bob in Waverley and we drove together to collect Ian from his room in a seedy terrace in Glebe. There was no back seat in the Triumph Herald and poor Ian had to sit on the carpeted space behind the two bucket seats. He sat with his knees drawn up, his hands on his knees, and his chin resting on his hands. I still remember his trusting brown eyes, eyeball to eyeball with mine every time I glanced backwards.

I drove. Neither Bob nor Ian had a licence.

By sunset we were on the highway going west from Parramatta. There was a lot of traffic. It didn't occur to us that there might be heavy traffic every day, or every Friday afternoon. We were convinced that we were part of a mass exodus from impending disaster.

Penelope Nelson, *Penny Dreadful*, pp. 185–6.

Van Gogh's chair

Helen Garner (1942–) reflects on what a creative artist can do with a small room of her own — or his own. She is well aware of the seemingly modest scale of her fictions.

I used to think, why can't I have a war or a revolution or something? And then I'd think, but I don't know anything about those things, and I won't be able to write about them until I do, and I may not ever, and I can't go out and look for them. There's a lot of that in it, the feeling that women's concerns are small or less important or secondary in some way. I don't think that myself. I think they're really crucial. I love novels about families. I suppose everybody does. Look at *War and Peace*—that's about a family as well as being about war. When I was writing *The Children's Bach* I felt very strange and anxious from time to time because the scope of it was so small and domestic. And one day I was walking past a print shop. In the window of the shop was a print of a Van Gogh painting, that famous one of the chair in his bedroom. I looked at it and I thought, this is a wonderful painting, a painting that fills you with hope and life. And I thought, what is it? It's a painting of the inside of his bedroom and there's not even a person in it!

Helen Garner quoted in *Rooms of Their Own* (Jennifer Ellison), pp. 144–5.

The heart of the matter

As Australia's best-known playwright, David Williamson (1942–) is acutely aware of the making and shaking of careers or of reputations.

Another night we went back to my place in Camden Town and there watched one of the episodes of *David Copperfield*. He hadn't read any Dickens so I recounted the plot. 'It's about this boy,' I said, 'who fights his way upward out of grinding poverty into the English middle classes. And then he becomes a writer.' 'Ah', he said, his eyes lighting up. 'And does he make it as a writer?'

Bob Ellis, 'David Williamson and the Eiffel Tongue', in *Days of Wine and Rage* (ed. Frank Moorhouse), p. 209.

Careful with the dressing table

Williamson tells the raw tale from which one of his most success- ful plays developed. He is celebrated for working very close to per- sonal or observed experiences.

The plot of *The Removalists* is based on a story told by a removalist who shifted furniture for me. It was cheaper if I helped him load and cart the furniture, and so I found myself, during the journey, listening to this story of the 'great day' he had had last Friday. He'd helped shift the fur- niture of a wife leaving her husband, and a 'couple of cops had to come to help the girl and her sister, and when the husband got stroppy, they gave him a bit of a thump.' What interested me as much as the story was the clear identification of the removalist with the policemen. He was glad to see the husband get a thump, and thought the police had every right to do so. He really enjoyed the afternoon. When I wrote the play I let the situation run through to its ultimate conclusion. The husband is killed. I did this to intensify the human tragedy — and the humour — of a situation in which three essentially limited men perpetrate a murder, not from viciousness and sadism, but from sheer bad management on the part of all of them.

David Williamson, 'The Removalists: A Conjunction of Limitations', in *Meanjin* 4/1974, p. 415.

The oysters of Yass

The 1968 productions of Alex Buzo's first play, Norm and Ahmed, *led to prosecutions for obscenity, both in Brisbane and in Melbourne. Yass, allegedly famous for its seafood, lies a long way inland.*

Later in 1969 the play was performed in Melbourne by La Mama, and the actor playing Norm, Lindsay Smith, was arrested after the first performance. He was told by the detective concerned that the police were acting on a complaint made by a member of the audience at a previous performance. 'But this is the first performance,' Lindsay pointed out. 'That may well be,' said the unfazed detective, 'but we're following up a complaint made by a member of the audience at a previous performance.' Lindsay Smith and the play's director, Graeme Blundell, were later fined, Smith for using obscene language in a public place and Blundell with aiding and abetting the commission of a summary offence, as neat a definition of the role of the director as you could hope to find.

My next play, *Rooted*, contained no four-letter words, and seemed set for a non-controversial career when it opened in 1969. When it was on a tour of the NSW country in 1972, however, it ran into trouble in the shape of the Mayor of Wagga, who said the play could be performed as arranged in the Wagga Civic Centre, but the title of the play could not be advertised. The touring company protested that they couldn't announce that 'a play' was going to be performed, as the public had grown just a teensy-weensy bit more discriminating since television had come to Wagga. His Worship held firm, however, and so the company announced that they would go to Yass instead, where they performed the play under its given title. Yass still stands to this day. In fact, it not only stand, it flourishes, and if Barry Dickins is to be believed, serves the freshest seafood in Australia.

Alex Buzo, 'My Survival as an Indigene', in *The View from Tinseltown*
(ed. T. Thompson), p. 28.

The back of his head was flat

Blanche d'Alpuget (1944–), novelist and biographer, is now married to former Prime Minister Bob Hawke, whose biography she published in 1982.

A year later I met L.

Between leaving school and beginning university I had a salesgirl's job in Grahame's bookshop, then in Elizabeth Street, not far from David Jones. Grahame's was one of the acceptable work places for eastern suburbs girls. A colleague on the gift-wrapping counter that year was the beautiful, large and stately sixteen-year-old Marie-Christine von Reibnitz, known to her friends, with only slightly derisory affection, as 'the Baroness'. She improved on her title later by marrying Prince Michael. I did my best to have a bad influence on her, persuading her sometimes to accompany me to Lorenzini's, a wine bar further along Elizabeth Street. It was a long narrow room with mirrors on one side and a bar on the other where artists, poets, sculptors and men working in shoe factories only until a commission for a mural came through, drank plonk sold by the glass, argued, ate octopus sandwiches and tried to seduce young women. In retrospect I think they were mostly snakeoil artists, but at the time they seemed dazzling. I first went there with L.

One afternoon in Grahame's I was straightening a rack of paperback novels when, glancing up, I found myself looking at a man who was looking back at me in a way that was eerie. It was as if our glances, meeting, had chimed.

He was a little less than six feet tall, with lank dark hair combed straight back from a widow's peak and slicked down. There was a slant to his cheekbones and eyes. His skin was a sallow colour, like a northern Chinese, and the back of his head was flat, which was also oriental, although obviously he was European. I thought he was dramatically handsome. He had strong even teeth and a broad smile. I don't remember how he was dressed that day. His clothes always had a solemn artiness that I discovered later was Iron Curtain chic. He was twenty-eight years old.

We kept looking at each other, as if in recognition. I think he bought one of the novels he was skimming and, while I wrapped it up, he asked me in hesitant English to have a drink with him when I finished work.

With an entrée to Lorenzini's I suddenly found myself *inside* the cake shop of the adults. But the exotic displays of the interior overwhelmed me, and I felt small, dim and inadequate in its rich atmosphere. Although I became an habitué for several months, I remember almost nothing about the place. The glasses of red wine I drank probably have something to do with poor recall. I met at least a dozen artists but remember only one, Joe Szabo, who seemed charming and kind and shocked me speechless by mentioning that, in order to eat, he was painting houses. I had never met an adult who admitted to being short of money.

Blanche d'Alpuget, 'Lust', in *The Eleven Deadly Sins* (ed. Ross Fitzgerald), pp. 107–8.

An apparatchik

Former lecturer in Russian and broadcaster Robert Dessaix (1944–) has in recent years published two remarkable books, one an autobiography and the other, Night Letters, *a powerful blending of different kinds of narrative.*

One day the cloakroom attendant at the university library said: 'They've written something about you in the paper.' And indeed 'they' had. A small article had appeared in the weekly news magazine *Nedelya* explaining to its readers that the Australian authorities had sent to Moscow an exchange student with anti-Soviet ideas about Soviet literature and that this could not be tolerated. There was a quote from a Soviet professor who'd met me at the ANU in Canberra and found my views totally outlandish. (No such conversation had ever taken place.) The same week this article appeared, the good professor and I met on a marble staircase in the old university building in the centre of the city. He was sweeping down and I was in the milling crowd at the bottom in the damp. (Russian vestibules are always damp. There's always a sort of foul steam in the air.) He hailed me from several steps above. 'The Australian!' He was jovial today and looking very *soigné* as usual. Like apparatchiks everywhere, he was basically a large zero, a blank space, and, like Chichikov in *Dead Souls*, he could fill the space with whatever cardboard cutout of a man circumstances required — the grandfather, the thug, the roué, the romantic — it didn't matter.

'Well, we've talked about your case,' he said, swivelling in his fine silk suit to nod at this one and that, 'and decided you'll study Dostoevsky while you're here. With your attitudes to Soviet literature it's inappropriate for you to work here in that field. Dostoevsky.' He beamed. 'Agreed?'

It wasn't a question.

Robert Dessaix, *A Mother's Disgrace*, pp. 60–1.

Double or quits

Sasha Soldatow and Christos Tsiolkas have, bafflingly, published a double autobiography with no clear signposts. This anecdote belongs to one or other of them.

I stole four volumes of *Das Kapital* from a party at Tim Rowse's. That was at the time lesbians were all getting their obligatory dog. I had no wish for a dog, but felt left out, so I made all four volumes of *Das Kapital* into dogs. It's easy. Glue on four cardboard legs, cut out a dog's face (don't forget the ears — I did once and my dog was derided), push the face through the middle of the book and stickytape the boards. Attach a piece of string and drag the dog about behind you. Of course you call it Karl.

My four Karls became very sophisticated. One could bark, another stand on its hind legs, the third fell on its side and the last, the very slim one, could not only fall on its side but could also roll over. I finally threw them out after everyone had seen their tricks.

It reads like a parable, but it isn't; I was only sending up Marxism and the recent mania for dogs.

Sasha Soldatow and Christos Tsiolkas, *Jump Cuts: An Autobiography*, pp. 108–9.

The return of the lyric muse

Arnold Zable (1947–), a highly versatile teacher, is probably best known for Jewels and Ashes, *in which he records his return to the Poland of his Jewish ancestors. In this anecdote, he records his father's re-enchantment.*

1936. Wellington, New Zealand. An immigrant. One of a mere handful of Yiddish speakers. Where was there an audience for a Yiddish poet in New Zealand? And when father moved to Melbourne with his family, to connect with the much larger Yiddish-speaking population there, when was there time for a Yiddish poet to practise his craft? There were three children to raise, no alternative but to work in factories, and eventually at the Victoria market. For over twenty years father sold socks and stockings, 'seconds' they were called, which he collected from hosiery mills in Brunswick, and which mother, a seamstress, spent many hours mending on the Singer sewing machine she had brought with her from Bialystok via New Zealand.

My enduring childhood memory of father is of a quiet man, somewhat bent and despondent. In the evenings he disappeared into the front bedroom. He seemed to find his greatest pleasure in reading his volumes of Yiddish poetry. I sometimes glanced into the room, and I would see him sitting by the dressing table, which he used as a desk, swaying over his books like a pious Hassid at prayer. He seemed immersed in another world, in the poetic dreaming he had carried within him since his Bialystok days.

Father retired in 1975. He was depressed for several months as he stumbled towards new ways to fill in his days. Towards the end of that year, his spirits soaring, Meier showed me the first Yiddish poem he had fully completed in just on half a century! Others followed soon after. The muse had returned in father's old age.

The first cycle of new poems was imbued with longing for a vanished past, and for the fire of youth. To paraphrase one of them:

> Among strangers, thousands of passers by
> Among faces, indifferent
> A hand, so warm, reaches out
> And no longer the city seems so strange

Arnold Zable, 'Singing Eternity', *Australian Book Review*, 151, June 1993, p. 41.

For Australia, read New York throughout

Cultural imperialism is not dead, as Kate Jennings (1948–) found in New York.

The book editor was gracious, charming, self-possessed, the kind of woman, I joked to myself nervously, that I would like to be when I grew up. I had used my somewhat forlorn New York network to gain an interview with her; I had, I thought, a 'hot' book proposal. My idea was to do a travel book on my native Australia — not a guidebook but one modelled on the elegant, inquisitive writings of people such as Eleanor Clark, Kate Simon, and Bruce Chatwin.

The book editor listened patiently to my outline. 'There isn't a market for that kind of book about Australia in the United States,' she said.

'Americans are in love with Australia!' I protested.

She shook her head. 'A British publisher might be interested.' And then she smiled. 'What do you think of New York?'

'Ah, it's okay, I guess,' I replied, nonplussed.

'There is room for a book on New York with the approach you described,' she explained.

'I haven't given New York much thought,' I said. Honest but lame. The book editor gave me a long look. 'How long have you lived here?'

'Six years.'

'You live here now,' she said. 'Forget about Australia.'

Kate Jennings, *Save Me, Joe Louis*, p. 51.

The two cultures

Laurie Duggan (1950–) uses a classical Roman model to contrast the Sydney lifestyles of fellow poets John Tranter and John Forbes (1950–98).

John Forbes rents a decrepit flat
a block from the Tranters' lush terrace,
so he eats and drinks from a well-stocked freezer
and sleeps soundly on a broken mattress.

Laurie Duggan, *Epigrams of Martial*, XI, xxxiv, p. 46.

Getting the legs right

Doctor, poet, novelist, Peter Goldsworthy (1951–) is also a wicked wit. Fortunately he has remained good-natured.

Ever since I treated a fractured right leg in my first year out of medical school by putting a plaster on the *left* leg I've had a feeling that life held out something else for me beyond medicine. Fortunately no harm was done, except to my ego. I removed the plaster, red-faced, and reapplied it to the other side. Creative medicine? Or gross negligence? I blame a wandering mind, a mind too often occupied elsewhere. I like to jot down ideas between patients in a notebook I keep for that purpose. Recently a chemist around the corner returned a prescription to me with the note that while he enjoyed the poem, he did not think it one of my best.

And here is one of the advantages of writing as a career: you don't need to know the difference between a right leg and a left leg, for instance. Or if you *do*, then you've got a few weeks or even months to think about it, and make up your mind which is which.

Peter Goldsworthy, 'Ask Not for Whom the Bleeper Bleeps', in *Toads and Australian Writers: Other Work, Other Lives* (ed. Andrew Sant), p. 38.

With the naughty bits

Sally Morgan (1951–) is known not only for her autobiography, My Place, *but also for her prints and paintings with their vivid reinterpretation of Aboriginal traditions.*

Towards the end of second term, Miss Glazberg told us there was going to be a night when all the parents came to school and looked at our work. Then, instead of our usual sheets of butcher's paper, she passed out clean, white rectangles that were flat on one side and shiny on the other. I gazed in awe at my paper, it was beautiful, and crying out for a beautiful picture.

'Now children, I want you all to do your very best. It has to be a picture of your mother and your father, and only the best ones will be chosen for display on Parents' Night.'

There was no doubt in my mind that mine would be one of the chosen few. With great concentration and determination, I pored over my page, crayoning and detailing my parents. I kept my arm over my work so no one could copy. Suddenly, a hand tapped my shoulder and Miss Glazberg said, 'Let me see yours, Sally'. I sat back in my chair.

'Ooh, goodness me!' she muttered as she patted her heart. 'Oh, my goodness me. Oh no, dear, not like that. Definitely not like that!'

Before I could stop her, she picked up my page and walked quickly to her desk. I watched in dismay as my big-bosomed, large-nippled mother and well-equipped father disappeared with a scrunch into her personal bin. I was hurt and embarrassed, the children around me snickered. It hadn't occurred to me you were meant to draw them with clothes on.

Sally Morgan, *My Place*, p. 19.

Indians

Morgan's mother hid the family's Aboriginal origins from her daughter for a long time.

The kids at school were amazed to hear that I shared a bed with my brother and sister. I never told them about the times we'd squeezed five in that bed. All my class-mates had their own beds, some of them even had their own rooms. I considered them disadvantaged. I couldn't explain the happy feeling of warm security I felt when we all snuggled in together.

Also, I found some of their attitudes to their brothers and sisters hard to understand. They didn't seem to really like one another, and you never caught them together at school. We were just the opposite. Billy, Jill and I always spoke in the playground and we often walked home together, too. We felt our family was the most important thing in the world. One of the girls in my class said, accusingly, one day, 'Aah, you lot stick like glue.' You're right, I thought, we do.

The kids at school had also begun asking us what country we came from. This puzzled me because, up until then, I'd thought we were the same as them. If we insisted that we came from Australia, they'd reply, 'Yeah, but what about ya parents, bet they didn't come from Australia.'

One day, I tackled Mum about it as she washed the dishes.

'What do you mean, "Where do we come from?"'

'I mean, what country. The kids at school want to know what country we come from. They reckon we're not Aussies. Are we Aussies, Mum?'

Mum was silent. Nan grunted in a cross sort of way, then got up from the table and walked outside.

'Come on, Mum, what are we?'

'What do the kids at school say?'

'Anything. Italian, Greek, Indian.'

'Tell them you're Indian.'

I got really excited, then. 'Are we really? Indian!' It sounded so exotic. 'When did we come here?' I added.

'A long time ago', Mum replied. 'Now, no more questions. You must tell them you're Indian.'

It was good to finally have an answer and it satisfied our playmates. They could quite believe we were Indian, they just didn't want us pretending we were Aussies when we weren't.

Sally Morgan, *My Place*, p. 38.

Enkidu keeps the books

Here Shane Maloney (1953–) carries the hard-bitten tone of his detective fiction over into Anatolian prehistory.

I found it in a glass case in the Museum of Anatolian Civilizations. It was a clay tablet, 5000 years old, the handwriting still as fresh and legible as the day it was baked. It spoke to me, I swear it did, through all the intervening ages. In the beginning was the word, it whispered. Keep the faith, baby. Always take notes. On the other hand, maybe it just said that the annual income figures for the Gilgamesh Grain and Grape Company were better than projected. Hard to say. My cuneiform isn't what it used to be.

Shane Maloney, 'This Man is No Donkey', *Eureka Street* 6(8),
October 1986, p. 21.

Horace or St Francis?

In this vivid evocation by Alan Gould (1949–) of the landscape around Assisi, fellow poet Kevin Hart (1954–) is pursuing a very different kind of illumination.

The hermitage itself rises sheerly from the cleft between two hills as though it is an extension of the rock. A stream issues from its base, and the windows mark the steep face of the building at irregular intervals. The interior is a honeycomb of cells and corridors that shrink on occasion to the height and breadth of a child. I pass under a low arch and stand on a patio on which there are two wells. Downward and outward the view from the parapet is stupendous. All the noise and under-noise of traffic is absent. Paths lead away into the woods along which crude shrines have been erected, Christian shrines of course, but more pantheistic, more Horatian in aspect than Christian. An exhilaration invades me — of what? Of nothing more than those moments and this particular arrangement of space, the now-ness and hereness of it, free from other significance or hypothesis, the delicious hazard that these mountains, these woods and their flashing colours, this hermitage and its labyrinthine passages and cells, this wind and the burgeoning blue stormcloud over the Plain of Perugia should conspire for me as they do, now and now only, and that this exuberant Umbrian wilderness should give witness to itself and itself exactly.

I turn to say something of this to Kevin, but he has disappeared. A search reveals him sitting in a small and dark chapel staring intently at a crucifix and a pointed violet light above an altar. I murmur something but my remark fails to interrupt his meditation. I have the sense of having intruded in a drama quite outside my curiosity and sympathy, indeed a drama that is the obverse of my recent musings. There is a strong odour of burnt wax. I leave him and wait on the patio, my sense of exhilaration somehow defiled.

In the evening I pursue a desultory argument over a poem he has written about mountains and God.

Alan Gould, 'This World and the Next in Assisi', *Quadrant*, September 1981, pp. 35–6.

A strong reading of the village

Hart has long been friendly with the overwhelming American critic Harold Bloom, whose New York is everywhere marinated in poetry.

No sooner am I talking to Bloom on the telephone than he is reciting stanzas of Feinman that he knows by heart, has known for thirty years. I barely have time to thank him for the book. Before I know it, we are deep in conversation about American poetry. This is a man for whom poetry matters: not as a nice arrangement of words, but as something prophetic, visionary, charged with power. For Bloom the modern poet (that is, the American poet) stands a breath away from solipsism: what is drawn from within, from the spirit, is the only truth that can edify. Culture, history, institutional religion — all these are evasions of that truth, mere fallings, vanishings. Rampant individualism, the Marxist critic could say; but what is Marxism for Bloom but a misreading of Hegel, and what is Hegel but a prolix misreading of that sublime poet Heraclitus? Bloom's politics turn on prizing the individual while flaying proponents of possessive individualism.

Even arranging to meet Bloom for lunch is an event charged with literature. 'Corner of Bleecker and La Guardia Place, my dear', he says. 'La Guardia and where?' '*Bleecker*, my dear … as Hart Crane says, you know, in "Possessions" …' And he chants into the telephone:

And I, entering, take up the stone
As quiet as you can make a man …
In Bleecker Street, still trenchant in a void,
Wounded by apprehensions out of speech,
I hold it up against a disk of light —
I, turning, turning, on smoked forking spires,
The city's stubborn lives, desires.

Possessions: the word resonates in my ear as I walk down to
the Village for lunch. What does one really possess? My self?
Never quite. As I walk around New York my self is beautiful-
ly submerged: perhaps there are only two cities, London and
New York, where I don't speak with a foreign accent.

Kevin Hart, 'America, America', *Overland*, 122, 1991, p. 40.

The last great story

Our concluding anecdote comes from John Hughes, whose tale
contains a fairy tale, memorably handed down by his grandfather.
Australian culture is made up of stories from many times and
many places.

Occasionally, when I return to Cessnock, I go into the base-
ment to look for a book I hope I will not find. The truth is,
I like to think it doesn't exist. In our first house my grandfather used to sit behind my bed and read me stories from
the book. As I could see neither my grandfather nor the book
I began to believe the stories were his own. In the lamplight
there was only his voice.

He 'read' from what he said was a collection of Ukrainian
folk tales. My favourite was a tale about a Prince who does
not know his name. He has a strange idea. He decides on a
competition and sends messengers to every corner of the
kingdom. Anyone who desires can try to guess his name. But
the prize is unusual. The Prince will give a chest of gold coins

to anyone who gets his name wrong, but death to the person who guesses correctly. This is what he thought: only someone who tried to get his name wrong might come up with a name queer enough to be right; a name he could not think of himself. And so the people came forward, drawn by the prospect of easy treasure. They called him Salmon and Trout, Oak and Mahogany, Birdskin, Lionskin, Stone. None of the names were right. 'No one alive is more unfortunate than me,' the Prince thought. He truly believed he would die without ever learning his name.

Then one morning a woman arrived at the castle. No one had seen her before but all agreed she was beautiful. The Prince fell in love with her instantly and forgot all about his name. He asked the woman to marry him. He had never felt so happy.

The woman agreed to marry the Prince on one condition. She had heard about the competition and wanted to make a guess herself. The Prince tried everything he could to change her mind. He was frightened. But the woman would not give in. She would marry the Prince only if she were permitted to guess his name. And if she were right the Prince must swear to uphold his oath and put her to death.

'Why?' I'd interrupt my grandfather.

'That's just it,' he'd say. 'The Prince couldn't understand why she insisted so strongly on his promise, but he saw that she would not marry him unless he agreed.' My grandfather paused and I could hear him breathing. 'On the morning of the marriage the woman came to the Prince before his people. She was dressed in her bridal gown and looked more beautiful than ever. "I will have my guess," she said. The people waited. It was terribly quiet. "But I don't know *your* name," the Prince said. The woman smiled mysteriously. "Then you might guess as well. If you guess right I will marry you now and never think again of your name." The Prince stared at the woman's face blurred beneath the veil and for an instant his heart lifted. He recognised his bride. And in that instant he backed away in fear. "That's right," she laughed, "I have given you your name. And now you must fulfil your promise." "No!" the Prince cried.' I started at the sudden loudness of my grandfather's voice. There was a long silence before he continued. 'A great buzz went around the crowd,' he said, 'for no one knew what had happened. They could see their Prince on his knees and they could hear the woman's laughter ...'

'What was the name?' The story had not turned out as I had expected and I could not understand what had happened. I blamed my grandfather.

'I don't know the name,' he said softly. 'No one heard it spoken.'

Over the years I've tried many times to account for the story's hold on me. I couldn't work out why it so terrified me when nothing seemed to happen.

John Hughes, 'My Mother's House', *Heat*, 3, 1997, pp. 74–5.

Sources and acknowledgments

The editor and publisher wish to thank copyright holders for granting permission to reproduce textual extracts. Sources are as follows:

Michael Ackland, *Henry Kendall: The Man and the Myths*, Miegunyah Press/Melbourne University Press, Carlton, 1995. **Glenda Adams**, in *Inner Cities: Australian Women's Memory of Place* (ed. Drusilla Modjeska), Penguin, Ringwood, Vic., 1989. **Phillip Adams** in *As the Twig is Bent: The Childhood Recollections of Sixteen Prominent Australians* (ed. Terry Lane), Dove, Melbourne, 1979. **Patsy Adam-Smith**, in *Birth, Death and Taxes* (ed. Dinny O'Hearn), Penguin, Ringwood, Vic., 1995. **Peter Alexander**, letter to the editor, 13 January 1997. **Don Anderson**, *Hot Copy*, Penguin, Ringwood, Vic., 1986. **Judith Armstrong**, *The Christesen Romance*, Melbourne University Press, 1996. **Connie Barber**, poem published on menu for Poets' Lunch and Wine Tasting International PEN and Centre for Studies in Australian Literature 1987, from the author. **Anne Baxter**, *Intermission: A True Tale*, W.H. Allen, London, 1977. **Bruce Beaver**, *As It Was*, University of Queensland Press, St Lucia, 1979. **Randolph Bedford**, *Naught to Thirty-three*, Melbourne University Press, 1976. **Bruce Bennett**, *Spirit in Exile: Peter Porter and His Poetry*, Oxford University Press, Melbourne, 1991. **Ann Blainey**, *The Farthing Poet: A Biography of Richard Hengist Horne, 1802–84, a Lesser Literary Lion*, Longmans, London, 1968. **Martin Boyd**, *Day of My Delight*, Lansdowne Press, Dee Why West, NSW, 1964. **Mary Grant Bruce**, *The Peculiar Honeymoon and Other Writings* (ed. Prue McKay), McPhee Gribble, Melbourne, 1980. **Jyoti Brunsdon** (ed.), *I Love a Sunburnt Country: The Diaries of Dorothea Mackellar*, HarperCollins Publishers, Sydney, 1990. **Vincent Buckley**, *Cutting Green Hay*, Penguin, Ringwood, Vic., 1983; *Memory Ireland: Insights into the Contemporary Irish Condition*,

Penguin, Ringwood, Vic., 1985. **John Button**, *On the Loose*, Text Publishing, Melbourne, 1996. **Alex Buzo**, 'My Survival as an Indigene', in *The View from Tinseltown* (ed. T. Thompson), Penguin, Ringwood, Vic., 1985. **Fiona Capp**, *Writers Defiled: Security Surveillance of Australian Authors and Intellectuals 1920–1960*, McPhee Gribble, Ringwood, Vic., 1993. **A.R. Chisholm**, *Men were My Milestones: Australian Portraits and Sketches*, Melbourne University Press, 1958. **Axel Clark**, *Christopher Brennan: A Critical Biography*, Melbourne University Press, 1980. **Manning Clark**, *A History of Australia*, vol. 2, Melbourne University Press, 1968; *The Quest for Grace*, Penguin, Ringwood, Vic., 1991. **Sharon Clarke**, *Sumner Locke Elliott: Writing Life*, Allen & Unwin, Sydney, 1996. **Charmian Clift**, in *Self Portraits* (ed. David Foster), National Library of Australia, Canberra, 1991. **Blanche d'Alpuget**, 'Lust' in *The Eleven Deadly Sins* (ed. Ross Fitzgerald), Minerva, Melbourne, 1993. **Helen Daniel**, *Double Agent: David Ireland and His Work*, Penguin, Ringwood, Vic., 1982. **Robert Dessaix**, *A Mother's Disgrace*, HarperCollins Publishers, Sydney, 1994. **Brian Dibble**, Don Grant & Glen Phillips (eds), *Celebrations: A Bicentennial Anthology of Fifty Years of Western Australian Poetry and Prose*, University of Western Australia Press, 1988. **Bary Dowling**, *Mudeye: An Australian Boyhood and Beyond*, Wakefield Press, Adelaide, 1995. **Laurie Duggan**, *The Epigrams of Martial*, X, xxxv, *Scripsi*, 1989. **Geoffrey Dutton**, *Kanga Creek: Havelock Ellis in Australia*, Picador, Sydney, 1989; *Kenneth Slessor: A Biography*, Viking, Ringwood, Vic., 1991; *Snow on the Saltbush: The Australian Literary Experience*, Penguin, Ringwood, Vic., 1985. **Brian Elliott**, *James Hardy Vaux: A Literary Rogue in Australia*, Wakefield Press, Adelaide, 1944. **Bob Ellis**, 'David Williamson and the Eiffel Tongue', in *Days of Wine and Rage* (ed. Frank Moorhouse), Penguin, Ringwood, Vic., 1980. **Louis Esson** to Vance Palmer, November 1920, from *The Writer in Australia* (ed. John Barnes), Oxford University Press, Melbourne, 1969. **Beverley Farmer**, *A Body of Water: A Year's Notebook*, University of Queensland Press, St Lucia, 1990. **Robert D. FitzGerald** (ed.), *The Letters of Hugh McCrae*, Angus & Robertson, Sydney, 1970. **Miles Franklin**, *Joseph Furphy: The Legend of a Man and His Book*, HarperCollins Publishers, Sydney, 1944; quoted in *My Congenials: Miles Franklin and Friends in Letters*, vol. 2 (ed. Jill Roe), HarperCollins Publishers, Sydney, 1993; quoted in *As Good as* a Yarn with You: Letters Between Miles Franklin, Katharine Susannah Prichard, Jean Devanny, Marjorie Barnard, Flora Eldershaw and Eleanor Dark (ed. Carole Ferrier), Cambridge University Press, Melbourne, 1992. **Ann Galbally**, *Redmond Barry: An Anglo-Irish Australian*, Melbourne University Press, 1995. **Helen Garner**, quoted in *Rooms of Their Own* (Jennifer Ellison), Penguin, Ringwood, Vic., 1986, pp. 144–5. **Peter Goldsworthy**, 'Ask Not for Whom the Bleeper Bleeps', in *Toads and Australian Writers: Other Work, Other Lives* (ed. Andrew Sant), Allen & Unwin, Sydney, 1992. **Alan Gould**, 'This World and the Next in Assisi', *Quadrant*, September 1981, pp. 35–6. **Oriel Gray**, *Exit Left: Memoirs of a Scarlet Woman*, Penguin, Ringwood, Vic., 1985. **Germaine Greer** in *Ferretabilia: Life and Times of Nation Review* (ed. Richard Walsh), University of Queensland Press, St Lucia, 1993. **Michael Griffith**, *God's Fool: The Life and Poetry of Francis Webb*, Angus & Robertson, Sydney, 1991. **Rodney Hall**, *J.S. Manifold: An Introduction to the Man and His Work*, University of Queensland Press, St Lucia, 1978. **Keith Hancock**, *Country and Calling*, Faber, London, 1954. **Frank Hardy**, *The Hard Way: The Story Behind Power Without Glory*, Australasian Book Society, Melbourne, 1961. **Kevin Hart**, 'America, America', *Overland*, 122, 1991, p. 40. **Gwen Harwood**, *Blessed City: Letters to Thomas Riddell* (ed. Alison Hoddinott), Angus & Robertson/Harper Collins, Sydney, 1990. **Anthony J. Hassall**, *Strange Country: A Study of Randolph Stow* (rev. edn), University of Queensland Press, St Lucia, 1990. **Gerard Henderson**, 'Anger', in *The Eleven Deadly Sins* (ed. Ross Fitzgerald), Minerva, Melbourne, 1993. **Dorothy Hewett**, *Wild Card: An Autobiography*, McPhee Gribble, Melbourne, 1990. **Michael Heyward**, *The Ern Malley Affair*, University of Queensland Press, St Lucia, 1993. **A.D. Hope** and Curtis Brown (Aust.) Pty Ltd, *Chance Encounters*, Melbourne University Press, 1992; Notebooks in the National Library of Australia, Book XV, 1973, pp. 87–8, and Book XXI, 1980, p. 82. **R.H. Horne**, letter to Robert Bell, cited in K.J. Fielding, 'R.H. Horne: Letters from Australia', *Meanjin* 2/1954, 243–4. **John Hughes**, 'My Mother's House', *Heat*, 3, 1997, pp. 74–5. **Barry Humphries**, *More Please*, Penguin, Ringwood, Vic., 1993. **Geoffrey Hutton**, *Adam Lindsay Gordon: The Man and the Myth*, Faber & Faber, London, 1978. **Ion L. Idriess** in *Self Portraits* (ed. David Foster), National Library of Australia, Canberra, 1978.

Clive James, *Unreliable Memoirs*, Picador, London, 1981. Kate Jennings, *Save Me, Joe Louis*, Penguin, Ringwood, Vic., 1988. Elizabeth Jolley, 'My Sister Dancing', in *Sisters* (ed. Drusilla Modjeska), HarperCollins Publishers, Sydney, 1993. Barry Jones, in *Patrick White: A Tribute* (compiled by Clayton Joyce), Angus & Robertson, Sydney, 1991. Ann-Mari Jordens, *The Stenhouse Circle: Literary Life in Mid-Nineteenth Century Sydney*, Melbourne University Press, 1979. Alfred Joyce, *A Homestead History: Being the Reminiscences and Letters of Alfred Joyce of Plaistow and Norwood, Port Phillip, 1843 to 1864* (ed. G.F. James), Oxford University Press, Melbourne, 1942. Paul Kane, e-mail to Chris Wallace-Crabbe, 7 February 1997. Garry Kinnane, *George Johnston: A Biography*, Nelson, Melbourne, 1986. Rudyard Kipling, *Something of Myself, and Other Autobiographical Writings* (ed. Thomas Pinney), Cambridge University Press, Cambridge, 1990. Christopher Koch, *Crossing the Gap: A Novelist's Essay*, Angus & Robertson, Sydney, 1987. John Lahr, *Dame Edna Everage and the Rise of Western Civilization*, Bloomsbury, London, 1994. John La Nauze, *Walter Murdoch: A Biographical Memoir*, Melbourne University Press, 1977. Bertha Lawson and John le Gay Brereton (eds), *Henry Lawson by His Mates*, Angus & Robertson, Sydney, 1931. Henry Lawson, 'A Camp-Fire Yarn', in *Henry Lawson: Complete Works 1885–1900* (ed. Leonard Cronin), Lansdowne, Sydney, 1984. Sylvia Lawson, *The Archibald Paradox*, Penguin, Ringwood, Vic., 1987. Jack Lindsay, *Fanfrolico and After*, Bodley Head, London, 1958; *Life Rarely Tells*, Bodley Head, London, 1958; *The Roaring Twenties*, Bodley Head, London, 1960. Norman Lindsay, *Bohemians of the Bulletin*, Angus & Robertson, Sydney, 1965. Graham Little, 'Counting Myself', *Australian Book Review*, 161, June 1994, p. 19. Mary Lord, *Hal Porter: Man of Many Parts*, Random House, Sydney, 1993. Harold Love, *James Edward Neild: Victorian Virtuoso*, Melbourne University Press, 1989. Ann McCulloch, *A.D. Hope: The Dance of Language*, Deakin University, Geelong, Vic., 1995. Graham McInnes, *The Road to Gundagai*, Sun Books, Melbourne, 1965; *Humping My Bluey*, Hogarth Press, London, 1966; *Goodbye Melbourne Town*, Hamish Hamilton, London, 1968. Humphrey McQueen, *Suspect History*, Wakefield Press, Adelaide, 1997. Shane Maloney, 'This Man is No Donkey', *Eureka Street*, vol. 6, no. 8, October 1986. Brian Matthews, *Oral Dreams*, McPhee

Gribble, Melbourne, 1991; 'My Demidenko Story' (column), *Age*, 3 October 1995, p. 13. **Mrs Charles Meredith**, *Notes and Sketches of New South Wales*, John Murray, London, 1844. **Alan Moorehead**, *A Late Education: Episodes in a Life*, Hamish Hamilton, London, 1970. **Frank Moorhouse**, *Days of Wine and Rage*, Penguin, Ringwood, Vic., 1980; 'The Path of Excess, the Balance of Wisdom', *Adelaide Review*, June 1997, p. 16. **Sally Morgan**, *My Place*, Fremantle Arts Centre Press, Fremantle, 1987. **Jan Morris**, *Sydney*, Penguin, Harmondsworth, UK, 1992. **John Shaw Neilson**, *The Autobiography of John Shaw Neilson*, National Library of Australia, Canberra, 1978. **Penelope Nelson**, *Penny Dreadful*, Random House, Sydney, 1995. **Nettie Palmer**, *Fourteen Years: Extracts from a Private Journal*, Meanjin Press, Melbourne, 1948; quoted in *Nettie Palmer* (ed. Vivian Smith), University of Queensland Press, St Lucia, 1988. **Vance Palmer**, 'London Days', *Meanjin*, 2/1959, p. 220; (editor), *A.G. Stephens: His Life and Work*, Robertson & Mullens, Melbourne, 1941. **Ruth Park**, *Fishing in the Styx*, Viking, Ringwood, Vic., 1993. **Nancy Phelan**, 'Messing about with Words', *Australian Book Review*, 159, April 1994, p. 33. **Hal Porter**, *The Extra*, rev. edn, University of Queensland Press, St Lucia, 1987. **Katharine Susannah Prichard**, 'Contrasts: Meredith and Marchesi', *Meanjin* 3/1961, pp. 388–91. **Henry Handel Richardson**, *Myself When Young*, Heinemann, London, 1948. **Kevin Roberts**, letter to Chris Wallace-Crabbe, 7 February 1997. **Roland Robinson**, *The Drift of Things: An Autobiography 1914–52*, Macmillan, Melbourne, 1973. **Betty Roland**, *The Devious Being*, Angus & Robertson, Sydney, 1990, pp. 97–8. **Herbert Schlegel**, 'Etaonshridlu', in *This Game of Ours: Supporters' Tales of the People's Game* (ed. Peter Burke and Leo Grogan), Schlegel Estate, St Andrews, Vic., 1993, p. 143. **Alan Seymour**, letter to Chris Wallace-Crabbe, 24 May 1996. **Bernard Smith**, *The Boy Adeodatus*, Penguin, Ringwood, Vic., 1984. **Sasha Soldatow and Christos Tsiolkas**, *Jump Cuts: An Autobiography*, Random House, Sydney, 1996. **Stephen Spender**, *Journals 1939–1983*, Faber, London, 1985. **Jane Sullivan**, *Age*, 28 August 1980. **Lucy Sussex** (ed.), *The Fortunes of Mary Fortune*, Penguin, Ringwood, Vic., 1989. **Roland Sussex**, letter to Chris Wallace-Crabbe, 7 November 1994. **John Thompson**, 'Remembrance of Things Past', *Meanjin*, 1/1964, p. 98. **Chris**

Wallace-Crabbe, 'Character Isolated by a Deed', *The Literary Half-Yearly*, July 1996, pp. i–vi. **George Wallace Crabbe**, *Scottish History, Songs and Lore*, George Robertson, Melbourne, 1908. **K.E.I. Wallace-Crabbe**, 'Pens and Yarns, Wings and Wheels', unpublished manuscript in private collection. **James Walter**, *Tunnel Vision*, Allen & Unwin, Sydney, 1996. **Patrick White**, 'The Prodigal Son', in *The Vital Decade: Ten Years of Australian Arts and Letters* (ed. Geoffrey Dutton and Max Harris), Sun Books, Melbourne, 1968; *Patrick White: Letters* (ed. David Marr), Random House, Sydney, 1994. **W.H. Wilde**, *Courage a Grace: A Biography of Dame Mary Gilmore*, Melbourne University Press, 1988. **David Williamson**, 'The Removalists: A Conjunction of Limitations', *Meanjin*, 4/1974, p. 415. **Arnold Zable**, 'Singing Eternity', *Australian Book Review*, 151, June 1993, p. 41.

Index